The Game Fowl: Its Origin and History
Game Fowl Chickens Book 9

by R.A. McIntyre

with an introduction by Jackson Chambers

This work contains material that was originally published in 1906.

This publication is within the Public Domain.

This edition is reprinted for educational purposes
and in accordance with all applicable Federal Laws.

Introduction Copyright 2016 by Jackson Chambers

Introduction

I am pleased to present yet another title on the breeding of Game Fowl.

This volume is entitled "The Game Fowl Its Origin and History" and was authored by R.A. McIntyre in 1906.

The work is in the Public Domain and is re-printed here in accordance with Federal Laws.

As with all reprinted books of this age that are intended to perfectly reproduce the original edition, considerable pains and effort had to be undertaken to correct fading and sometimes outright damage to existing proofs of this title. At times, this task is quite monumental, requiring an almost total "rebuilding" of some pages from digital proofs of multiple copies. Despite this, imperfections still sometimes exist in the final proof and may detract from the visual appearance of the text.

I hope you enjoy reading this book as much as I enjoyed making it available to readers again.

Jackson Chambers

Disclaimer

This book was written in an age when cock-fighting was widely acceptable throughout society. In many places throughout the world, cock-fighting has been made illegal.

The material presented herein is intended to be strictly for educational purposes with the purpose of enlightening Game Fowl breeders about the history of their breed. Publication of the material is neither an endorsement, nor a criticism of its contents. This book is presented as part of large series of educational material on the history and raising of numerous chicken breeds for utility or exhibition purposes.

As the reader, please consider it your duty to become familiar with local, state, provincial and federal laws relating to the subject matter contained herein before attempting to utilize any of the information presented.

As the author, publisher and retailer cannot control how the reader utilizes the historical information presented in the pages herein, they hereby disclaim any liability to any party for any loss, damage, disruption or other liability that may be incurred by the reader's misuse of this material.

SUPPLEMENT TO The Feathered World.

DUCKWING. PILE. BLACK-BREASTED RED. BIRCHEN. BROWN-BREASTED RED.

GAME BANTAMS.

(Specially drawn to illustrate Mr. Proud's article on Bantams.)

PREFACE.

The growing demand for a text book on breeding and fighting game cocks has enticed the author into the pleasant task of writing this work.

Although game fowls have held the interest of learned prominent and wealthy men for several hundred years, in Great Britian and in America, to a degree of enthusiasm unequalled in any other line of sport; yet the investigator is surprised to discover how few the sources of information on that subject are and how meagre is its literature. Thus, in the preparation of this book, it has been necessary to draw freely from tradition and memory. Excepting a few reminiscences published here and there in the "game papers," there is nothing to cover the entire history of cocking in America, from the first settlement at St. Augustine to 1869, when Dr. Cooper published his work. There has been no review of the field since that book was published, except in a few pamphlets containing personal observations of the authors.

With such incomplete records at hand, it has been impossible to write the first part of this book with a degree of satisfaction and a fidelity to historical truth so much to be desired. Thus the author has been compelled to draw largely from a diversified experience extending over twenty-five years of contact and communication with the many distinguished and successful game fowl fanciers in this country and in others. In fact, it should be admitted that the entire book, with the exception of but few pages, is nothing but the actual observation, and practice of one man. The reader is told in these pages how a successful fancier has selected his brood stock; how he has bred that stock to get

PREFACE

the best results; how he has walked his stags, fed his cocks, and handled them in the pit.

Accepting the impossibility of writing a book on this subject which should be at once simple enough to be within the grasp of the least favored reader and at the same time so profound as to gratify the exacting tastes of a philosophic mind, the author has chosen to follow the advice of Ovid, and he has "steered towards the middle course." This effort, therefore, may prove as difficult to the one class, as insufficient to the other; but it is given to the public with a confident faith in its usefulness to the greatest number of game fowl fanciers throughout the English-speaking world.

INDEX

Origin and History	9
Famous Strains and Breeders	12
Cocking in Ireland	16
Cocking in Spain	20
Oriental Cock-Fighting	21
The United States	23
Famous Pits	25
Breeding	28
Brood Stock	28
The Cock	28
On Getting Breeders	36
The Hen	48
The Size of the Game Fowl	51
Mating	53
Influence of Previous Sire	54
Breeding to Feather and Color	58
Oddities of Color	61
Inbreeding	65
Crossing	73
Importation	76
Breeding Places	81
The Hen House	84
Eggs	86
Caring for Chicks	89
Marking	90
Stags and Family Fights	92
Dubbing	94
On Walks and Walking	97
Cocking Mains	101
Form of Articles of Agreement for a Cocking Main	106

INDEX

Picking Up Cocks for a Main	108
On Feeding Coops	111
Matching for Battle	113
Cock House and Equipment	117
On Feeding Cocks for the Pit	118
Exercise	121
Preparing Cocks for Battle	125
Conditioning for Long Heels	126
Cock Bread and Its Use	133
Feeding for Short Heels	133
Jakey Magruder's Receipt	134
Extending the Feed	136
Heels or Gaffs, and Heeling	136
Heeling	140
Ring Tactics	147
Grist's Keep	152
Southern Rules	160
Philadelphia Rules	164
New York Rules	165
Western Rules	169
Baltimore Rules	172
Diseases of Game Fowl	174
Game Fowl Literature	184
Writing and Reporting	189
Famous Strains and Breeders of Recent Times	197
White Hackles	198
Warhorses	203
Shawlnecks	206
Grist Games	208
Red Horses	210
Black and Tans	213
Hansborough Fowl	215
Kennedy Redquills	216
Aldrich and the Mugwumps	217

INDEX

Red Cubans	219
Roundheads or Flatheads	221
The Wingate Fowl	223
Allen Cocks	226
Tassels or Toppies	226
Hammond Gordons	227
King Cocks	228
Huddleston Fowl	229
Shufflers and Champions	230
Dominiques	232
Hennies, or Hen Cocks	235
Pyle Cocks	237
Muff Games	239
Gulls	240
Ginn Cocks	240
Orientals	241
Well Known Feeders of this Generation	243

ORIGIN AND HISTORY.

If we accept the Biblical account of the Flood, in which we are told that every person and animal on earth was destroyed except one pair of each kind, then we are compelled to admit that there was a time when there was but one pair of fowl in existence. What that pair looked like or whether they were dominiques, games, or Cochin Chinas the Good Book does not say, but certain it is according to divine authority, every living kind of chicken must have been evolved from one pair that Noah brought out of the Ark.

However unlike different breeds of chickens may appear, observation and experience teach that all came from a common stock. This is not remarkable when we come to remember that, by the ingenuity of modern scientists such as Darwin, all sorts of pigeons have been evolved from our ordinary loft birds. For instance, how little does the pouter or the fantail resemble the homing birds, yet all came from the same pair to our certain knowledge. Therefore, the simple fact that the game fowl looks so little akin to the Langshan is no evidence that they are not of the same origin, however ill-disposed we are to accept the truth.

Going back to those pre-historic times, some writers attempt to derive all so-called barnyard fowls from the jungle fowl of Asia; if they are correct, all the satisfaction game fanciers can derive is that their favorites—the lordly game fowls of the present day—resemble the original more than any other fowl in our knowledge. But it is true that he is totally different from his progenitor in all other respects, most particularly in courage.

It would be absolutely impossible to give the exact manner in which the game cock was evolved from the jungle fowl, but quite probably through intelligent selection, as all other fine stock have been developed. At first, the most spirited and pugnacious specimens were selected as brood stock from those domesticated, and the best from these down the ages, till the fowl we admire so much was developed into a fixed type. As to the game fowl's coming from the pheasant, I attribute no importance to the claim; it is neither logical nor sustained by science so far as scientific discovery can throw any light on the subject.

The origin of color is no doubt subsequent to the evolution of the species. I consider color in all domesticated fowl, largely a matter of accident. This is easily understood by calling to mind the similar sporadic cases of variation that have come to the notice of everyone. We would naturally, for instance, consider the common black bird one of his own kind, and naturally black; yet I have seen two white ones in the same drove. Let us suppose these happened to be male and female, why could not a man have bred these together and perpetuated a strain of white black birds? These sporadic variations occur among all animals, and are often due to locality and vegetation.

The purpose of this book is not to go beyond the limits of authentic record. It is not my intention to approach my subject as Dr. Cooper did, with burning eloquence, on those many instances in history where *chickens* are mentioned, not even that sad story of Peter's perfidy, but I think it more in the scope of my efforts to confine myself to cases where *Game Chickens* are mentioned.

There seems to be little doubt that cock fighting originated certainly as far as history teaches, with the Anthenians. The study of ethnology teaches us that all people well advanced in culture and civilization have been devoted to sports of all kinds, indeed their worship often took the form of a literary and athletic kind. Hence, they were entertained as we are of the present day; though a gulf of years separates us, yet we know from the ancient records that the Greeks bred and fought a particular species of fowl, and they spoke often of "the haughty cock" from which we might infer that they bred a courageous breed of fowl especially to fight. However, it is not improbable that the Greeks themselves learned the sport from some oriential race they had conquered, perhaps, through their colonies in Asia Minor. Greek literature gives us cases in which the fighting cock was held up to armies by the generals as a model of courage worthy of emulation, and there is at least one case in which cocks were used to fight in the presence of the whole army, whereupon the commanding general enforced the lesson intended by observing that if these brutes would show such pluck and ambition only for the sake of victory, how much more should men fight both for the sake of victory and for their native land.

There are also many references in Roman history to cocking, and there is little doubt that Caesar could have taught later-day heelers a lesson or two in tying on the gaffs since that he did not find it hard to locate words to explain cock fighting as he found it among the Britains when he invaded the island, 55. B. C.

In as much as this form of sport was found in England fifty years before Christ, there is no telling how ancient this form of sport is among the English speaking people. Little doubt there is that the inhabitants of England inherit the practice of fighting cocks from the ancient settlers of the island, who are identical in blood with the Welsh people of the present day. The Angles, Saxons, Jutes and Danes do not appear to have learned to fight cocks before they settled in England in the fifth century. The evidences are strong that from some Celtic branch as the Welsh of ancient times, the Irish people had learned to fight cocks before Caesar invaded Britannia. There is no question the Welsh and Irish of today are among the most ancient cock fighters in the world and they have developed the sport as they have all other lines of sport, to the present point of perfection; they have the proud record of having preserved these customs and traditions of their races through war and revolution, against the vicissitudes of national life.

FAMOUS STRAINS AND BREEDERS.

The first mention of this form of sport is of the time of Henry II, when history places cocking among the most popular recreation.

It was not then looked upon in any other light than bird hunting is at the present day. This was the construction of the sport by the general public for several centuries; and although some legislative restrictions were passed by parliament early in the Seventeenth Century, the pits of England were never in a more flourishing condition than during the Reign of Charles II. The king frequented the pit at Whitehall, and his own strain of Pyles were among the best game fowl in the country. They were known for years as "King Charles' Pyles."

During the Commonwealth, true to the genius of puritan institutions, laws against cock fighting were passed, and while the sport was hampered, it did not cease and never will. Those laws have not been repealed, and others have been pessed making the practice even more difficult, but it is perfectly futile to attempt to eradicate the natural instinct that has been inherited for thirty centuries. Parliament had just as well pass a law requiring all Englishmen and Irishmen to have black hair. It's a thing they themselves could not control.

The most noted man in the history of cocking in England was the old Earl of Derby. His memory is as fresh today as that of any of the greatest statesmen that adorn the pages of British history, and as long as cocks are bred, the name of Derby will be an inspiration to ambitious breeders. His favorites were duckwing reds with white legs and white beaks streaked with black. Besides these, the Earl had many other colors, such as duckwing greys, yellow-leg duckwing reds, very dark reds with black eyes. Some of the latter he sent to Governor Floyd, of Virginia, and this blood runs in the veins of the "Black and Tans" and all the other black-eyed Redhorse fowl of our day.

Lord Sefton also enjoyed great distinction as a breeder. His birds were mostly very rich duckwing reds with yellow legs and those I knew had the most beautiful coloring of any light reds I have seen; while they were red like any other duckwing fowl, they were different from others across the back, being of a perfect violet color, which contrasted with the other rich colors was both novel and beautiful. Numbers of Lord Sefton's fowl were imported to this country, and as far as we are informed, always gave satisfaction.

Sketchley, the great English authority, wrote his book in 1814. There was a great demand for a work written by one so well qualified. The book became the practical cockers' guide and has remained so ever since, although very rare at the present day. Sketchley tells us that the standard colors in his time, which went back to 1760, were Black-Reds, Greys, Blacks, Spangles, Furnaces, Polecats, Cuckoos, (Dominiques), Gingers, Red Duns, Duns, Smoky Duns and his own strain of Pyles originated from crossing a ginger or light "Custard" hen on Duns. He claims that they of his day found it almost impossible to preserve a Pyle color for any length of time. The breeders of the latter part of the Eighteenth Century avoided mixing colors. They bred more to standards than breeders of the present day. They found it easy to perpetuate Dark-Reds, Dark Blackbreasted Reds, Dark Breasted Greys, Ducks, Dark Blackbreasted Birchen, Silver Blackbreasted Greys, Clean Mealy Greys, and Red Duns. The English always called their blues "Duns."

Sketchley had clearly apprehended the necessity of a feeder's becoming well acquainted with a strain of fowls in order to feed them successfully. He records the fact that he whipped Cussons, a cocker of his time, six out of seven mains, he having John Beastall every main; Cussons using a new man for each main. David Smith was the only living man that understood Cussons' fowl and for some reason did not feed them. As a strong indication that cocking was looked upon entirely in a different light in the beginning of this century, than it is now, the Rev. Mr. Brooks, of the established church of England, bore as good a reputation as a breeder of fine coks in those times as any man in the country. This sporting parson gained his reputation about 1786. His birds were the famous Shropshire Reds. In this connection, it may not be out of place to mention the fact, too, that in those times, a regular pastime at school Friday evenings among the boys was cocking. The boys brought their cocks and the teacher was judge of the hacks, almost every Friday evening.

There was a strain of Mealy Greys in 1764, considered the equals of any birds in all England. They had nearly white breasts and ran from 4.06 to 4.08. In this connection, I will remark that cocks were not nearly so large as they are now. A cock in the palmy days of the White Hall pit, weighing 5 lbs. was considered above the average by several ounces. These Mealy Greys won their reputation in some famous mains between Sir Charles Sedley and

Hugo Maynell, Esq., two of the best known cockers of that day.

Another well known strain in the early part of this century was bred by Lord Ware and fought by Mr. Thomas Wilson, of Burton, Staffordshire. These fowl were black with sooty faces and black legs. They were extremely popular in the pit and odds were always in their favor, until Wilson made the fatal mistake of breeding the old stock together too long.

Dr. Barnes, of Staffordshire, had a remarkable strain of fowl about one hundred years ago. They were tall, lanky, thin-bodied birds; notwithstanding they whipped everything in reach. These birds were called by the English, "Cuckoos." We call them Dominiques.

Beastall, the great feeder, always preferred a strain of fowl bred by one Sant. These were very dark black-reds, trimming perfectly black in the hackle, with black beaks, black legs, and of fine station. It is said that Sant would never let a hen go to anyone.

Sketchley says that the best feeder in England in his day was Thompson. He had a way of taking off more weight and still fighting cocks strong, than any other man in the business. He also takes an interesting quotation from the Nottingham Journal containing mains reported between Heap and Harrison, in which Heap is credited with 22 in 32 fights.

From old cuts we can see that pits were not arranged as they are at this day. Our pits are level with the floor, theirs were raised about three feet above the floor, on a platform. Cocks were handled artistically and according to rule, just as they are now. However, when the amount to be fought for was as much as five pounds, the match was fought in silver spurs.

Of the feeders in more recent times in England, the best

known is William Gilliver, now an old man. He is still fond of the sport and makes a specialty of the white-leg reds, so well known in the days of the Earl of Derby. Among the others well known in cocking circles is "Dick" Haydon, who enjoys the peculiar distinction of having won more money on one cock than any other man in the history of the sport, and also of having refused about $2,500 for one cock—his famous "Peter Jackson." Herbert Atkinson stands well among the cocking fraternity and is well known on both sides of the pond. It may be of interest too to the the "Henny" fanciers to know that the greatest breeder of that feather is Lord Lonsdale of England. He has kept this strain pure for years and they are sonsidered the best of that feather in the world. They are generally black or of a perfect rich grouse color so popular among the Henny cranks. My recollection is that "Dick" Haydon's "Peter Jackson" was of the Lonsdale stock. Of course there are many first-class cockers in the old country, but my space is limited and I must forbear further mention.

COCKS AND COCKING IN IRELAND.

CONTRIBUTED BY MARSHALL WHEELER, ESQ.

Owing to the indiscriminate crossing of the various breeds of game fowls native of and imported into Ireland, it has got to be that very many of their fowls cannot be said to belong to any breed, and take their names solely from their various colors. To so great an extent has this crossing been carried, that should a cock be obtained of a certain color which it would be desirable to perpetuate, no dependence whatever can be placed on results, for it might turn out the thing desired and it might not. A brown-red cock might turn out a spangled, a gull or a white. It were an almost endless task to name over the different kinds of that country, a few, therefore, of the most prominent will have to suffice, to-wit:

Brown-reds,	Black-reds,
Thrush breasted,	Spangles,
Piles,	Blue duns,
Duns,	Gypsies,
Gulls,	Birchen grays,
Whites,	Skinners,
Henfeathers, and	

Highflyers, composed of the golden and the silver pheasants.

Of all these varieties the brown-reds are in Ireland the "first favorites" among most cockers, on account of their general superiority as to health, strength and gameness. The black-reds stand next in favor, and sometimes successfully dispute the palm of superiority with the brown-reds. Instances of extraordinary good cocks are not unfrequent, however, among those of other colors. A white cock was once thrown out from a blue skinner; his owner fought him for three successive years against others of all weights from all the surrounding country and never lost a battle. He was finally poisoned. A cock of the henfeather variety in a main in Dublin of 21 cocks, won nine fights in succession and the main. At another main fought at Dungannon, in Tyrone county, one of this breed won fixe successive battles and the main. Though no positive dependence can be placed on results as to color, yet it is generally true that a brown-red cock with a black hen will produce his own color; and the same is also true of a black-red with a yellow hen. The thrush-breasted varieties are results of a cross between Irish and English fowls; Spangles and Piles of certain Irish crosses; Blue Duns are from black- or brown-red cocks with blue hens; the Gypsies are an Irish cross, and are so called from a certain appearance of their countenances, which are smutty looking, and feathers around their faces like a hood; the gulls come of a blue cock and black hen; so also the Birchen grays; whites are usually thrown from the Piles or Spangles, though sometimes from other kinds, they are milk white; the Highflyers *it is said* by some enthusiastic sportsmen come of a cross between the Golden or Silver pheasant of Ireland and a game hen, though the tradition is worthless when it is known that such a cross can no more perpetuate itself than the mule, being barren; and the hen-feather variety are so called because the cocks have tails short, like a hen, and the feathers all stick forward.

Thirty years ago cock-fighting in Ireland used to be carried on to a great extent. In Dublin a cock pit was erected enclosing an acre of ground, the roof being entirely of glass. Thither resorted the high and low breed of the land, standing upon a common level, and carried cock-fighting to the height of perfection. And in the rural districts cock-fighting flourished without let or hindrance, bringing all classes to a democratic level. Noblemen there were who kept the game cock keepers and feeders, as much so as a groom for their horses. Many curious anecdotes might be told of these high ones and their game cock trainers, for be it known, that the latter occasionally took the liberty of using their masters' feathered bipeds without any special permission. A noble whom we will call Cook for the nonce, once kept a large number of the purest, best games for fighting. Well, his keeper (whom we will call John), one day took it into his head to bring on a half dozen of Cook's cocks to a fight that was coming off near Dublin. He did so, and bet his pile on them. Just as the fight was about to begin, in came Cook, and without knowing his own cocks, put up a heavy sum on them. The fight went on, Cook's cocks came out victorious, and Cook told John to bargain for the lot, as he had nowhere before seen cocks which he thought were so near the equals of his own. John hesitated, turned red and stammered out the truth, when Cook was so pleased thereat (for the cocks had whipped a rival noble's), that he had a coach-and-four got up, and took John and the birds home in triumph, and afterwards employed a painter to take the pictures of the cocks.

The system of feeding for a fight was and is much the same that is practiced in this country. Sometimes in cases of sudden necessities, a fat cock which it was desirable to bring down as soon as possible, would be put upon a swinging rope over night and not allowed a moment's rest, which, together with the usual purgative, usually brought several ounces lighter in 8 to 12 hours, though the practice was not a good one, and never used when it could be avoided.

After the law had been passed against cock-fighting, the practice had to be followed more privately, and many amusing scenes were the consequence. At a cock fight in Dublin one night the police came in upon the crowd and "sich a gittin up stairs you never did see" by all of the crowd, except one fellow, who was one of the main men at the main, and who ran about the pit catching the cocks, putting them into bags and handing them over to the police, as if he had just come in with them and was anxious to break up the whole concern. "We don't want the cocks," said a police. "But what the d———l shall be done with them—they will get them and go to fighting them again if they are left here," replied *the stranger*. "Then we deputize *you* to take care of them," said the chief of the party; and thus did the *proprietor* save his own and his opponent's cocks, and they fought them afterwards.

But the palmy days of this sport are among the things of the past. Still cock-fighting may one day revive in all its pristine vigor and glory under new influences and new laws.

It shall be so when the people of Ireland as a mass shall so determine.

COCKING IN SPAIN AND OTHER COUNTRIES.

The Spanish people in all probability got their first game fowl from Egypt, through the Moors. Their methods of fighting have been noticeably different from that of the English as far back as history goes. They have always fought their cocks in natural spurs, and their fowl are very small. A cock that weighs over 4 pounds is considered of doubtful blood by the Spanish. Next to bull-fighting, the Spanish races, no matter where they are found, are fondest of cock-fighting. The ladies take as much interest and lay their bets as freely as the gentlemen, and the laws of society do not prohibit cock fights any more than theatres, bull fights and horse races. Indeed, Duval tells us in his book of travels among the Spanish-Mexicans, that he had seen a priest celebrate mass and shortly after start for the cock pit with a bag of money under his arm.

The people in Spain do not fight cocks so much as those in the Spanish countries of the world. The Cubans are passionately fond of the sport, and have been for years.

The *Porto Ricans* are as fond of cock-fighting as the Cubans, and their methods have been identical from time immemorial, simply through Spanish influence. It is the Filipinos that have developed more originality than any of the other countries settled by Spaniards. Cock fighting is their national sport and a Fillipino values his game cock above all other worldly possessions.

This work would be incomplete without reference to cocking in *Mexico*. The Mexicans are far ahead of any other Spanish cockers in the world. Certainly for a hundred years they have been reducing the sport to a sceince, and today a man may see some extremely scientific fighting among the rich and enthusiastic cockers in "Old Mexico." They fight their cocks in "slashers," a kind of razor strapped like a gaff to the leg—generally the left. This "slasher" is an inch to three inches long and inflicts the most ghastly wounds. I saw a letter in which a gentleman from the City of Mexico reported a main, in which one of Mr. R. C. Davis's Whitehackle cocks, a 5.14, won after fighting twenty-eight minutes with a leg *cut off!* and died immediately after winning. Talk about "the razor flying in the air," a "coon" dance is doubly discounted! The Mexicans fight for more money than any other people, and it stands to reason that they will (if they have not done so) develop the art of cock-fighting to a degree of skill unknown anywhere else in the world.

The *French,* especially those in the north of France, and the *Belgians* are devoted to cock-fighting. They are, however, far behind the English. They use a breed of cocks known as *"Combattant du Nord,"* and Flemish breeds. These cocks are of enormous size—8 pounds is small; they run in weight as high as 12 pounds. They are fought in the crudest kind of steels, and everything pertaining to the art of cock-fighting is in the rough, as yet. One of the most popular paintings at the Columbian Exposition, department of French art, was "A Cock-fight in Flanders."

The French and Belgians prefer fighting in clubs, and they like tournaments. The pits are largely attended, and the French laws are liberal, as they are all subjects of amusement.

ORIENTAL COCK-FIGHTING.

The most particular style of cock-fighting is practiced among the Japs, Chinese, Indians and Malays. These use a kind of bird indigenous to those countries and totally different in appearance from game cocks anywhere else in the world. They are known in America as "Japs," and "Aseels." These cocks are built on the same model, being very strong in the neck and are armed with tremendous parrot-like beaks. This comes from having been bred to bill from the time, no doubt, of Confucius. Montressor, a British officer in India, gives us a description of a cock fight in the East. It appears the birds are confined in closed boxes with their heads protruding from a hole. The money at stake is put on the boxes, which, at the signal, are placed together so that the cocks can bill each other. These fights are extremely brutal and it is wonderful to see how much of such punishment they will take before either is exhausted or quits.

Many of these cocks have been imported to this country, and some of our more inquisitive cockers are conducting expensive experiments. For my part, I have found them useless for our style of fighting, but less so as the Oriental blood is crossed out. Laying all other objections aside, their instinct to bite without kicking even in the most distant cross renders them useless for steel fighting. This I have seen emphasized repeatedly. Elsewhere will be found pictures of these Orientals, in which may be noted their muscular build, drooping tails, big heads, strong beaks, and scanty plumage. In the pure blood the plumage is so sparse that there is a naked spot on each wing and on the breast, generally as red as blood. They come in all colors. Dr. H. P. Clarke, of Indianapolis, Ind., and Anthony Greene, of Sacramento, Cal., are the most noted advocates of Oriential infusion. Since they began their experiments, these breeds have been scattered over the United States in crosses of almost every known strain of game fowl. As to the merits of these crosses, I might refer my reader to the game fowl papers for the last ten years.

THE UNITED STATES.

Cocking in the States began before the Revolution. General Washington, we are told, had a fine strain of game cocks at his home on the Potomac, and Andrew Jackson later on was a great admirer of game fowl. He is credited with having originated an excellent strain called the "Jackson cocks." They were said to be the best blind fighters on record, being, as some said, more dangerous without eyes than with them.

There are families scattered throughout the Union that have bred and fought cocks from father to son for generations. Notable among these are the *Arringtons,* of North Carolina, who handed down to posterity the "Stone Fences;" the *Eslins,* of the District of Columbia, who have handed down the "Race Horses;" the *Elises,* of Pennsylvania, who have transmitted the "Black Hackles;" the *Rhetts,* of South Carolina, who gave us the "Rhetts,"—a strain whose blood is in the veins of many of the best Southern fowl of our day; the *Chappels,* of South Carolina, famous for years as breeders of "Dominiques," still popular in the South; the *Singletons,* of Georgia, the *Botelers,* of Maryland, the *Smiths,* of Maryland, represented in this generation by Mr. Geo. E. Smith, of Washington, D. C., and many others with whom we are less acquainted.

There are also many men still prominent in cocking circles, whose biographies would be a history of cocking in these States for the past thirty or forty, and in some cases, fifty years. In this list are Mike Kearney, of New York; Wm. Morgan, of New Jersey; Walter Hopkinson, of Georgia; Steve Moore, of Georgia; Alfred Aldrich, of South Carolina; F. E. Grist, of Georgia; G. Park Huddleston, of Tennessee; Tom O'Neal, of Kentucky; Perry Baldwin, of New Jersey; Dick Lee, of Washington, D. C.; John Evans, also of Washington; F. W. Maddux, of Virginia; M. M.

Green, of Virginia; C. F. Dumuth, of Iowa; Mike Garrigan; Holly Chappel, of Michigan; Joseph Wingate, of New Hampshire; W. L. Morgan, of New Jersey. These are men that have come within my scope of observation; of course there are others, but I do not care to assert without personal knowledge.

The States have been famous for strains as follows:

Georgia—Shawlnecks, Grists, Warhorses.
South Carolina—Rhetts, Morgans, Bacons, Warhorses, Mugwumps, Chappels.
Alabama—Claibornes (or Mobiles).
Kentucky—Dominiques and Blues.
New York—Kearney's White Hackles, Genet Pyles, Gingers.
New Jersey—Morgan's White Hackles.
Arkansas—Travelers.
Mississippi—Allen's Round Heads.
North Carolina—Arrington Stone Fences.
Maryland—Shawlnecks, Baltimore Muffs and Top Knots and Greys.
District of Columbia—Redhorses and Redquills.
Virginia—Redhorses ond White Hackles.
Pennsylvania—Black Hackles.
California—Japs.
Tennessee—Huddlestons.
Massachusetts—Casey's Roundheads and Stone Irish.
Indiana—Trans-Atlantics.

It is safe to assert that the Union was stocked with fowl from this list of States, which seem to have been peculiarly favored in giving birth to strains of extraordinary merit. Among these, South Carolina, Georgia and Alabama at the South, and New York, Pennsylvania and the District of Columbia in the more Northerly sections, have exercised the greatest influence over game cock history in the United States.

The most extensively bred fowl in the world are Shawlnecks and Warhorses. If I were to say there are over one million in the United States, I would not exaggerate the truth. There are thousands of chickens bred in the Union every year under other names, but they are to a great extent nothing but Warhorses or Shawlnecks. By this I do not mean to claim that these fowl are the best, but it is due them as a peculiar distinction. It cannot be denied, either, that they must possess high merit as a reason for their popularity.

FAMOUS PITS.

The most successfully conducted pits in recent years have been run in New York on Long Island by Mike Kearney, the celebrated importer ond breeder of the White Hackles. This pit was run in the interest of the better element and was patronized by a class of men from New York city that not only have the money but are willing to put it up. Therefore some of the largest moneyed mains in the history of America have been fought in Kearney's pit. Unfortunately this famous retreat has been forced to discontinue on account of the blue laws recently enacted for political effect and put into force by the most unscrupulous band of robbers ever licensed by governmental authority; they are fully equal to Algerian pirates. Their regular plan of campaign is to wait till the sport is about over, and then "pull" or "hold up" the entire audience while pockets are picked.

Many fond recollections cluster about Johnnie Erb's famous resort in Newark, New Jersey. Johnnie was himself an enthusiastic sportsman; he made everything attractive to his visitors and mains were always conducted in the most orderly manner with little probability of outside interference. This pit was freely patronized by wealthy sportsmen from New York and the States south of Washington, and there are few places where more money has changed hands in a few hours.

Johnnie Erb bred a strain of Irish Greys that were held in high esteem; the finest and handsomest duckwing grey cock the writer ever saw was bred by Johnnie. This bird weighed 7.04 and no four-pounder had longer plumage. He was the most superb looking cock I ever saw. He also got good ones. These cocks are still fought around New York and New Jersey.

Johnnie's place is suspended for the present, owing to the pique of some petty official who demands more than he is worth as "hush money." No man is better fitted to run a pit than Johnnie Erb, and his many friends hope before long to see him doing a big business at the old stand. Pat Garvey's place in Baltimore has been the scene of as much fighting as any in America. The Baltimore people love cock-fighting and not a week passes that there are not a number of fights, if not a main, in Garvey's pit. Maryland Rules make quick fighting and as a result, there is always time for much hack-fighting, which is entered into with great zest by a jolly lot of fellows that will fight anybody for fun if not for a few dollars. Most of these men are orderly citizens and Pat is loved as well as respected by them all. He runs his pit in a most orderly and honorable way, and there is never any room for toughs or rowdies. The result is that the most desirable class of cockers frequent this pit and some of the largest and most famous mains in the history of cocking have been fought in it.

O'Leary's place in Chester, Pa., is by no means the least important among the *rendezvous* of Eastern cockers. O'Leary is a genial host, fond of the sport, and has a reputation for keeping order. Some of the largest monied mains in this country have been fought in O'Leary's place. It was here that the famous Shenandoah Club of Pennsylvania was so badly beaten by the "Black and Tans" for $200 and $2,000, in 1898.

Among the places that have recently come into prominence among cockers is Steubner's Road House, not far from Washington, D. C. This is at present the most roomy and best patronized pit in the East. The place is convenient in every way, comfortable, accessible, and kept in an orderly manner. Several important mains have been fought at Steubner's, and the place has a very bright future.

In the South many mains have been fought in Charleston pits, also at Ten Mile Hill. The "Old Spanish Cockpit" of New Orleans is known all over the cocking world. In recent times the new pit between Florence and Mars Bluff, S. C., has sprung into considerable prominence.

BREEDING.

BROOD STOCK.

The general plan of this book will follow the course of correct breeding, walking and fighting of game fowl. Miscellaneous matter will be added after this plan shall have been perfected.

In pursuit of this arrangement, our first object is a concise discussion of all those matters that are of greatest importance in the breeding and perpetuation of a strain. Let us say at the very threshold of this attempt that the greatest care and nicest discriminations are necessary in the selection of Brood Stock. Here is the foundation of all success—*that you start right and keep right.* The breeder can never keep right unless he starts right. For the present let us consider therefore those things that are essential to start in this most fascinating of all sports engaged in by the English races. Let us first talk together at sufficient length to determine: What is a suitable cock for a stock-getter? and, what is a suitable hen for the purpose?

THE COCK.

Two things must always be kept in mind in the choice of a Brood Cock— Spirit and Body. The matter of first importance is *Spirit,* or what is generally termed "gameness." This, we will consider later; for the present we will write of those things that go to make a fit cock physically to be lord of a brood yard.

Without *constitution,* no strain of chickens can ever be successful; many will die while chicks, what are raised will give extra trouble; many die after being carefully walked, undergoing the first cock moult, and many go under, or are not able to stand the physicing and other hardships of feeding for the pit. They mince in the coops and do not throw off their food, running often into roup, heart trouble and consumption. It is a waste of time to breed from delicate specimens, besides the many disappointments that must follow such a foolish course. Therefore, in the choice of a brood cock look first for *constitution*. Pick a cock with excellent wind power, broad breast, big, strong wing butts, and one that stands with legs well apart, broad in the back and flat. His head should be rosy: a scaly face indicates some radical derangement of the system, no matter how merry the cock may be. He ought not to feel loose and flabby, with feathers like a sick turkey hen. He must have a clear, bright expression of the eye, and a willingness to eat without being gluttonous. There is always something wrong with a cock on a good walk that piles over top of the hens to get the most feed. There is always something unsound about a cock that never offers to share his food with the hens. In short, the chivalry of a game cock is a safe index of his physical condition. The habit of gluttony, the cock being on a *good* walk, stamps a cock as unfit for a stock-getter no matter how much his pedigree may be prized, or how many battles he has to his credit. He may get fairly good stags over vigorous hens, but chances are against him.

It is not generally safe to breed from a cock that has been "thrown out" because he failed to throw off his food in the feeding coop; a cock thrown out by an experienced feeder in culling out for an important main is not to be trusted in a brood pen—there is something radically wrong, either in *spirit* or in *body*. But badly *impaired constitution* in cocks once perfectly vigorous is also to be avoided. This comes in most cases from 1. Old age; 2. Being battered on the walk; 3. Wounds received in the pit. Any one of these makes a cock less fit for brood purposes than before his health was impaired. Sketchley, the greatest English authority, in his book on Game Fowls, published in 1816, insists that cocks four years old have decreased in vitality and are no longer first grade brooders. He prefers a blooming forward stag or a two-year-old cock. On this point of age: there are many of the best breeders in the world that have bred from the same hens and cocks as long as the birds lived, and have done so with good results. I have known cocks eight years old to get good, hardy, strong, chickens that developed into excellent fighters. I have one case in mind of a brood cock *fourteen* years old; he was said to be a good getter. However, these phenomenal cases do not disprove the fact that, as a general thing, age diminishes the vitality of a cock and renders him less suitable for brood purposes. None of the old Pensioners, we must all confess, can get as perfect chickens as they could at two years of age.

However, if the breeder insists, because of special merit, in breeding from an old cock, he should always be careful to breed him to very few hens—not over three, and these should not be over two years old—forward pullets are better. I have had cocks from pullets and a five-year-old cock to make a remarkable record; but the pullets from this cross with a cock three years old, did better still.

I cannot come to believe that a stag once badly battered, ever makes the same cock he would have been: with better reason, a cock badly beat up on his walk, having had such a shock to his system is not a first-class brooder. No matter how valuable he may be, a full brother that has never had such a strain on his vitality is better and will produce a greater number of fine specimens.

Wounds received in the pit are of a variety of kinds; some unquestionably discapacitate a cock for brood purposes, and the authority quoted before claims that a cock that has been prepared for battle cannot be set down as a first-class brooder for that season, though he never fought. I must agree with the proposition as far as short heel fighting as practiced in New York is concerned. Such men as Howard, Rogers and Kearney, give their fowl a heavy physicing and a twenty-one day feed of an extremely artificial nature. Rarely a cock may go through and come out sound enough, but only rarely would cocks from a New York feeding coop make first class brooders the same season they were fed. Of course it would be still worse if the cock had been shown in the main and more or less cut up. It is different in Southern Rules. Many cocks are fought South after a seven or nine day feed, never over fourteen, and the dieting is very simple, such men as Col. Grist not using physic at all, nor any of those patent dishes that have given rise to the current comparison,—"to live like a fighting cock." Hence, cocks from a Southern feeder's coops are often fit for first class brooders; but if they are shown in the main and cut the case is different. No badly wounded cock in any heels can ever be graded as first class for breeding purposes. Slight flesh cuts do him no permanent damage, and are not sufficient cause for discarding a good cock.

The three cardinal points in the physical make-up of a cock are: 1. Constitution; 2. Conformation; 3. Feather.

By conformation we imply the entire form of the cock, from his toe nail to the tip of his beak.

No one is capable of judging the form of a cock but one who has had sufficient experience to recognize his defects and fine points. An intelligent breeder will show his wisdom by leaving this part of the business to a man of generally known ability—a man who has made a decided success of breeding game cocks for the pit. However it is best to avoid a hobbyist; his opinion is not safe. Some men become married to false ideals and as usual are all the more blind to the defects of their spouse. However successful a breeder may have been, his judgment is not trustworthy if his beou ideal is contrary to models that have been established on the experience of the cocking fraternity for a hundred years. Therefore I should give little credit to any one who advised me to breed from a very squatty cock, and I would be equally deaf to one who urged the use of a leggy, slab-sided specimen. Such men are hobbyists, and while their intentions are good, they are unsafe counselors.

It is impossible in most cases to get the assistance of persons of experience, and the breeder must exercise his own judgment, directed by written instructions. I submit the following:

1. Avoid all kinds of freaks, such as three spurs, an unusually drooping tail, an enormous beak, eyes of different size, extremely duck-legged, very leggy.

2. Avoid defects, such as gouty feet, rough legs, crooked beak, defective breastbone, crooked toes, very short prop-toe and turned in—what is called duck footed.

3. Avoid bad or impaired constitution.

4. Very short and brittle plumage.

The points of a good specimen are:

1. Strong toes of medium length, and smooth bone, showing nearly the same size from knee joint to foot.

2. Shank should *never* be long—a long thigh and short shank always does the most execution. Long shanks are most undesirable.

3. Medium station. By all means avoid extremes. A medium stationed cock has the advantage over a low-set bird and he will easily light off and wear down a leggy cock in equal fix, provided he is bred right. A leggy cock,

all things being equal, could not win three fights in ten against such cocks as Kearney's Whitehackles in short heels, and the chances are more than equal in those birds' favor in long heels.

There are few points on which the breeder is more open to err than on this question of station. He naturally falls into the error of thinking that height gives a cock the advantage, but he forgets it only gives him the advantage provided the cocks are going to bill all the time, and he forgets that while a medium stationed cock rarely ever is weak on his pins, a very leggy one is always so, and if the stilty bird is fought off two or three rounds, he is invariably whipped. The breeders of stilty cocks hope to win in the go-off; they *expect* to lose if it comes to several pittings. A medium cock in condition can roost as high as a leggy one, his blows are stronger by reason of natural laws, he can stay strong on his feet longer, and being bred with fire and a dashing spirit, he is the most dangerous fighting machine known to nature.

4. To prove the *form* of a cock he should be set upon the open right hand, his head to the right and the fingers extending up towards his belly. In this position, his *breast* should fill the palm well, and should be a round, well filled out form, not hollow between the thigh and breast bone. The breast bone should not be flat, but gently curved from the craw to the belly. A cock should have a fine, broad, full bosom, and very thick from his back to the edge of his breast bone he is termed "deep in the keel," and is not a good specimen. Next, consider the bird's *back*. This ought to be broad at the hips and flat, by which we mean not arched from the root of the tail to a point above the hips. In this case, cocks are said to be "roached." Cocks that have one hip higher than the other are called "hunchbacks." Both

"hunches" and "roaches" are unfit for brooders, though they have been known to win. I know of one hunchback that won nine battles, but his success was never credited to his deformity. The *neck* should be at least medium in length, not short, and, if strong, the longer the better. The neck should not be curved so much as to make the cock look bow-necked. The *head* ought never be long; for practical cocking a short, thick head is best, although in the show pen a long, slender head might take the prize. There is a vast difference between the whip-tailed degenerate seen in show pens of the present day and the sturdy fighting cock with his luxuriance of plumage and indomitable pluck. The *beak* should be not over medium in length, and strong at the base. The *eyes* should be lustrous, wide open, standing well out, not sunken in the face. I like, if the cock's beak is turned away, to see the clear eye stand out—a pop-eye is not a defect by any means. A pop-eyed cock can see almost in every direction at once, he is hard to blink, and the blood in battle cannot obscure his sight; this is not true of a hollow-eyed bird. The cock's *shoulders* should be broad. You can never get them too broad. He is a feathered pugulist and requires the essentials of a human fighter. No man has ever held the belt any length of time that was not proportionately larger than the ordinary man about the shoulders. Game cocks cannot be first class without good shoulders. The *thigh* is never too large; cannot be. The power of a cock depends largely upon his thigh, just as a man's striking ability depends upon his arms. I have seen an old castaway blinker whip thirty-seven turkeys. He could hit a full grown gobbler square in the breast and knock him over. Upon examination I found this old cock had a thigh like a man's forearm.

The third cardinal point of criticism in a cock is his plumage. It is not my purpose to go into the question of breeding to a color at this place, though that subject will be discussed elsewhere. Our present desire is to examine the cock's feathers, no matter what his color may be.

Toughness of quills is highly desirable; brittle feathers are a constant source of annoyance in a strain. Rarely can stags enough of such a breed be picked up to fight a main, on account of defective plumage. Often cocks come in with quills broken in the wing from simply flying up and down the roost, and if they come in sound, they are likely to lose too many feathers even in the spar. I have seen Redhorse cocks whose quills were almost like whalebone. They might be twisted entirely out of shape without any injury whatever. This is a great advantage. *Length* of plumage goes further towards making game fowl show their blood and win admiration than anything else. There is perhaps on the whole earth not another living thing so beautiful as a game cock in full feather. Other virtues are not to be sacrificed for feathers, but if two cocks were equally well built and perfect in conformation, I should always prefer the one with the longest and most beautiful plumage. Nor is this a mere whim; long feathered fowl, experience teaches, usually have tough quills, and furthermore, when trimmed out for battle the wings are so much more ample and strong, being filled with big, hard, tough quills. I have often seen a six pound cock that could not fly ten feet from the ground on account of short wings, whereas I have just had trouble with a famous six pound brood cock of my own that got out of his pen by flying through a hole in the roof twelve feet from the ground. Such cocks have well developed wing muscles and power of propulsion. *Healthy* feathers never look dingy. They should have a nice, clean look and a life-like gloss. No cock is fit to breed from if his plumage has a dull, lifeless look. *Tightness* of feather is necessary, but by this I do not mean the kind of tightness seen on a show bird, as if the feathers had been saturated in glue and then pressed against the body. The feathers should simply lie to the bird's figure so as to bring out his symmetry of form. It must not be fluffy as it is on the ordinary yard fowl.

ON GETTING BREEDERS.

It must be admitted that many are the requirements of perfection, and it must often happen that very fine cocks fit for breeders cannot entirely come up to the standard in every detail; but the nearer any cock approaches the full letter of the standard the nearer he is to a perfect cock, and correspondingly more desirable as a getter over favorite hens. Certainly, unless a cock can show 90 per cent. of these points he is not a desirable fowl.

The inquiring mind at this point naturally would seek information as to how such cocks are to be gotten. The way is clear. There is scarcely a thing in this world that the human mind can crave, but that it can be gotten. To secure satisfaction of a desire we must first *find* the thing and then *pay* for it. Different from the times when no reputable cocker would sell his fowl, almost any cocker now will part with them at a reasonable price. I know of only two exceptions and one of these men could not whip a coop of ducks, while the other has been repeatedly licked by men who *will* dispose of fowl. So that the best in America and in Europe are purchasable, and the breeders of world-wide reputation are well known to the public. Therefore, it cannot be hard to *find* what the searcher may desire. The next thing is to *pay* for it.

I must appeal earnestly to the ambitious purchaser's reason. Can any man in any branch of business expect the best at the lowest price? Could anyone expect a famous breeder and successful cocker to sell him his favorite brood cock for $10.00? He may get the favorite brood cock of a hundred breeders at such a price and then not get more than his money's worth, whereas, he might have saved money by giving the first man $100.00 for a brood cock. The best is the cheapest, no matter what the price. It is the same with cocks as with horses. Why is it that a famous stallion whose get have won the large majority of their races sells for 100 times as much as his own brother? perhaps $50,000 when his brother goes for $500? Would not the same thing be expected in the cocking business? But the purchaser replies, "I cannot afford to pay such a price for a cock." Plainly the man who holds such views either is too poor to follow up the chicken business, or his heart is not warmed up to the situation. But, I assert with confidence, that I can name a dozen men in my acquaintance any of whom would promptly send a buyer a cock that would score over 90 per cent. on the standard set forth, if he were forwarded a postoffice money order for $25—a mere song. Yet he might send the same man $10 and get exactly what he paid for. What man in any line of business is fool enough to send his best out at an ordinary price? I know men who advertise that would send a man a $10.00 cock for $10.00 and a $100 for $25.00. I don't begin to believe that anyone can afford to sell a cock reasonably near my standard for less than $25.00. In every case that I recall where men have found what they wanted in the hands of trustworthy, reputable breeders and paid for it without stint, they have gone promptly to the front and very shortly recovered and made money. I give no names but know it to be true of a Warhorse breeder in South Carolina. Likes get likes, and a trio of fowl costing $5.00 will generally get trios worth $1.50. Pay for the best and start right!

GAMENESS.

I have preferred the word *spirit* to *gameness* in considering the other half of a game cock's composition, because it is broader—it includes not only indomitable persistence but all there is of freshness, life, and energy in the bird's nature.

On the walk, I like to see a cock full of motion, scratching, calling the hens, and rarely still enough to give you a snap shot with a camera. When a hen cackles I like him to respond and give the impression generally of "fondness for the ladies." Nature has so decreed that chivalrous men are usually brave, and I believe the same rule holds with game cocks John Evans, a well-known cocker, said of a brood cock of mine once after feeding him two weeks to fight in a main for $200 and $2,000, which he won easily: "Here is a cock that has *more heart* than any cock I ever saw," meaning no matter how much he was physiced or worked he never failed to come up merry. I have often noticed that this cock known for his gameness never lost his temper with a hen, even when penned, and though hungry, he is a knight at all times. As a usual thing, Chevalier Bayard in his palmiest days was no more of a gentleman than this same beautiful brown-red game cock. I do not wish, however, to be understood as impeaching the courage of a cock that fights hens; some good ones do it, but the habit is very annoying and often disastrous. Their gaffs should be sawed off close to the leg. The *best* cocks I ever owned, or bred, never pecked or struck the hens with which they were mated.

In hand, I like best a cock that is tight-fisted, i. e., lifts his feet up close to his body, fans out and holds up his tail well, and carries his head up, with a suggestion of power and vigor in his entire composition. Some elegant cocks are very restless in hand, chatting and kicking all the time, while others handle to perfection and are comparatively quiet. The former are usually very nervous and savage fighters and if provoked may become man-fighters; the latter are generally easier to handle, less liable to become man-fighters, and are not by any means slow in the pit. One of the best strains of cocks I ever saw were extremely gentle in the hand, but perfect cyclones in the pit. Between the two styles, it is hard to choose—either is good enough. The first must be handled with more tenderness to avoid their becoming man-fighters, in which event they may turn on the pitter and give their antagonist the advantage.

Many persons attach much importance to the *crow* of a cock. Of course the noise a cock makes with his vocal cords cannot indicate anything as to courage. I like a short, spirited crow, proportionate in depth to the size of the fowl. I have no question that some strains can "out crow" others. From what I have seen I believe the Gulls are the most attractive fowls along this line, in my knowledge. There is something strained about the crow of all the Redhorse fowls, and I have never heard cocks crow with as much mellowness as the Irish I imported in 1893. They crow longer than I like, but always the same liquid mellowness. I have never noticed any regularity in this respect among other strains.

Gameness is that quality of spirit which sustains a fighting cock no matter how badly he may be punished.

No other subject engages the attention of amateurs and fanciers as the question of gameness, which is so closely connected with the other essentials of fighting fowl that, to understand the subject in hand, it is necessary to revert to what might be termed characteristics.

There is no question in the writer's mind that the country is full of men seeking impossibilities in game fowl as in other lines of effort. There are numbers of men who cling to the idea that although every known strain of chickens has shown a runaway, there is somewhere a breed of cocks that cannot be stopped by any course of inhuman treatment known to inventors of persecution; they spend lives and fortunes in a futile search like that they ridicule in Ponce de Leon. If the tyro would submit at once to the inevitable fact that his standard of gameness does not exist, and address himself to the improvement and perpetuation of some good strain already famous and easily procured for a mere bagatelle, he would take up the work at its highest point of development, and soon be richly rewarded for all his labors.

I have often heard a novice remark after a few weeks' experience, "Oh, the Warhorses are no good, the Shawlnecks will run away, and the Whitehackles are not what they are cracked up to be." Does he stop to think one instant how many thousands of these birds are bred every year, how broad his statement is, and how illogical? I shall make a strong and surprising statement, and it is this: There is no living breed of chickens that does not show a runaway now and then—what I would call a cull—even in the hands of the best breeders! This statement will not surprise such men as Grist, Smith, Aldrich and Kearney, but it may prove a serious shock to Mr. Jno. Brown, who has been testing the stags from his first trio.

Sometimes, for mysterious reasons, the best game cocks in the world will do the most unaccountable things. Get some old "stager" to give you a few of his experiences, young men. He may tell you how he has seen a cock as well bred as any in the world run away in one week and whip all the cocks in the vicinity the next; how one just as good refused to fight a gray cock, but whipped every red you could find, and finally died the gamest he ever saw.

At Paris, Ky., some years ago, a celebrated breeder, who shall be nameless, but who is known all over the cocking world, showed his brood cock in a very important main, and the rascal ran away, after having the other cock licked, with over $400 on his back. I recall a case where a favorite cock of Blucher Hansbrough's refused to fight a dunghill, and actually went under in his presence, and Hansbrough was known to be the most careful breeder and greatest stickler for gameness in the Middle States.

These are only a few instances. Now if these gentlemen had been like the average beginner, two of the greatest strains of fighting cocks on American soil would have been exterminated. As it was, the first named bred from the full brother to the runner, and raised cocks that were seen, after fighting an hour with both legs broken, to drag themselves with their wings across the pit to the other cock. The last named knowing the strain and pedigree of his fowl, no more thought of killing off his brothers than the state would think of hanging a whole family because one member had committed murder.

For these reasons, it must appear thoroughly unreasonable to judge a whole strain of game chickens by the acts of one specimen. It must furthermore appear that pedigree is the rock of safety on which the beginner should build, and he ought not to lose faith because of something he cannot understand.

Well, then, how about this "testing habit," common among those who seek to discover, to their heart's content, what may serve only to mislead and confuse? Let me say, not one man in a thousand, even of experience, can tell one thing of value by what is called private testing. The only rational testing known to the writer has been disused for fully sixty years and, as far as he is informed, never was used in this country. The plan was simple, and sound. Sketch:-

ley, the great English authority, who wrote his book in 1814, advocated it. His experience ran back to 1760, and his influence is plainly felt in England today.

According to this plan: Suppose the beginner purchases a trio from some breeder and wishes to discover the gameness of the progeny. He picks up a whole main of his birds in proper health and feather, they are put through just the same tedious and painstaking course of feeding and exercise as for a main, and are fought according to rule. Each bird is closely watched, both for fighting qualities and for gameness. If the whole main compares favorably with the best known to the experimenter, they most probably are worthy of further attention, otherwise the whole "get" goes into the pot.

Cutting out single birds, and, as is frequently done out of condition, is no satisfactory test. The writer would say, that if the breeder would like to make a convincing and reasonable test, he had better make a main to show as many as possible of the new stock, for a small amount, and fight them off in condition. If a main and hacks cannot be arranged, Welsh-main the whole business, i. e., match them against one another, and match up the winners till nothing is left except, perhaps, one.

Everyone anxious to rise and prosper can, however, congratulate himself that it is really within his power to purchase such stock as will not require these severe, expensive tests, and with composure he may sit by the pit where his stock are battling for honors and profit, free from all anxiety and with a certain sense of security that makes one comfortable in a crisis.

A very satisfactory test on depth of gameness may be seen in cock houses during the cleaning out of the coops after a big main. All the cocks that have been fought are cold and stiff; they have reflected on their troubles and are suffering from a general relaxation and collapse of the whole system, if not from serious or fatal wounds. Each cock is examined and if found unfit for any future use, his head is taken off. No matter how sound, hacked cocks are of no use. To clean the coops of rubbish the fought cocks are taken out and one by one presented, and if they refuse to fight they go to the executioner's block. The proceedings are highly instructive to a beginner. He will see that a half dozen cocks wounded in different ways, bred by one man will all "refuse," while a similar number bred by another man and even worse hurt, will all bristle up and show an eagerness for battle. From which of these breeders would a thoughtful man prefer a brood cock? Some men claim that if a cock makes a good game fight and tries his best to win, they don't care if he refuses next day. I cannot agree with this view for an instant. I should feel deeply disappointed if mine refused to *show* after cooling off, even though they were blinded in both eyes and badly cut up in a long battle. But if they *show fight* under these circumstances, I do not deem it necessary to put a fresh cock on them and batter them around. This I have sometimes done with my own privately, just to see how much they would stand, and have even chopped them with gaffs, but I want to put myself on record as denying that any such thing is a fair test. If a man claims that his own fowl are game, he has no right to expect more of the fowl of others than he demands of his own.

One of the most dangerous habits of unreflecting breeders is the choice of brood cocks for *individual perfomances*. These people have no power to resist temptation and if, at a main, they see a fine looking strong cock come into the pit and literally riddle the opponent's favorite, without knowing anything more about the cock they pay a good round price for him and place him over their best hens. The blasting of more prospects comes from this cause, perhaps, than any other. In the first place, the cock may be a dunghill, in the next he may be the only brother in ten worth bringing to a pit. Impressions at a pit are as deceptive as they are at an auction. When Casey of Boston, was fighting Mackin, of Chicago, for $200 and $2,000, in 1899, it had been give and take to the fourteenth battle in fifteen matches. For the deciding battle Casey produced a beautiful rich black-breasted red with yellow legs, to all appearances an elegant bird fit to battle for the $2,200 and gate money, about $200 more. The fight dragged on for an hour with the Casey cock badly wounded and totally blind, but still claiming. He became the object of general admiration, and some of the best men in the business were bidding for him as a brooder. Just as he had a good show to win out a great fight, he turned completely, dropped his tail and ran away. It was found afterwards that this cock was a quarter Jap. Had this cock won after a gallant battle some one of those bidders would have hundreds of chickens from him in this time, and his reputation and pocket book would suffer for the next twenty years. A dear friend grown gray in the cocking business, after ridiculing the writer for some experimenting with Oriental blood about ten years since, had to be held at Garvey's pit afterwards to keep him from buying a quarter Jap that made an excellent fight. I could fill this book with instances of errors made by selecting brood cocks for individual performances. If there is an authentic pedigree and a distinguished history behind this individual performer, the ambitious breeder, if he discovers merits of a superior order, may be justified in purchasing, otherwise he may commit an egregious blunder from which he cannot recover in ten years, except by the extermination of a whole yard of elegant fowl to reach the rotten spot. Like consumption and lunacy in the human kind, it may not break out for several generations, and then you can't tell where it comes from, so the whole flock must go. An ounce of prevention is worth a pound of cure.

If after all, it seems wise to select a cock that has fought in a main, by all means prefer a winner. No matter how game a fight a loser may make, he does not get the money. You must endeavor to propogate not only gameness but winning ability. Some cocks produce a fine impression on an audience and yet lose, simply because they drum like a pheasant with their wings while their feet are idle; the gaffs are not tied on a cock's wings. You must have an instinctive kicker. This quality is bred into some strains so deeply that they as naturally throw their feet at another cock as a man would strike with his fist. Hence, it often appears that a cock in battle must lose when to the surprise of everybody it is discovered that the *winner* is the loser. It is impossible to get too much of this foot fighting propensity. Too much billing is a suicidal practice, especially in long heels. This was well illustrated in the twenty-one cocking main between Dr. King and Mr. R. C. Davis at Mars Bluff, S. C., December, 1899. The doctor for the top weight showed a cherry-red, yellow legs, with an Oriental cross in him. Mr. Davis produced a straight Whitehackle. The fight was a long and bloody one. The Whitehackle was rattled till blue in the face and too weak to stand, but by good nursing recovered somewhat; still, choking with blood, he could not bill, but he kicked every time the King bird billed him. The Oriental cross beginning to bill after the birds were well fatigued, the doctor's cock kept biting, and every time he did the Davis cock kicked. The outcome was the Whitehackle, though almost dead, finally broke the King cock's neck.

The *style* of fighting deserves careful attention. Some

cocks are disposed after a few blows to root under and try to protect their heads. If the cocks are equally matched this is very objectionable, and may be due to being in the cock's nature, in which case he is unworthy, or it may come from having been walked with turkeys. A cock that "gives the head" is unfit for a main. You must remember that you are not the only man betting when your cock is in the pit. The confidence and money of friends may be squandered. A constitutional "ducker" is useless for any purpose, but the best cocks become such if allowed to fight turkeys. They will also "give the head;" that is, fail to strike on the other cock's bill hold and "break" with an antagonist.

A *"wheeler"* is a cock that after becoming somewhat fatigued runs away like a quitter, but renews the battle if his antagonist lags. They often weary the other cock down and win; although one of the best judges in this country told me he never saw one lose, yet I would not breed from a constitutional wheeler. But it must not be forgotten that when cocks are overmatched they very often wheel by instinct. They do this as a deliberate *ruse de guerre*: a little Redhorse cock decided a main in Philadelphia in the winter of 1899 by wheeling from a big strong Pyle. He worried the Pyle down and killed him. The Spaniards who frequented the New Orleans pits in 1885, produced cocks *trained* to wheel. They fought these little 3.08 cocks in natural heels against cocks of any size armed with steels. The cunning little fellows would light running and keep it up till the big cocks were completely exhausted, then turn and kill them.

A *shuffling* cock is one that wallows all over a cock in a vicious attempt to give him body cuts. A shuffler helps his feet to keep in motion by struggling violently with his wings. These cocks are exceedingly dangerous during a mix-up in long gaffs, but if they are given to this style of fighting they will in equal condition lose seventy-five per cent. of their fights in short gaffs, because short heel fighting calls for good high work and injury to the head and neck. It is wrong, however, to suppose that body blows are not desirable in short heels. In short gaffs a good cock is prepared to strike a telling blow anywhere. For instance, blows across the back are especially dangerous, and as bad rattles as I ever saw were given by one and a quarter inch gaffs, while couples are frequent. It follows, then, that purely shuffling cocks can win only in long heels.

A *sparring* cock is one that flies high and makes no attempt to get a bill hold for several rounds. These cocks often take runaway cocks by surprise and win at once by "hooking" their opponent. After the first few rounds they have no advantage, as they invariably settle down to the standard way of fighting.

A *buckling* cock is an elegant fighter in any length of gaffs. These cocks fight with their eyes wide open and generally drive in close enough to get a bill hold upon which they give the foe several violent kicks with all the power in them. They are a kind of composition of the *sparrer* and the *shuffler*.

An *infighter*, if swift enough and handy with his feet, is by long odds the best style of fighter. He is furious in all his movements, skillful, and irresistible. He will overpower a shuffler, he will crowd a sparrer and slay him. There is no way to keep him off. This kind is rarely seen, but I never saw one get a scratch either in long or short heels, and the battles are always short. All I ever saw were medium stationed cocks. They are worth all the money you have. In attempts to describe this kind of cock, they have been called by such names as, "jig-saws," "buzz-saws," and "cyclones," but nothing gives an adequate idea except the thing itself. They combine all the virtues of the shuffler, sparrer and buckler with an irresistible power and dash.

No matter how good a fighter you may have, he may come against his equal in which case there will be need for something else besides leg work—he must be an unceasing "claimer." That is if it comes down to a fight in which both cocks are terribly distressed and cut to pieces with, maybe, both eyes out and the battle dragging on for two hours, your bird should always try to "keep the count;" he ought to snap to the very last. The pits in New York are good places to see this virtue illustrated. New York Rules are very severe. The gaffs are large and blunt, and the pitters are not allowed to nurse, cluck, or do anything to make a cock bite. The count is comparatively short and unless a cock is an incessant snapper he is almost sure to lose. A game cock in poor fix will in most cases win against an ordinary cock in prime condition. I have seen cocks after having both eyes out for an hour, snap viciously at the sound of a foot on the tan. I once saw a Redhorse stag totally blind fly entirely across the pit at the sound of the opposite pitter's voice. There is no way on earth of whipping this kind in Philadelphia Rules, except out and out killing. Cocks may get along with out this quality in long heels, but they cannot win without it in short.

Having discussed at length the standard of a brood cock it is now in order to pay our respects to

THE HEN.

Often she is foolishly ignored in the make-up of a brood pen, and there is more hazard risked, in many cases, than with the cock. If the breeder will simply keep in mind the fact that all of the exclusive breeders from time immemorial who have attempted to keep their fowl out of the hands of others have made it a rule never to let a man have a hen or a pullet, while now and then they would give away a stag or cock. This is because it has been held for a century that the characteristics are transmitted more readily through the female than the male. It follows, then, that the female must have the most painstaking consideration.

Three things are to be cared for in the choice of a brood hen: 1. Pedigree; 2. Form; 3. Constitution. As hens cannot be tested for gameness, the only guide to purity is pedigree. You must know the record of all the male members of her family. What her father did, her grandfather— as far back as you can, then her brothers, her uncles, her sons and own nephews. If they have proved game fighters and most of them winners, she is a good hen. The reader cannot prize too highly a well formed, healthy hen, full sister to ten brothers that have won under every form of persecution incident to the pit, whose father was a game fighter and winner, whose mother was sister to game winners, and whose sons have all won, both as stags and cocks, or died in the attempt. Such a hen is easily worth $50.00. They are few and hard to get, because miscellaneous breeding is the order of the day. Most men put a cock with "ten or fifteen good hens," and of course the exact pedigree of any one of the chicks is wrapped in mystery, and no individual hen has a chance to make a record.

Second is the hen's *form*. She ought to point very much *like the cock* as to breast, back, bone, station, head, eyes, beak, neck and shoulders. A hen that is too fat cannot be judged well. The best time is before she begins to lay or directly after she begins to set. *Defects* named in cocks must be avoided in hens. They transmit defects and blemishes more freely than a cock, especially roached backs and rough legs. Very seldom does a fluffy, soft, hen with small bone get first class stags.

Much has been written on the *disposition* of a game hen as affecting her sons. Some claim that a hen ought to be very cross, spiteful, hard to manage, always in trouble, talking in hand like a cock, and ambitious to run out all the other hens. Such a hen undoubtedly produces a good impression for pugnacity, but such propensities, I wish to assert with emphasis, do not constitute essentials in a first class hen. Certainly all game hens are very alert, quarrelsome and energetic when they have young, but otherwise some of the best hens I have ever seen were gentle, kind and tractable, sometimes even timid and indisposed to fight. They remind me, as game fowl often do, of our own species. While the men of a family may be as brave as lions, the women may be modest and gentle like doves. I have an old hen now that never struck over two licks in her life, and her four sons of the last season are the most noisy, nervy, and pugilistic fellows I have raised for years. Yet pugnacity is pronounced in some hens. I used an old black hen as brood stock for several years and still breed her progeny freely, that killed her mother in battle, and I have had hens that could not be backed either while laying or with chickens. These hens would crow in hand like a cock. Some of my Irish hens are the most terrific fighters. I loaned one—a big brown-red—to a friend and he informed me that she would be queen of the ranch if she had to whip a hundred hens!

I will say this, nevertheless, that while this pugnacious spirit is not essential, yet if a hen does fight, she should be shifty, swift and strong. I had a specially well bred pullet that was the finest fighting female I ever saw. I bred her to my best cock and got the finest fighter I ever bred.

Careful breeders often bring up the question of breeding

from pullets. After a thorough trial I am convinced that hardy, forward pullets are just as good as three-year-old hens. This stands to reason: a pullet hatched in April and bred the following April is quite the same as a young woman of twenty summers with her first infant. A first class March or April pullet with a two year-old-cock of the right stamp comes pretty close to the high-water mark in mating.

THE SIZE OF THE GAME FOWL.

In expounding the points of a standard for cocks and hens, I have avoided the question of size. If they are not too small nor too large, size is of little importance. Our present purpose is only to lay down some facts that will help the breeder to foretell about what weights he will get, and this might be deferred to a later head, but for the fact that the purpose of selecting brood stock may influence the choice. The plan may be to rear heavy weights, light weights, or middle weights.

A cock that weighs over 6 lbs. in condition is termed a "Shakebag," and is fit to fight any cock regardless of size. Barring accidents, a six pound cock that is in good fix and active will whip one a pound heavier but without activity. It is the rarest thing that a big cock is lively on his feet and swift enough to keep himself warm. When a cock weighing 6.14 say, in condition is active, quick, and strong in proportion, he is simply irresistible; but such are very few and far between. No matter how carefully some fowl are bred, almost invariably, if bred for size, they degenerate, become coarse, and are not even approximately equal to their smaller and more refined relations. The prettiest fighters in American pits average from 4.04 to 5.08. Yet, the eternal cry is for big cocks! In Lord Derby's heyday, five pounds made a cock of fine size. The Spaniards of today consider anything over four pounds too common to keep. For brood purposes cocks running from 5.04 to 6.04 make the best for stock getters. Of course now and then a 4.12 or 7.0 cock may be found fully up to all requirements, but the little cock must be bred to hens of good size and the big one to hens not over the average; that is, if you want cocks that are easily matched, such as are neither sparrows nor ostriches. The following table is approximately correct:

Cock	Hen	Male Offspring
5 lbs.	4 lbs.	4.12 to 5.04.
5.08 lbs.	4 lbs.	5.04 to 5.12.
5.12 lbs.	4 lbs.	5.08 to 6 .
6 lbs.	4 lbs.	5.12 to 6.04.
7 lbs.	4 lbs.	6 to 6.12.

Using this table as a basis, if the size of the cock, or hen, or both, be increased there will be a proportionate increase in the size of the male offspring at full maturity, that is, in their second suit of feathers.

Quite an interesting formula of mine for getting the average weights of cocks bred from hen and cock of a given weight is the following:

Add the cock's and the hen's weights together, add one, then add the ounces or pounds the cock is over five pounds, and the hen over four pounds, then divide by two: the result will give the average weight of cocks you may expect from your matings. Thus in the table above, add the second cock's 5.08 to his hen's 4.0 and you have 9; add 1 lb. and the 8 ozs. the cock is over 5 lbs; this gives you 11 lbs; now divide by 2 and you have 5.08, which means that if you breed a cock weighing 5.08 to a hen weighing 4.0 lbs. you may expect cocks averaging five pounds, eight ounces.

Suppose a second case: The cock weighs 5.04, the hen 4.04:—5.04 plus 4.04 plus 1 plus 4 plus 4 equals 11 lbs; divide by 2 and the result is 5 lbs, 8 ozs.

THE GAME FOWL.

Another: Cock is 6.02, hen 4.06: 6.02 plus 4.06 plus 1 plus 1.02 plus 6 equals to 13; 13 divided by 2 gives 6.08.

While outside crosses may bring about considerable variation, this formula is reasonably accurate and is a safe guide. One more case: Cock is 6.0, hen 3.10: 6.0 plus 3.10 plus 1 lb. plus 16 ozs. equals to 11.10; divide by 2 and you have 5.13.

The breeder will, of course, wish to know what he is doing, and he may as well understand in this connection that in preparing for battle a cock in fair flesh loses according to size, from 4 to 20 ounces, if he comes from his walk in proper condition. As a general thing, a cock that runs about 5.08 on his walk should be fought at about 4.14. He can be fought in long heels at 5.02, in good fix. A cock running 6.08 can be fought in elegant condition at 5.10, though he would more than likely come to 5.13 in perfect health, with less risk. In Philadelphia Rules it must not be forgotten that three ounces will be given a cock for the hood and feathers. Thus a cock actually weighing 5.10 can be fought at 5.07. It is, therefore, possible in these rules to fight a 6.08 in perfect fix at 5.07. I have seen a cock weighing 7.06 fought in thirteen days at 6.04 check, and win, in Maryland Rules. Cocks are fought from two to four ounces heavier in long heels than in short. However, I have seen a fine cock win a long dragging fight in long heels, after being reduced from 7.02 to 6.0 lbs. More will be found on this subject in a later chapter.

MATING.

Mating is unquestionably one of the mysteries of successful breeding. It is a striking fact that no matter how excellent may be the record, pedigree and conformation of a cock and a hen, they may not prove a *hit*. A safe rule is never to mate specimens that inherit the same defects. It must never be overlooked that by breeding you can never do more than preserve a virtue, but you can double a vice. Any man who breeds a cock with scruffy legs, to a hen with the same blemish, must not be surprised if *every* chick makes a rough-legged specimen.

Game fowls are like all other animals—they inherit constitutional weaknesses; hence in breeding from new and unknown stock, one takes chances little less uncertain than throwing dice. Some of these radical defects may not render the fowl unfit for a getter, but others cannot be subjects of compromise. If a strain is constitutionally roupy, for illustration, their days are numbered. To breed from them is bad enough but to mate them with roupy stock is murder!

INFLUENCE OF PREVIOUS SIRE.

Some problems in game fowl breeding have never been solved to the full satisfaction of all breeders, although proofs may be of the most convincing nature. One of these problems is: *The influence of previous sire.* That is to say does the sexual intercourse of a cock and a laying hen leave the blood of the cock in the veins of the hen?

At first flush it would be natural to say "No," but let us consider. Time and again we have had positive proof that copulation has influenced the blood of the females, not only in the lower animals, but even in human beings. This has been made as plain to view as the stars that people the sky.

Those that have bred dogs know that if, by way of illustration, a setter bitch has her first litter of pups by a bull dog, every litter she has thereafter will have one pup that shows the bull blood, thus indicating that the blood of that bull dog is in the bitch as long as she lives.

It is a well known fact that a mare bred to a jack always

throws mulish colts thereafter, even if bred to the finest stallion in the world. Her colts always show a dark streak down the back and their ears are larger than they would be if she had never been bred to a jack. Furthermore, some mares so bred either become difficult to get in fold, or altogether sterile. This proves conclusively that the jackass blood is in the mare the remainder of her life.

The writer recalls a case even in the human family showing the influence of a sire upon the female. A lady of pronounced blonde type with auburn hair and blue eyes married a gentleman who was a pronounced brunette. They reared a family of five children—all blonds. This lady has now dark-brown eyes and black hair! Why such a marvelous change?

A professor of biology in Oxford University, England, reports an extremely significant case. A farmer near the city bred one year a white drake to white ducks, and all the ducklings came white. The following year the same ducks were bred to a black drake. The ducklings came mixed in colors. The third year the same white ducks were bred back to a white drake, but every duckling came black! This illustration of the influence of previous sire is too convincing to be questioned.

But coming nearer still to our subject, an experienced and intelligent Texas breeder of game chickens reports a case directly in point. He discontinued breeding game fowl and allowed a Leghorn rooster to run with his game hens. The game chicken fever overcame this gentleman the following year and he took up one of these hens known to be the gamest of the game, let her lay out her litter and set. At the proper time he mated his hen with a first class game cock, and got a lot of stags. Several had large white faces of Leghorns, while some did not. He fought all, and those with the Leghorn faces ran away, while the others fought gamely. Does this not show to the satisfaction of the most skeptical that the blood of that Leghorn rooster got into the blood of that game hen, and was she not ruined for life? Again, if such were the case with this hen, is it not safe to conclude that any game hen is worthless for breeding game cocks if she has ever been bred to a dunghill rooster?

Indeed, do not all of the illustrations, which are based on the very best of authority, point to one conclusion, viz: That the blood of any female is forever affected by that of every male by which she has been impregnated?

"Caesar's wife must be above suspicion," is a maxim that aplies with special force to a game hen, and that although (we had better accept the ungarnished truth) they are instinctive whores. The rule of human conduct laid down by writers on moral philosophy is, "When you do not know whether a thing is right or wrong—do not do it." If there is, then the slightest doubt about the virtue of a game hen, she is not a suitable mate for the most chivalrous of all knights—a thoroughbred game cock!

Many years ago I had a favorite black hen that threw those popular "bobolinks" of that day—black cocks with brass wings-butts, and fighters they were, desperate heelers and the hardest hitters I have ever seen. I bred this hen one year to a black-red cock and in after years, though she ran with bobolink cocks, she would throw as many dark-red cocks as black brasswings.

Such then is the extreme caution necessary to be exercised in the exact art of breeding thoroughbred, dead game cocks, that, need I say, any individual that is the object of suspicion is a dangerous element in a brood pen.

These observations will be received with disfavor by that class of breeders who have old favorites that have met with some misfortune of the kind I have named; indeed these views may be condemned by those that I seem to persuade to destroy a special pet—a fine, well bred game hen that has sometime been running at large with common fowl or that has met an appointment with some neighbor's Plymouth Rock rooster in times gone by. But the object of this work is to set down facts and accept the truth without favor or prejudice; and we can scarcely come to think that any man, be he ever so blind and deaf, could ignore entirely the proofs we have that the blood of a game hen is affected for life by copulation, while laying, with a dunghill cock.

It must follow that a game hen's blood is also influenced by every cock that impregnates her eggs. So that it is a great misfortune to breed a fine, valuable, pet game hen under a so-called game cock. Thus to be perfectly safe, a breeder who values highly some favorite hen certainly takes some risk when he mates his choicest females under an *experimental cock,* and if possible it would be safe to try sisters under the new cock, such as could be discarded without such heavy loss. How often we see even experienced breeders go on trying cocks of new strains, year after year on their choicest hens, and in time discover that runners came from the straight old stock! Can this not come from the influence of previous sire? May not the sprinters come from the blood of some of those experimental cocks you have been trying over your old hens?

I have seen pet hens bred for eight years, to different cocks each year, some to more than one cock in a year. We can easily imagine that such a hen is no more her original self than that woman Dean Milman tells us of in his notes to Gibbon's Decline and Fall of the Roman Empire, who was married twenty-three times. Such females come to resemble a composite photograph in which there is a blurred picture of many faces.

Let us conclude this subject by impressing upon the

breeder the great importance of protecting the virtue of game hens; of guarding them against experimental matings; and finally, of never forgetting the extreme susceptibility of a game pullet to life-long influence of the first male to which she lays an egg. If pullets are not to be mated or bred from, a perfectly safe plan is to run them under their father, uncle or full brothers, if they are to be used for perpetuating the full blood of their strain.

BREEDING TO FEATHER AND TO COLOR.

Danger lies in the path of that man who sacrifices utility for beauty. In breeding game fowl we would do well to remember what Holmes said about choosing a wife: "I chose my wife," said he, "as she chose her wedding dress; not for a glossy surface, but for the qualities that would wear."

The primary object of a breeder should be to breed strong, healthy, highstrung, well built, hard-fighting, bloody-heeled, dead game cocks. Color is the last consideration. Every strain produces an exceptionally beautiful specimen now and then, but my experience has been that these Adonises are rarely up to the standard of a breed. Why? I do not know, but such has been my observation.

It is, then, an extremely difficult task to breed "to a feather" without sacrificing more valuable qualities. By breeding *to a feather* we mean that fine art practiced by the show-pen people, whose first aim is to produce a strain so much alike in markings that only the most experienced eye could detect the difference between two specimens. According to these experts, a cock would be barred and would have no show to win whatever if he were in the black breasted Duckwing Red class and had one brown feather on his thigh. It would be an unpardonable sin to show a cock with a grey feather on his craw in the Silver Duckwing class, no matter how fine a cock he might he. It is next to impossible to breed a game winning strain of fowl *to the feather*. The attempt means a sacrifice of utility for the aesthetic taste. Perhaps the nearest approach to successful breeding to the feather was the Earl of Derby's white legs and streaky beaks. Yet, those fowl were never to that exact standard required in the show-pen. They only approximated a standard. It was quite a common thing for the cocks to show brown in the breast, while the hens varied in color considerably. The reader must not jump to the conclusion from the general description given of famous breeds or strains of the present and of the past, that these fowl were bred *to a feather*. By more careful examination it will be discovered that those famous breeds were of a general color but were only uniform as to color. Thus, "Ginn's Greys" may be all shades of grey. The "Black Devils," recently come into popularity, are not all black by any means; not any more so than the Blackhorse Cavalry of Confederate fame was a body of men who rode black horses. Times were when a blackhorseman was glad to have any horse at all—bay, roan, or even white; certainly after the novelty of war vanished before the serious reality of fighting Yankee regulars.

Breeding to a color is entirely different from breeding *to a feather*. The former is easy and feasible. Refined and successful breeding requires judicious in-breeding, which in most instances results in a fixed color. That is to say, the Kearney Whitehackles are *light reds,* with white or yellow legs. If ten thousand are bred there will never be a single one with black legs or dark plumage. Yet the Whitehackles vary widely in shades and markings, and are not of such standard as show judges demand of winners. So it is with the pure Warhorses. While they are dark-reds, no man expects every cock to be of the same shade of red. In fact, some may come very dark duck-wing reds, and even brown-reds. The legs are sometimes blue and sometimes green, while eyes vary in color widely. The Allen Roundheads are an in-bred strain, also, yet while they are reds, they are of no particular description of red. Nor is it true of course that in-bred strains are necessarily of one color. Col. Grist's fowl are all in-bred and line-bred, and yet from the "Champion Family" he often gets a grey from red parents. From his Grady Family he gets a blue sometimes.

It is easy to fix a type in pit game fowl and just as easy to preserve that type. For this purpose brown-reds are easily bred. This is a strong color, characteristic of many of the finest cocks that ever feathered a pit. Varying from mahogany, which makes an extremely handsome fowl, to a bright golden ginger, they make a fascinating breed and give little trouble to retain that color. No matter how long bred, they remain brown-reds. This is not true of Pyles. In attempting to breed to a color in Pyles it often happens that they vary so much as to fade out, so to speak, while Dominiques easily, after long years of in-breeding, run into "Smocks" and Pyles.

The introduction of fresh blood often destroys a standard of color, though if it is desired to retain a given color nothing is easier, if a little caution be exercised. To illustrate: Let us suppose that a breeder of Gulls desires fresh blood and wishes to retain the color; the plan to pursue would be to secure a breeding pen from some thoroughly reliable breeder, of as nearly the same general markings as the Gulls;— say a pen of Whitehackles. After the blood had been mixed there would be a fresh infusion of blood but no change in color. Hence, a good Heathwood cock would answer for the infusion of fresh blood into any family of yellow-legged bright-reds. The method for making out-crosses has been discussed elsewhere.

ODDITIES OF COLOR.

Some observations are in point as to peculiar colors so much fancied by many fanciers and some practical cockers. I do not believe the Dominiques come up to the high standard of such fowl as the dark-reds, brown-reds, and light-reds. Quite an interesting article appeared in July Grit and Steel of 1904, in which a tabulated record of colors was given with the battles fought by different colors for one year. In forty-nine battles the Dominiques lost nine more than they won. However, it is foreign to my plan to criticise any color or strain. There can be no question that as far back as I can discover any authentic history of the Dominique feather, about the year 1750, when they were called "cuckoos," in England, they had devoted admirers, as they have in America at the present day, especially in Kentucky. Those gentlemen are not so much interested, of course, in what the writer may think of Dominiques as they are in some useful information as to the perfection and preservation of their favorite feather. I have experimented extensively with this color and set down such safe conclusions as I have gleaned after many years' labor. Elsewhere I have stated that the Dominique, in some respects, is a mystery. No matter how little of the blood may run in a cock's veins, if he be of the Dominique color he will throw his color bountifully, both stags and pullets, but far better marked in brown-red and black hens. The rock upon which Dominique breeders often split is breeding to long and persistently in and in or line breeding the feather which caused them to become whiter and whiter the longer they are so bred. The same error is in the selection of the wrong color when fresh blood is infused. If the simple rule—avoid light colors to save the Dominique feather—be implicitly obeyed, it will prove easy enough to retain Dominiques of the prettiest markings. Put a Dominique cock over brown-red hens with dark legs and the offspring will be many red Dominique stags of a fixed type, as well as Dominique pullets with red Dominique necks. Legs are always white, yellow or spotted. No Dominique cock ever has green, blue or black legs. Put the same Dominique cock over solid black hens of a breed that throws solid black or black-breasted cocks, and the get will be the best, clearest marble Dominique stags and pullets. It seems to be settled beyond dispute that the clearest and best marked Dominiques result from a clearly marked cock or hen crossed on a black hen or cock. If the desire is to get a lot of perfect marble Dominiques, put a clearly marked Dominique cock with no red feathers, or as little as possible, with a yard of hens that throw black cocks. As to color of legs, the handsomest results will be gotten by using a white-legged Dominique stag or cock marked clearly, over a yard of black hens that usually throw black cocks—dark-legged hens preferred. *Breed away from light colors always to dark colors to perfect and preserve the Dominique feather.*

I have advised the use of a Dominique *cock* in fixing the color, because the most singular results come from the use of a hen. It is impossible to get a Dominique pullet from a Dominique hen under an *off-colored* cock. Put a black cock over a Dominique hen and the offspring will be, *all stags Dominiques; all pullets other colors—not one a Dominique.* While this has been stated to be true of greys, it is not absolutely true of any other feather besides the Dominiques.

However, the choice of color in your fowl must be governed by the same rule as the culture of fruits; select that which best suits the locality. Black bears thrive in the tropics, but the polar bear is white; grapes that thrive in Greece would die in New York. So it is with game chickens. It has been well known to cockers for nearly two hundred years that certain colors did best in certain localities. Wm. Sketchley tells us in his work that a strain of reds in his day (1814) from one part of England were worthless when bred in other parts of that island. By a sort of "survival of the fittest" on this same principle, Kentucky has become the home of the Dominique, Maryland produces the best Grays (black), the Southern States the best dark-reds, the Northern States the best Pyles and Light-reds. Very rarely is it true that deep black-reds of the Warhorse color thrive in the North. There can be little question that a greater variety of colors reach a high degree of excellence in the Southern States, especially in South Carolina, Georgia and Mississippi. While the North produced the different families of Whitehackles and the Gulls, that won a world-wide reputation as well as other strains of the light colors, with the single exception, perhaps, of Joe Wingate's brown-reds and Jarv Ellis's Blackhackles of Pennsylvania, no dark-reds have won anything more than local reputation, certainly in modern times. There is little to pass down to posterity from the great sporting State of Kentucky but the record of her blues, which is already history, and her Dominiques. But South Carolina, Georgia and Mississippi produce the highest grade of deep black-reds, grays of all shades, brown-reds and light-reds of all shades. While a breed of Pyles known as "Cotton Bolls" have won some distinction, they have never merited a place with the colors named before, as bred in the South. The Kearney Whitehackles of New York are said to be just as good in the hands of R. C. Davis, of South Carolina, as they are in New York. Dark-reds thrive in the Middle States, Maryland and the District of Columbia. Reds, grays and muffs reach a high degree of excellence in Maryland. The best muffs and grays bred in America are unquestionably in and around Baltimore.

Returning to the subject of mixing colors: While it is unwise and dangerous to breed for a feather or too much with an eye to color, yet it must not be forgotten that indiscriminate mixing is also a source of disappointment. Wm. Gilliver seems to be the most indiscriminate breeder located in England at this day. His fowl appear to be bred very much as are the Irish fowl, "just any old color." But the best of old English breeders opposed the Irish practice and claimed the mixing of colors showed "a lack of refinement in breeding." While the essentials must never be sacrificed to color, there can be no doubt that in a majority of instances certain colors do not "nick," and will not produce satisfactory results. I have observed a complete failure come from breeding a yellow-legged Irish Grey cock over green-legged Kentucky blue hens. Some crosses of blue and grey produce fine blue-gray cocks, but only certain colors seem to nick. Perhaps it may be safe to say that darkblues and grays with dark legs will produce the best results. I do not care to breed from reds with dark legs and Pyles nor grays over Pyles. Blacks rarely nick with Pyles. In fact very few colors do "hit" with the Pyle feather. Some regard must be had as to the color of legs and beaks. Dark legs over yellow or white often produce what is called "terrapin,," or "tortoise-shell" legs. Some admire legs of this color, but few. The prettiest terraipn leg comes from a cross of black legs and yellow. Dark-legged fowl do not give good results if mixed with white-legged ones, unless the young come as a cross I once saw made of a Kearney Whitehackle cock with white legs over a yard of brown-red hens. The chicks divided; about half took the cock's color while the other half came to the hen's color, though somewhat lighter. This was the result of crossing two in-bred strains.

One more consideration as to feather. By examination of several individuals it will be discovered that they differ widely in the number of feathers in the fan of the tail. Some cocks and hens show only six, some seven, rarely over eight. Cocks often have six sickle feathers in the tail and six in the fans. While cocks do not fight with their tails, yet, as between equally good individuals, I would prefer a cock and hen with seven or eight feathers in the fan of the tail. This gives a cock a much handsomer appearance when trimmed for battle and gives him better support when 'throw upon his tail in battle. Fowl so feathered usually carry a pretty, spread tail and are more gamey looking—less like the cowardly, whip-tail show birds that are a slander on the name of a game cock.

INBREEDING.

In-breeding consists not only in breeding over his pullets and hens under his stags, but the mating of close relations, such as brother and sister, uncle and niece, aunt and nephew, or the same in the half blood, also first cousin back and forth.

It does not take many generations for a strain to become strictly an in-bred strain of fowls. For instance, if a cock is bred to his own daughters and the get mated together, they are closely in-bred at once, and will show the characteristics of all in-bred fowl.

There are many points of interest to be considered in this subject. In the first place, there is no other way to fix a type; in the second place, what is the effect on the constitution of the birds and on their spirit; also, what results, good and bad, flow from it.

A progressive farmer in Kansas has brought to perfection a breed of Poled Hereford cattle in the following manner: He was breeding a short-horned bull over registered Hereford cows, and among the young one season he got a bull calf *without horns*. He at once conceived the desire to originate a breed of hornless cattle and made a start by mating this young bull with his old stock. Afterwards he put this bull over his own get twice, then went back to the old stock for fresh blood. He has now two herds of elegant, large, healthy, fine hornless cattle, for which he is getting fancy prices.

This illustrates how *types* can be fixed in any kind of animals. It was in this way that pouter pigeons, rufflers, tumblers, and fantails were developed from the original common pigeons. Almost any type can thus be fixed in a strain of fowl by judicious in-breeding, and that without destroying the constitution and without any deterioration. In this particular we must not confuse man with the lower animals. Those opposed to in-breeding often refer us to the fallacy of in-breeding as shown in the case of too close inter-marriage, or incest. It is true that the human race would be idiotic degenerates in perhaps two generations if brothers and sisters married and the laws of nature did not prohibit incest. But this does not prove the same to be true in the lower animals. For instance, all the English sparrows in America sprang from one little cage brought to this country a few years ago; yet these little mischief-makers are just as noisy, happy, strong and aggressive as the old stock in England. The Chinese pheasants and quail of the West sprang from only a few specimens imported in recent years. We are also aware of the fact that our own quail almost always mate within the flock, but they look just the same to me now as they did when I was a boy, and very old men give in the same experience.

These illustrations go to prove that incest is not against the natural law in the lower animals as among men. Therefore no analogy can be discovered, and proofs against in-breeding cannot be drawn from comparisons with the human race.

There is no question that domestication tends to degrade an animal's constitution. While they may by scientific crossing and feeding increase in size and beauty, their natural hardihod is vitiated *to a certain extent*. Suppose any domestic animal were compelled to shift for a living like wild animals; for instance, even a Harlem goat turned loose in the Rocky Mountains, how long before that goat would be all hide and whiskers? If our finest Jersey cows were let go in the forests, what would be their condition in a few months? If our most beautiful and largest game fowl were turned adrift, how long before they would perish or degenerate? You who have put your stags on bad walks can answer this question. I loaned a condensed idiot twelve thrifty hens and a stag once, but they were required by the rules of his house to prepare their own bill of fare. This essence of lunacy complained to me that he was "not getting a single egg." I went to see what the trouble was and it took me just one hour to find the birds (following cows in a field half a mile from the house). A strong breeze would have carried the whole flock into the next county. I did not receive a single hen; all were ruined by neglect. But pheasants and wild turkeys were thriving in the same vicinity. Domesticated animals become less active and self-reliant, instinct weakens and the natural constitution is degraded. I have never heard of a wild turkey's having the "gapes," and such diseases are unknown among wild chickens.

Therefore the difference between in-breeding among wild animals and those that are domesticated consists in the fact that tame animals are more liable to have some constitutional vice than wild ones, and for this reason greater care is necessary to avoid breeding to a fault. To be plainer, if a cock with a roached back is bred to a hen with a roached back the tendency to roach-back chickens is doubled. Thus if the hen's back is nearly flat and perfect she will throw defective chicks, if she is a sister or daughter of the cock, more freely than if she were no kin to the cock. Fowls closely related inherit the same defects and when in-bred those defects will be doubled. For this reason, a cock with constitutional roup bred to his own sister will more than likely produce roupy chicks, because the sister has the same tendencies in her blood as the cock. And here is the chief objection to in-breeding, viz: Brood stock that are closely akin are likely to have the same constitutional tendencies, hence when bred together must produce chicks even more defective than their parents. If, then, for generations, such fowl are bred together, can it be surprising that very few good specimens appear?

Granted that all fowl have some serious constitutional derangement, and it must follow that in-breeding is bad; but it is not true that all strains of fowl have *serious* constitutional troubles, hence in-breeding cannot be condemned. On the other hand, as many benefits may flow from in-breeding; *when the breeders are free from defects* it would not be logical to condemn in-breeding.

It must follow that in-breeding is advisable if done with good, sound stock and with discretion. In fact, certain benefits flow from the practice that are impossible otherwise.

One of the desirable results of in-breeding, besides the fixing of a type, is the greater *uniformity* secured. Fowl crossed out frequently are very irregular in appearance, formation, and behavior. They inherit in too many directions at once. By actual experience it has been observed that in-bred game fowl not only are physically similar, but they are strikingly alike in characteristics. I have seen strains so long in-bred as not only to become as sure as night and day in color and general make-up, but they all even crowed alike; while there might be a difference in the *pitch* of the voice, there was always something that suggested those strains. I have noted this in Smith's Black and Tans; they all have similarity in their crows. I have followed these same fowl to a number of pits and seen them show more uniformity in fighting than any other strain of dark-reds I have ever known.

There are many most valuable points in uniformity. In the first place, you soon discover whether a uniform breed is worthy of perpetuation for, if they are bad, you will be fully convinced, for nearly all will show the fatal defect; whereas fowl that are not uniform deceive and encourage the breeder till he is led into great trouble. I have seen this illustrated repeatedly. Mr. Morgan tried a cross on his Whitehackles, in-bred for years and thought from excellent results in one main that he had made a "hit," but before the winter was over he was completely disillusioned by having the same cross ignominiously defeated and their worthlessness entirely proven.

It is, all things being equal, much safer to stake large sums of money on a uniform strain, because you can, in the first place, before you ever agree to bet, form an opinion as to your chances; you know what you are doing, because when you see one fight you can generally form an idea as to what the rest will do. If one quits they are usually all unsafe; if one goes in right, follows up right and wins a game fight, the prospect is you have a good show to win. In equal condition in-bred cocks are more than likely to fight alike. If one is a high-flying, clean-sparring, and aggressive bird the others will show the same characteristics. If one shuffles low to the ground, expect to see all fight to that standard.

Again, cocks that are uniform in characteristics and constitution are much easier to condition and give much less trouble in the feeding coops. If a feeder is compelled to treat every cock in his house differently he has such a job that he can but despair of winning unless the other fellow is in equally as bad a fix. It is for this reason that the great feeders have usually fought the same strain. For instance, Dick Lee made his reputation fighting Redhorse fowl. These were inbred chickens and uniform. Tom Rogers, Wm. Morgan's feeder, usually loses when he is not fighting Morgan's Whitehackles; whereas, with Whitehackles he has won nearly all the mains he has fought. Morgan's fowl have been in-bred for years. I have seen numerous cases where good feeders with motley coops of fowl have been whipped by ordinary feeders with coops of in-bred fowl of one strain. The fact is cockers generally expect trouble when an opponent shows a whole main of the same feather. Why? Because they are usually uniform in quality and likely to come to a high standard, they are likely all to be in the same condition, and if one is a good, game fighter all will be. In this connection it is a striking fact that no great feeder has ever made a reputation but by fighting in-bred strains of fowl. If we start back with the days of Sketchley, whose memory ran back to 1760, we find not one feeder mentioned in the history of cocking except in connection with some in-bred strain of fowl, and today every man of national reputation in the pit is associated with some strain of in-bred fowl, that has done its part in making him famous.

By in-breeding it must not be forgotten that not only feathers and form are fixed, but mental qualities as well. There are certain inevitable, and yet most desirable, traits secured by in-breeding. If the birds were worth perpetuation on account of some superior virtues, these will be characteristic of the strain. The fowl become more nervy, quicker, of a higher temper, and therefore, they are apt to fight a sluggish, cross-bred cock to death before he wakes up.

Speed does not hurt cocks in any gaff if they are good at the heel; but it must follow that, for long heels, judiciously inbred cocks would be decidedly superior to miscellaneous crosses, because being more high-strung and of a violent temper they have a lightning-like rapidity that soon ends the battle. In proof of this position, I believe it is true, certainly as far as I am informed, that every distinguished breeder in the Southern States has his own in-bred strain of fowls. I believe Col. Grist has not made an outcross on his fowl for years; McGinty claims always he hurt his Warhorses by trying the experiment; Mr. Allen, of Mississippi, has in-bred his Roundheads for years; and Hopkinson, who spread the John Stone Irish over the South, has in-bred the original stock to the present time. It is certainly significant to a thinking man that all these strains of fowls as well as those at the North, that have made a national reputation, have been in-bred. In the way of general summary, the greatest fowl in the recent history of American cock fighting are: Redhorses, Black Hackles, Warhorses, Grist's Shawlneck breeds; and Whitehackles—all in-bred!

However, no matter how careful and expert a breeder may be, certain evils are unavoidable in the course of time, and must be rectified, or the strain will retrograde and become degenerate. I hear men say now and then, that they have game fowl not crossed out for forty years! I think there must be some error in such statements. It may be possible to in-breed forty years successfully, but I think not. If game fowl were of the same uniform constitutional perfection as Jungle Fowls, this would be possible, but, as domestication vitiates natural vigor, there are so many risks to be run a man could scarcely avoid them all for forty years. It must not be forgotten that the slightest deefct that appears in a strain of in-bred fowl is ineradicable and increases every generation. So that in course of time, every specimen in an in-bred flock will show this defect, and by it they will be rendered worthless. Roup is generally found among fowl in-bred for many years, and unless something is done to diminish the constitutional tendency, the whole flock will be ruined.

The old English rule for keeping in-bred fowl up to the standard was: Breed only soundest specimens, and always youth to age, or youth to youth. Therefore, especially should we avoid breeding an old cock over old hens—all being closely related. If old stock are bred, cocks must be bred to pullets and old hens under good, strong, healthy stags. Two-year-old hens under a yearling stag, in my opinion, all things being equal, will bring the very best results, although I have had fine fowl from an old cock over yearling pullets. One thing I have noticed plainly: the get from an old cock on pullets, while they may not appear to better advantage as stags, will have much more vigor and live longer than the get of the same cock over hens. An old stud gets sleepy colts—you have heard it; suppose the mare is also old. I candidly believe in-bred fowl will give the best results if youth is bred to youth. Therefore, I would breed closely in-bred fowl—*a strong ,healthy, forward stag over two year old hens or yearling pullets.* While cross breeders may breed from all sorts of old *pensioners*, in-breeders cannot safely run the risk, because old fowl are more likely to have vices of constitution than young ones, and they have less vitality. The only thing a man can do with a very old cock that has become a great favorite is to put aside prejudice and place the old fellow on his pension roll; he may do for a pet, but he is out of business as a getter.

But with all this, the time will come when fresh blood is necessary. Here is the rock on which nearly all of the old breeders have been wrecked. There is no question that striking the right thing is *purely luck*. I *have* thought it wise to breed to similar feather and while I struck it once and got fowl just as good as the old stock, an acquaintance of mine has tried it with disastrous results. On the other hand, I have seen an outcross made of entirely different feather with most satisfactory results. I have seen the Redhorse crossed on Whithackles and produce game winners from the start. Then bred back, they were always good; but there is no unfailing rule for securing fresh blood. You must take your chances. You had better try to get fowl just as much like your own in *mental* traits as you possibly can, regardless of feather, and those you know to be game. Make your outcross on the very best of both, always using the best.

Even after you have gone back till you have only one-eighth, or even a sixteenth, of the fresh blood, your fowl may be entirely unlike the original stock, and then you may at the quarter not be able to distinguish the crosses from the pure stock. I notice this plainly in my fowl crossed on the Irish I imported in 1893. On the Redhorse blood, even in the thirty-second, I see the Irish plainly, while over my Whitehackles the Irish blood is hardly perceptible in the half bloods.

What I have written may not coincide with the experience of many of my readers; the conclusions I have arrived at are based on actual experience and I believe in the main are correct. While I have been lengthy the subject is of so great interest and importance that I hardly think I could have used my space to greater advantage. There are many discoveries to be made yet, and I am in hopes all troubles may soon be cleared away by the progress in biological science.

CROSSING.

However, fresh blood is necessary in the long run, not

because in-breeding cannot be successfully pursued for any length of time, but because breeders become too confident and careless to make judicious selections and obey the rules; because the best of men err at times. This necessity for fresh blood is the rock upon which most famous breeders have been wrecked. Some form the habit of outcrossing and never get over it; others make injudicious crosses and their stock degenerates; others still make a hit and utilizing the fresh blood to the greatest advantage keep to the front and continue to win.

Where and how to procure fresh blood as well as how to use it is the most important consideration.

I have already taken the position that the best is cheap at any price, while inferior stuff is not worth even the tenth part of what it costs. Deal with the men that fight their cocks, not in hacks, but in mains where large sums of money are at stake. The country is filled with hack fighters but there are in reality very few that fight mains. Men who will show twenty-one brothers in one coop and fight for $100 to $1,000 are, all things being equal, pretty safe men to deal with, if they are men of integrity. If your purpose is to secure most reliable blood for actual pit purposes, you must find a professional cock fighter of experience who will wager his last dollar on his birds against all comers. Sporting men are not in the habit of giving their money away, and they have always some good reason for expecting to win when they put their money up. Novices stake their money upon sentiment; professionals upon probability of success. A neophyte bets on a cock because he likes that cock; a professor of the sod because he thinks for good reasons, the bird can win. These are the reasons why *caeteris paribus* the stock of a professional is best. In the selection then, of fresh blood, I would first find the right man; in the next place I would pay for the best, if the stock is pur-

THE GAME FOWL. 75

chasable, or get it through some friendly influence. Having gotten the new blood, the next thing is how to use it.

It is to be hoped that the birds you have procured are as similar to your own in color and characteristics as possible —if not identical, the nearer the better. Now for the mating: Put the male with your females, and if you have a female of the new stock, put her with a male of your own. This gives you the advantage of trying the infusion from two directions at the same time, and while one may prove unsatisfactory, the other may prove superb, and your time is not lost. The second year put a strong, active stag of the cross, up to the standard, with a yard of not over six of your best hens, full sisters preferred. This will give you stags and pullets three-quarters your own and one-quarter of the new blood. At the same time you might have run a cock of your own over a yard of the crossed pullets. This gives you two yards of the one-quarter blood. At this point in your crossing, you should fight as many of the crosses as possible of your first year's breeding. If they measure up to your expectations, proceed to a more thorough commingling. You have some three-quarters in two pens. Put one of your own cocks three years old, free from constitutional defects, over a yard of your three-quarter pullets, and a hardy, forward stag of the three-quarter blood over a yard of your straight hens three years old. The following fall you will have two lots of birds with only one-eighth of the fresh blood in them, the other seven-eights your own blood. If you have done this judiciously you will find these birds of the seven-eights blood will be about free from the troubles that beset you in the start. You can now use the various crosses you have for fresh blood many years to come, and by throwing the birds in the seven-eights pen together you are practically at home again.

IMPORTATION.

In this connection it may not be out of place to say something on the question of importation. There are few men in the Union that have spent more money and more time in importation than the writer. He is, therefore, prepared to give the reader the benefit of practical experience. In the first place there is no more expensive practice in the business. I paid $50 for a pair, $50 for a trio, $33 for a single hen, and about $75 for another lot in a few months. These importations were made by a man full of experience of men and affairs, and he could readily see how easy a thing it would be for an enthusiastic novitiate to export his gold to Europe and get in exchange table fowl at the cost of $5 a pound. If it is so extremely difficult to find the right man here at home, how are your chances across the seas? Private correspondents, whose letters I am not at liberty to publish, write me that the laws in England are so rigid against cock fighting that sportsmen of that country cannot afford to have accounts of mains in England appear even in American publications. Very, very rarely does an English cocker of standing sell a cock; they never advertise, and we cannot frequent their pits. How, then are we to find the right man in England? It is plainly a task beyond the average man's ability. The difficulty is even greater with Ireland, and the French are so far behind us in the *art* of cock fighting we could scarcely be benefited by infusion of Gaelic blood. The French and the Belgian cocks weigh from eight to twelve pounds, and a cock of 4.12 in condition would be as great a curiosity there as a cock of ten pounds would be here. Their spurs are either horn or the crudest kind of steel *eperons,* and their cocks show a lack of refinement in breeding. From Spain we cannot hope to get desirable fresh blood, as their methods are totally different. Their cocks are bred to fight in natural spurs and are instinctive "wheelers." They are considered very course if they weigh over four pounds. There are apparent reasons, then, why we cannot expect much from Spain. A little more attention must be given Japan and China. In my humble opinion, there never has broken out among the breeders of any form of live stock a more disastrous and fatal epidemic than *Japamania.* To expect the best results from an infusion of this oriental blood is to expect the stream to rise higher than the source, and when any man places himself squarely in opposition to the axioms and proverbs of science and religion he is on untenable ground. It is astonishing how such men can apostatise the faithful and make converts in the face of truth, yet, through a small beginning in the state of California this country has become infected with what is known as "grade Japs." These Japanese chickens are some carefully imported from supposed cockers in Japan (who never saw a steel gaff in their lives), but most are brought over in steamers from China and sold to *gullibles* on the western coast for game fowls. Who in our land would breed on stock from a man that never saw a gaff? Even if the fowl were game according to our standard, they are not bred for our style of fighting and are totally different in every way from our pit game cocks. These fowl are bred in their own country to fight with their *beaks,* hence their predisposition to *bite* instead of kicking—a most dangerous fault in steel fighting; they have not feathers enough to hide their skin; they are tall and ungainly; lastly, while there may be game ones according to our requirements, in Japan, they have never reached these shores. Therefore, to cross good game chickens with those "Johns," as they are called in California, is to dispose of one-half of the merits of your old reliables for one-half of the biting propensity, the short feathers, and the lack of gameness according to our definition. This is a mathematical necessity, and all the eloquence and plausibility on earth cannot disprove it. But their advocates reply, "Try the quarter and the eighth." "Yes," we will add, "till you have the sixty-fourth." From their own mouths we have the confession that you want but a fourth or an eighth of the blood. Seems that it would be impossible to have too much of a good thing!

The fact is these birds have never done a single thing worthy of record in the full blood, and after fifteen years of promise and prophesy in the crosses, they have not accomplished enough to live at best. Further, it is quite significant that the very best men North and South condemn them to a man and do not breed Japs in any fraction of the blood. Sporting men are for winners; they have had ample time and opportunity to investigate this question. Why do they condemn and not contract Japamania? I will be bold enough to say that these observations are all made in a full knowledge of the subject gotten by careful personal investigation extending over several years with every opportunity, and upon a personal knowledge of the best men in the business, and the general condition of cock fighting in America.

It has really been amusing to follow up Jap enthusiasts conclusions; they often condone in these fowl what they would promptly condemn in our own fowl. Just after my contribution adverse to Japs appeared in Grit and Steel Vol. 1 No. — a gentleman who is absolutely wrapped up in these Asiatics complained that his sales had fallen off and proceeded to argue the injustice of proving these fowls a menace to the integrity of the American game fowl. He insisted upon their gameness with so great earnestness as to almost bring tears of repentance to my eyes, when lo, and behold, the very next paper I received, contained an account of a runaway Jap from this very same man. He has been silent since, but he will bob up serenely when the shock passes away and the charitable mantle of forgetfulness shall have hid his misfortune from memory. If, perchance, he identify himself, I beg of him and all of those who are similarly unfortunate, to remember that it is no ill will towards them that prompts me to urge the breeders of this country to avoid these Japanese crosses; my earnest hope is to get the prodigal to return and keep the other members of the family from going astray, as Brutus would put it: "Not that I love Caesar less but Rome more." Those of us to whom in the lottery of human life the duty has fallen to do the writing for the fraternity must be fully impressed with the weight of the obligation and of the duty they owe to those whose confidence they may inspire. If the day ever comes when this effort shall be a text book for the craft, I ought to be inspired by candor, fairness, and strict adherence to the lines of truth. These considerations prompt me to advocate what I know may bring financial injury even to those whom I am least disposed to injure, but, if there is to be grafted on this country an error in breeding, that with the progress of time, will unquestionably contaminate the blood of every game chicken in the Union, I should be false to my trust, were I to avoid a subject that is fraught with so much importance.

The writer has often been addressed on the subject of Aseels. He has experimented with two strains of them and while in many ways they are superior to the Japs and are evidently, according to Asiatic standards, finer far than the Johns, they, too, are unfit for crossing with our fowls. There are perhaps some Aseels that will chop out game in England and in the United States, but they have the other deficiencies of the Japs—too much bill fighting, feathers too short, and disposition to exceeding tardiness in battle.

The cocking fraternity, like law, religion, politics and letters, is filled with dreamers, and El Dorado hunters, but like Ponce de Leon, De Soto and the Alchemists, their lives are doomed to disappointment, and the only epitaph becoming their tombs will be the one word, "Failure." To those who will "lend me their ears" I will say that there are some elegant dead game breeds of game cocks in both Ireland and in England, but only in rare cases and at heavy expense can they be gotten. Even then they are no better than our best, so all in all, it is unwise for any but men of great experience and international acquaintanceship to embark in the business of making foreign crosses. My purpose is not to enter upon any encomium on our country, but ingenuity is inseparably connected with all that pertains to the game chicken business, and these States have easily distanced the world along that line. Hence, nothing but curiosity excuses the importation of game fowl. I confess having my share of that feminine virtue, but I am, also as a consequence, here to testify. If there is any one single thing of necessity and great importance that these States can learn from Europe, I am at a loss to discover that thing. From what Great Britain considered her *inferior* blood we have developed into a nation that has eclipsed the mother country; we got the *best* game fowl from Great Britain to start with, why should we not surpass them in cocks and cocking? I am aware that men of boasted experience do not need these suggestions, but they are penned with the best of motives, for those of the fraternity who are always willing to listen to honest counsel and for those aspiring beginners who are to take up the work where we put it down, and project into the future what is good and bad in the present.

BREEDING PLACES.

Granted that we have fit males and females, our next task is to secure a suitable home, where the surroundings will all combine to bring the best results. Sunshine, grass water, comfortable quarters, and proper food must all have careful attention.

Two systems of breeding are common—the *pen* and the *walk* system. In some respects the pen is superior to the walk; so far as individual attention, control of diet, and such details are concerned the breeding pen is best, but if a thoroughly suitable place is found where the birds can be bred in freedom, they are incomparably better off, and the labor of breeding is very much less. The conditions are for what I would call a *complete breeding place*.

1. Rather *rolling,* so that water does not stand in puddles long after a rain and stagnate about the premises. Damp places are usually very hurtful to both old and young game fowl, and stagnant water is very injurious to them.

2. *Woods* near by, where the hens can find both shade and plenty of leaves to work in. Industrious hens raise industrious chickens, but if the hens have no opportunity to work they will idle around and become sickly. Both laying hens and those with chicks find many forms of worms and *larvae* by scratching in the woods, and my rule is to run the risk of losing a few from varments rather than to be deprived of the advantages connected with the woods. A small body of woods will serve every purpose, and often is more protection against hawks than injury by way of foxes, minks, &c.

3. *Running water is* indispensible; if all your chickens have to be watered from an old pot or a trough, like pigs, your losses will be heavy; you are more than likely to have the cholera among the flock; the gapes will attack your young and what you do raise will not be of the best. There-

fore you must have a spring or running stream near by.

4. Close *proximity to a field of grain* works like a charm. Of course you must look carefully after feeding them until the grain ripens, but after harvest you will have a beautiful lot of birds if you allow them the freedom of a field of wheat, oats or rye. They thrive on any kind of grain, and those who are able to do so plant different kinds of grain in patches about the place, such as wheat, rye, oats, barley and millet. They are specially fond of eating millet from the stalk, and it is particularly good diet for the young birds. Corn is the best food for game chickens in winter, but almost any other kind of grain is better from springtime out.

5. A clean, well ventilated *house* supplied with ample nests and roost poles. But more on this point later. The fowls must be provided with perfectly healthful places to sleep and to lay. When the weather opens and is no longer severe, a good cedar tree makes the best kind of roost, provided the fowls are safe from thieves and varments.

6. *No other fowls* of any kind should be allowed to stay on the walk where you are breeding game chickens. Ducks and geese will poison them through the water; turkeys fight and bother them; and guineas tease the hens and often pluck the feathers from your brood cock and kill the young chicks.

7. *Isolation* is absolutely necessary. Disaster will surely overtake any breeder who trusts his brood stock to the risks of having them so near to other chickens that a strange cock can get with his hens. It has been said that a game hen is an instinctive whore. I dislike to slander the dear creatures, but we must protect their virtue, hence it is best to avoid all danger by having them at least half a mile from dunghill fowls. I have often known dunghill cocks to wander away from home a quarter of a mile; suppose one met a favorite

game hen! A friend tells me of a hen of his that he discovered in the suburbs of town meeting her engagements several hundred yards from home, in the most stealthy manner, with a Plymouthrock waiting at the corner for her. As soon as the harm was done, she slipped immediately back home; "And," he adds, "went right into the pot!"

There are many advantages in breeding fowl on places that fulfill these seven requirements, and, if combined with all that, the breeder lives on the place, and looks in person after every detail, he will surely be richly rewarded. The fowl should be allowed the freedom of birds and not housed any more than is absolutely necessary. When the weather is pleasant I doubt if anything should be done but call them up twice a day to look them over, give them a little food and keep them from becoming actually wild. However, it is not always possible to have such homes for brood stock, and it becomes necessary to resort to *pen* breeding. A good pen is by far better than a bad walk, and if the breeder understands his business there is little difference in the result except the labor. A man who breeds in pens must have both *experience and patience*. He must be *constant and accurate*. Feeding in pens, the chief trouble is overfeeding in nearly every case, combined in many with improper food. It is plain that brood stock in pens must be so handled as to give them every advantage they would have on a first class walk. It is wise to make them work as much as possible, therefore, the smaller the feed the better. They can pick up corn too fast, and it is very fattening. Corn is not a good constant diet for fowls in pens. I have one pen arranged in three compartments—one for roosting and nests, one for straw where I throw oats, wheat and small feed and let them hunt for it; another where there is grass and broken earth. They must have green food and they like to scratch and roll in fallow. This must be re-spaded occasionally. Another thing: not more than three hens ought to be kept in one brood pen for any length of time. Where they are not sisters I have stalls with little doors, into which I put them if all are laying, until each lays, when she is let out. These eggs are all carefully marked, not from end to end as is customary, but completely belt them with hen's mark and date. They are then put into bran in a place where they will not be subjected to violent changes in temperature. These eggs I usually set outside, under a game hen. Setting hens cannot do well in a pen, where breeders are. Fowls in pens ought to have a light feed three times a day and nice, fresh water every day put where no filth can contaminate it. Laying hens drink much water, therefore it should be accessible and pure. Another good thing for cooped fowls is plenty of *lime*. A big beef bone for them to pick on helps now and then. Tidbits of fresh meat at intervals will supply the place of worms and miscellany they might catch outside. Spurs should be sawed off all cocks and hens in the pens.

THE HEN HOUSE.

A suitable house for breeding purposes is very simple. We will go upon the idea that only six hens are to be allowed on a walk and three in a pen. On the walk my rule is to breed full sisters well selected.

For the six hens and a cock the house should be at least ten feet long, six feet broad, eight feet high in front and six feet high behind. The timbers should be well let into the ground and the house should not have a plank floor. It should be divided into two stalls, petitions running from front back. The first stall should be six by six, for roost poles, and the other four by six, for nests. The stall for roost poles must be lighted by a large window on the end and ventilated by stationary blinds front and rear about two feet by two. The house should have a door about four feet high and two and a half feet in front near corner post, to open inward. There should be a hole in the end at least four feet from the ground for the fowls to go in and out. Under the edge of this hole instead of a step ladder, as is customary, a round spur should be fixed so that the birds can fly up to enter. The advantage in this is that dogs, foxes, minks, etc., cannot get in and if the hole is left open there is no danger from this score. Just inside, under the hole, there should be a small ladder arranged up to the roosts, the foot of which should rest on a narrow platform from which the hens may fly down when they go to lay or fall from the roost. The roost poles should be about five feet from the ground, at least three in number, the entire length of the roost stall, and the same heighth from the ground, but no pole should be near enough to the wall to touch the cock's tail. These poles must not be too large or too small, but exactly fit the grasp of the foot, otherwise the fowls will become duck-footed. Unskinned saplings make the best poles; a rough surface is better than a smooth one.

The stall for nests should have an entrance about four feet by two and a half, with ventilating blinds front and rear, but no window; hens like to stay in the dark, and set much better in secluded dark places. There should be *twelve* nests. If there are not more nests than the hens need they will disturb one another, and setting hens will be constantly annoyed. Instead of blocking the nests along in a row they will give better results scattered about. This will lead each hen to have her own nest. Hens are like people, they readily form bad habits, and no habit does a hen harm more readily than piling in on other hens to lay or set. Nests must never be deep, for the hens will jump down on the eggs and break them; from this they will form the habit of eating eggs, and will begin to break them by design. Each nest should have a foundation of dirt, and then built up with dry grass or some soft material; oat straw or wheat straw well broken up will do. The limits of the nest should be just sufficient to furnish ample room for the hen to spread herself out on thirteen eggs, but make due allowance always for hot weather, and arrange everything so as to fight vermin in case they appear.

This house will not be specially attractive from without, on account of the flat top, but for a few dollars it may have neat ornamental roof and the general plan can be varied to suit the taste and means of the owner. On a rough estimate the house can be built for from $12 to $25. This house can be reduced in size or enlarged to suit the particular case. For a pen of a cock and six hens it cannot be excelled. Any intelligent carpenter can make out a bill for the necessary lumber and materials, and put the whole thing up ready for use in two days.

EGGS.

An egg is a very delicate organism; it cannot, therefore, stand jars, rough treatment of any kind, heat, nor cold. Hence, eggs should be taken in from the nest, carefully marked as directed before, and put in a suitable place for their preservation.

There has been much discussion as to several points on eggs. Some claim it is best to lay them on the side in the bran and turn them now and then; others prefer to stand them on the small end in the bran. Neither plan will save the egg if it is kept too long, but I prefer the first. It has been urged that the sex of a chick could be foretold by the shape of the egg. It has been held by many English and American breeders for over a hundred years that round, blunt eggs hatch out pullets while pointed ones hatch out stags. Sketchley, the English authority, claimed in his work published in 1814, and based on information running back to 1760, that he had discovered this thing to be true after faithful trial. I will be flat. I have no faith in it, because I have repeatedly had hens in my special breeding pens that invariably laid eggs of exactly the same shape and their eggs hatched both stags and pullets, regardless of shape. I imported a hen from England that lays a round, short, blunt egg every time and I got more stags from her than pullets.

Another claim peculiar in itself is that there is a dunghill in every clutch; so the evil is obviated by destroying the first egg. I have heard of one old breeder that ate the first four. Some also destroy the "cluck," or last egg a hen lays. There is sound philosophy in destroying the first and the last eggs; they are likely to be ill formed or lacking in vigor, but there is no deliberate design on the part of nature to afflict a game hen with dunghill progeny.

Many hold that one good tread from a cock will fertilize a whole clutch and if the cock be taken away the hen would go on laying, set and hatch just the same as if she had had the gallant attentions of her lover every day. There is a strong probability that this is correct, and yet it is also a very odd fact that if a fresh cock is introduced after, say, six eggs are laid, the eggs from that time out will hatch to the second cock. Biologists have never given any satisfactory explanation of this phenomenon. Some of the egg-wise tell as a great secret how valuable eggs may be indefinitely preserved. They dissolve shellac in alcohol then paint the eggs thoroughly, let them dry and put them away carefully. They claim to have gotten a fair hatch after keeping eggs over one year. This seems to be a case of suspended animation. I have never tried it, as I would not care for chickens hatched under such difficulties and hardships.

If a breeder wishes to market a surplus of eggs, he has only to grease them and they will never hatch; grease is destructive to the vitality of an egg by clogging effectually the pores that nature has provided to preserve the germ of life. I will pass over superstitions as to eggs, such as their not hatching if carried over running water, to more important questions.

In the choice of eggs to set, all that are of singular and peculiar shape must be discarded. All things being equal, I prefer to set eggs from a hen that lays every other day to those from a hen that lays every day. A cracked or punctured egg will not hatch; it will only rot in the nest.

A hen should never be set on over thirteen eggs; nine will be enough for a small hen. Don't be greedy. One first class bird is worth fifteen of depraved constitution. If a hen hatches and rears thirteen chicks, that is enough. If your six hens do this well you will have seventy-eight if the hens set but once, and every hen must be allowed to set once in the year. It is necessary to her health.

Be careful to set the hen so she cannot be molested, and by no means molest her yourself, in your eagerness to see how she is progressing. Mark on her nest the day she is set, and pay her a call one day before she should hatch. You are likely to see one or two pairs of little bright eyes peeping from under the mother's puffing feathers. You might lift the hen gently, but do not start her to stirring her feet among the eggs. She may mash some little fellow that is just struggling out of the shell. It is best, as the chickens get dry and strong, to remove them, but put them back with the hen at night. If she has not finished hatching next morning take the chicks out till the hen finishes hatching or the remaining eggs prove unfertile. Some times, just before the hatching begins, it is wise to sprinkle the entire nest well with tepid water while the hen is on it, lifting her for the purpose. Sometimes the nest becomes too dry and the hen cannot produce moisture neccessary to soften the shell.

CARING FOR CHICKS.

Hens with chicks should be handled in such a way as to follow the lines of instinct and nature as far as possible. Cooping the young ones unnecessarily is hurtful; also coddling and high feeding debilitates them. Let the hen work as much as possible and let the little fellows tug and struggle over the insects the hen scratches up. They should be reared precisely like children, with knowledge of honest labor, energetic and wide awake to opportunities.

Many fancy dishes are recommended for young chickens, even so great delicacies as bread sopped in chamber lye, with an appendix to the effect that the young birds are fond of variety! What is unnatural must be avoided; hence, salt meat and victuals seasoned for the table are unfit for young chickens. Nature provides birds with all the salt their systems require through the water they drink. Such things as are cooked without salt will not hurt them, but after all, feeding young chickens is a very simple thing. In the first place provide them with a bountiful supply of pure, fresh water, then provide yourself with a supply of wheat and tailings. Give them the tailings as a regular diet, and every now and then with corn bread well baked without salt. *Never feed young chickens raw dough.* A feed of cracked corn and clipped oats is excellent for the evening after they begin to feather well. Of course there will be but little need for feeding if the hens can be allowed free run in the fields of small grain, and she can beat you or any living man caring for her young, if she is given half a chance.

If it is necessary to coop the hen at sundown, prefer a roomy, clean, dry coop on the ground if practicable. Chicks contract troubles on their feet on plank floors—crooked toes, corns and such like. Do not place coops so near together that the chicken can get mixed, or the hens may kill each other's chickens, and the broods become confused.

MARKING.

No careful breeder fails to mark his chicks and the best time is just is they are taken from the nest. They should be distinctly marked in some peculiar way so that if stolen they can be identified; if you wish to make certain crosses or matings you can identify what you wish to use in future; and in mains you can tell your fowl from those of others who may have fowls in the same main. There is every reason for marking game chickens. They are exceedingly valuable property and are subject to many vicissitudes that may obliterate their identity and confuse their ownership.

Various plans have been adopted by different breeders; some mark by clipping the eye lid or the nostril; some have undertaken tatooing parts of the body and sewing silk in the skin of the wing; but no other plan is at once so efficient and satisfactory as marking the webs. My plan is to mark one web for the mother and one for the father. For instance, one favorite pen have a single cut in the outer paddle of the left foot for the cock and a double cut in the inner web of the right for the hen from which they are bred. Various combinations are possible in the four webs, but it is not advisable to mark wholly in one foot. There is certainly some objection to cutting a cock's paddles; if he is marked too deep he is weakened in his toes, if too shallow the mark is useless. I prefer at least one double cut made in each way so as to heal up in the form of an M.

THE GAME FOWL.

The following combinations are possible:
1. Right out single; left out single.
2. Right out single; left in single.
3. Right out single; left out double.
4. Right out single; left in double.
5. Right out double; left out single.
6. Right out double; left in single.
7. Right out double; left out double.
8. Right out double; left in double.
9. Right in single; left in single.
10. Right in single; left out single.
11. Right in single; left in double.
12. Right in single; left out double.
13. Right in double; left in double.
14. Right in double; left in single.
15. Right in double; left in single.
16. Right in double; left out single.

Besides these:
17. Single in left in.
18. Single in left out.
19. Single in right in.
20. Single in right out.
21. Double in right out.
22. Double in left out.
23. Double in right in.
24. Double in left in.
25. Single both webs of right.
26. Double both webs of right.
27. Single in both webs of left.
28. Double in both webs of left.
29. Single in out, double in in of left.
30. Double in out, single in in of left.
31. Single in in, double in out of right.
32. Double in in, double in out of right.

beginner had just as well close his ear to the declarations of enthusiasts that, perhaps, rear more fowls for the market than for the pit. A stag is a minor and he has no legal responsibility; no matter how well bred, while he may meet his obligations like a man, he may also, after winning your confidence, suddenly plead the law of infancy in a most important engagement.

After the young are weaned they cannot mature and reach perfection unless they have a proper range, where fresh water is bountiful, and they can find plenty of food. If the weather is not severe trees make the best and healthiest roost for young game chickens. If trees are not at hand, they must have ample room in a perfectly clean house kept free from vermin.

Pullets that are forward and begin to breed early should be kept with their full brothers for reasons discussed under "The Hen."

DUBBING.

Stags should be trimmed, if possible, on the run and allowed to heal up in freedom. I have known not one under five hundred stags to be injured for life upon the old idea that they should be trimmed and kept in coops till they heal and become gentle. I believe in the taming part, but the remainder is irrational. When a stag is dubbed he sheds much blood, his system is depleted, and cooping adds to his troubles. Therefore when his system is strained is when it ought to be assisted. Trimming and cooping together combine to weaken a stag's constitution. As to taming, if the stags, after thorough recovery from drubbing, are put into "feeding coops" and gently treated till they will come to the front and chatter at feed time and take feed from the hand, which can be accomplished in one week, they will be sufficiently tamed and ready for walks.

Stags should be trimmed when they are from five to six months old, provided the comb has matured. They should never be dubbed before they have a cock's comb. If dubbed too soon excrescences grow about the throat and the comb bunches. This gives the cock a rough and unattractive appearance and impresses the craft with the idea that the bird is the product of inexperienced enterprise.. In most cases stags are ripe for the shears at six months.

Dubbing is properly done only with shears, which should be stout and sharp. The use of knives and razors is as far behind the times as the reap hook is behind the mowing machine. The bird should be first rolled up in a bag, with his head alone left out. A string should be tied around the whole, not too tightly. The operator then begins by pulling out the ear lobe and clipping it off smoothly. Then the gill or wattle on the same side should be taken firmly between the fingers, pulled out well; beginning from the beak it should be cut off in conformity with the growth, being careful not to cut too far under the windpipe, for when the other gill is cut the throat may be left completely skinned. It is believed that cocks whose throats have been skinned have their breathing affected. Having gotten off the ear lobe and wattle from one side, proceed with the other side in the same manner; be careful not to leave "teats" under the beak nor back against the throat.

Dubbing combs is a question much discussed by practical cockers. The Northern cockers nearly all trim close and leave their cocks with keen, gamey looking heads, whereas the Southern cockers favor high combs, what may be termed "hatchets." The reason advanced by the Northern men is that in short heels, as the fight lasts long and there is bound to be much billing, everything must be done to do away with what might interfere with the sight; that a big comb by bleeding would fill the cock's eyes with blood and interfere with his fighting. The Southern men expect fights to be soon over in long heels and dub entirely with reference to heel work. They believe that a cock should shuffle in the other cock's bill hold and if the count is long an antagonist will lay hold of it, thus giving the long count cock a chance to shuffle; so, in any event, when the high comb cock has a bill hold he can shuffle and when he has not he has another chance by tempting him to lay hold of him. Some argue, too, that the cock upon striking places his heels nearer the head and neck of his foe.

The writer does not assume to take sides nor to champion the cause of either plan. His plan of dubbing the comb is not to cut the stag's comb so flat as a show bird nor give him a hatchet on his head, but to trim so as to leave just enough comb to protect the brain. He makes it a rule to take the stag's head firmly in hand, place the thumb between the mandibles, with the index finger behind the head and the second finger under the throat. Then begin from the rear close to the back of the head, and cut the back part of the comb off at an angle of forty-five degrees, with one clean cut. Now begin from the front close down to the beak, and cut perfectly squarely back, leaving enough to serve as a shield for the brain. This plan gives the bird a square, strong, gamey appearance, and leaves protection on the top of his head.

Of course if the stags go for each other after being trimmed they had better be taken up and walked as soon as possible.

I have heard of stags that bled to death upon being trimmed, but have always had an idea the first man who lost one that way did so in a dream. Cases are sighted that require stitches, but I have never seen one that could not be simply thrown into the air and left to be his own surgeon. I would not advise seering with a red hot iron under any circumstances, but some strong astringent like alum and tincture of iron can be used to advantage, while many use cobwebs, which are simple and efficient.

ON WALKS AND WALKING.

Your labor is futile unless your stags are properly walked. Unless you can get suitable walks it is by far the wisest plan to dispose of the birds, for they are worse than useless if put on such walks as we shall condemn in the following paragraphs.

A good walk conforms to the requirements set forth in observations already made on a breeding place. While it may be impossible to get forty or fifty such walks in one community, yet you can approximate as nearly as possible if you cannot get places entirely up to the standard. The following are essential and the man who walks stags should have his eye always cocked for them:

1. Pure water. 2. Healthy and safe roosts. 3. Accessibility to food. By all means avoid: 1. Sloppy, filthy places where a cock runs among hogs and can get at swill. A slop barrel is as destructive among game chickens as a bar room among Indians. They hang around just like old soaks, and becomes tetotally worthless. Hens and pullets stand it better than stags and cocks. 2. Too many hens exhaust a cock's virility; he becomes less chivalrous, slow, phlegmatic, and often degenerates into a eunuch. If a walk is otherwise desirable, a cock may be left on it although there are a number of hens, but he should have two or more dunghills under hack and sure to remain under, with no spurs. Of course no first class walk would have more than a dozen hens on it and one cock. Not once in a hundred cases can a first class cock be picked up for a main, if he is walked where there are forty or fifty hens and half a dozen or so dunghill roosters. 3. While a walk may be

too good to pass over on account of guineas, geese, ducks and pea fowls, it is never good enough to redeem itself for a flock of turkeys. No cocker with any experience will walk a cock with turkeys. Now and then a cock has no disposition to fight turkeys and no harm will follow, but in most cases the turkeys nag at a cock till he becomes desperate and a fight ensues, and the turkeys, being tall, stand over the cock, force him to duck, and being very strong, they get him by the head and hold it, often for a minute at a time, against the ground. This teaches the cock to "duck" and "give the head"; he is ruined. Even when you feel sure your cock will not fight a turkey you run a serious risk. Ducks and geese are chiefly injurious by poisoning the water, but guineas are very mean sometimes. They are the most consummate hypocrites in the form of fowls, and under the cloak of amity they often effect ruin. Avoid them if you can. 4. Proximity to other cocks, especially if they can meet and spar a lick or two every day. "Maiden cocks" are always best, and if a cock has been walked where he could never see a cock he will be watchful, aggressive, and full of fight. Such rarely "crow under" or hack in the feed. But well bred cocks that have had to contend for territory for several months are often bashful and may hack in the process of conditioning. 5. Barren places where the bird is forced to live on what is thrown to him are not good walks, no matter how well the cock is fed. 6. Distinguish always between summer and winter walks. A cock may thrive in summer where he would suffer in many ways or perish in winter. Winter walks are greatly benefited by horse stables. If a game cock has access to a horse stable in winter he will be able to thrive, both in the matter of food and of shelter from cold and snow in severe climates. 7. Dishonest persons are always to be shunned. There is no use to rear a fine fowl, put him on the best walk in the country just to be peddled off by the very man to whom you have trusted your property. Safety against robbers cannot be overlooked. There are a certain class of men devoid of conscience, who tell the truth from necessity and obey the criminal law only from the fear of corporal punishment. Such men in a community are destructive of good order and ruin industry. They cannot be relied on to walk a cock honestly and they cannot resist the temptation to dispose of your fowl to the first imitation thief that is looking up other men's cocks for a cross-roads chicken fight. 8. When stags are walked you should have an eye to the time when you are to take them in for use, and try to walk them so that you can conveniently pick up enough in a day to pay for a day's journey. As a general thing, to pick up twelve cocks that are main-worthy in a day is to do well.

The stags should be put into clean, dry sacks, head first, the bags well tied at the mouth, and placed in a vehicle roomy enough not to crowd the bags too closely together. The stags can bear being pressed in cold weather, but in warm weather many will die.

If possible trust the walking of your stags to no one except somebody better informed than yourself. If you get in fifty per cent. of the birds walked by a novice you will be doing well, whereas, those who understand the business take in from seventy-five to ninety per cent. Of course some fowls disappear from natural causes and die on walks just as they would have done at home. For several years I have taken in from eighty to ninety per cent. of the stags walked. I turn down many walks, and having secured valuable walks I pay a fair price for their use and hold them from year to year. Hence, when the winter comes I try to manage to have some stags always ready, and when I send or go for the cock I take a stag or two to drop in his place.

I have several walks where I have had cocks for eight years. Most of them I have held for four.

It is always safest when you walk a stag to rely upon no man's promise to dispose of his dunghills; the stag must be master from the start, and if he has to run under or fight his way up at the first he may be seriously injured. The laity do not understand the game chicken business, and their intentions may be ever so good, but from ignorance they ruin your fowl. I once gave a laborer a very young stag to walk and in the run of ten days I asked the fellow how the bird was getting along. His reply was, "That is the most friendliest chicken for a game rooster I ever saw. Why, him and Mary's rooster and the Banty never does fight and they lives together in the most peacablest way." I visited the walk and found the fellow's wife didn't mind violating his promise to kill the dunghills, and found my stag running under a big Plymouth Rock and a Bantam. So they would have remained till the stag was old enough to subdue the two bosses.

When the stag is comfortably walked take his description and weight (which you should have along) down in a book, and the full address of the party who is keeping him for you. It is necessary to take the pedigree and weight, so that when you wish to take up a main you will know where to find what you want. As a general thing stags develop into cocks several ounces heavier. If they are on first class walks a stag weighing 4.04 at ten months, will come in a cock weighing 4.14. A 5.0 stag will come in weighing fully 5.12. I once put out a stag weighing 5.09 and he came in weighing 9 lbs.! They may be relied on to gain from six to ten ounces, according to size. Very rarely will a 6 lb. stag fail to make a 7 lb. cock, if on a good walk. I put stags out last season weighing 5.14 and they came in weighing 7 lbs., and over.

What is fair compensation for walking a game chicken one year must be determined by surroundings. It is unwise to be stingy; but you will avoid much trouble by paying every man the same. I find they often come together, brag on their "roosters," and gradually swap secrets. If you are paying one more than another there is dissatisfaction at once. The best walks are gotten in parts of the South for the *use* of the bird, and that is unquestionably the best country for walking cocks. The game bird is so popular in certain sections of South Carolina and Georgia that you can ride for hours and hear nothing but game cocks crow. The farmers all keep game fowl for practical purposes. However, in the Middle States and the Northern States it is different. Walks in those parts cost from fity cents to two dollars.

The moral effect of an occasional visit is great, but you should never produce the impression that you are suspicious or lacking in confidence. These visits should not be often and should appear to be accidental rather than planned.

I will conclude these observations on the allied subjects of breeding by advising a careful examination of each individual stag and pullet you raise for imperfections. Such as are illformed in any way or constitutionally weak, ought to be disposed of at once so as to give the others a better chance. The more there are on a yard the less they thrive. Look out for broken or crooked limbs and toes, crooked breasts-bones, and defective sight from any cause. The perfect ones need all your care, and you have no time to conduct a chicken hospital.

COCKING MAINS.

The breeder is presumed now to be amply supplied with fine, healthy game cocks in their second suit of feathers. Any chicken is a cock after he has moulted and his plumage is grown—what is termed, "in his second suit of feathers." Early stags may be nearly two years old when the plumage is complete, while late stags may not be over fourteen months old. In some sections anything is considered a stag at twelve months or under, but this rule is plainly unfair, because many stags are hatched in March and will be *in the same suit of feathers* till the following winter, about twenty months, yet a stag hatched in July will be in his second suit of feathers by the following December one year—about seventeen months. The only safe guide is the moult; every moult means one more cock year regardless of the Gregorian calendar. Good stags hatched in July, if not very large, will make cocks fit for a main the following December one year. The nearer large birds are to three years old the better, when they are taken up for fighting. Dick Lee always claimed that a big cock was never at his best before he was three years old.

If, then, upon looking over your birds on their walks you find a sufficient number in fine health and feather you are prepared to enjoy the long coveted fruits of your labor —you are ready to make a main.

Making mains is exactly like all other forms of contracting. Each man tries to fix things in his own favor, and each endeavors to have even minor advantages on his side. Fair minded men don't take long to make mains if they really want to fight, but would-be sharps and professional blowers often negotiate months, and either fight a fake main or disappoint everybody altogether. Frequenters of the pit and men really fond of the sport should avoid men who are constantly scheming to gain some unfair advantage or to advertise themselves by negotiations as volumnious as the testimony in a murder trial.

Men are supposed to meet each other half way; if one party proposes a top weight the other should have the right to name the bottom. Thus if A offers to fight a main with B they generally toss for weights. If B wins he names the weight, say 4.04, for the bottom, and A names the top, say 6 lbs.; B simply gets the choice of weights. So with all details. Any dispute can be settled by toss of a coin. But no man in making a main should put himself, his birds, and his friends at a disadvantage. The result of a fair contest is to give each party *his share* of what he wants the agreement to contain.

The following essentials ought always to be provided for in the contract: First, the *number* of cocks to be shown. In the North mains of thirteen cocks and even eleven are common, though some as large as fifteen and seventeen are fought. Mains in the South run from thirteen to twenty-one cocks. The element of luck enters somewhat in any heels, but there is less of it in short heels than in long heels. In any heels the greater the number fought the less the risk is of deciding the main upon a cast of the dice. I do not consider a show of fewer than fifteen cocks and that between close weights where there will be as many as thirteen to fall in, a fair trail of the merits of cocks or of condition. In a very small main, it is possible for an amateur, by a happy combination of accidents, to win against superior cocks in excellent condition; but the probability of such things decreases as the number of matches increases. Therefore, if you have reason for great confidence in your feeder and your fowl, it is most advisable to show as many pairs as possible, and close weights. Second, the *weights*. The weights named by each party will influence the number of matches. Close weights will bring about more matches than wide weights. Hence if the top is 6.04 and the bottom 4.00, in a show of eleven cocks, there are likely to be but few matches—perhaps five which ought to be called no more than a *cock fight* not a *main*. Generally it is understood that all cocks catch in matching if they are in two ounces of each other, give and take. Further, if the top is 5.14 and the bottom 4.08 in a show of twenty-one cocks, there will be a *main,* for not fewer than fifteen matches will be made and perhaps nineteen. I have heard of one main in which seventeen were shown between close weights—4.08 to 5.11 and every bird fell in. A very pretty main would be to show seventeen cocks from 4.04 to 5.12. Between these weights, the birds make the prettiest fights, and there is likely to be a good number of matches. However, in making mains you should always have in mind the weights of your cocks as they run on the walk. An experienced eye can guess as closely to weight as a meat merchant. Having in mind the walking weights of your cocks and remembering that they can lose in the feed from four to sixteen ounces you well know how to choose weights. Plainly if your antagonist choose a top weight 6.08 in a fifteen-cock main, unless you named a light weight, about 4.12 or 4.14 there would not be much fighting. Therefore, his weight, 6.08, would be a disappointment if all your cocks were small. Then, if his cocks were large as his top weight would indicate he would show a bunch of cocks too big to match yours. If, however, you are well supplied with cocks and have every reason to be confident and really want all the matches you can get, name your bottom weight as near to his top as possible, not forgetting to allow margin to show as few of the same weight as you can. Hence, if he names 6.08, you will catch him well by substracting about one-and-a-half ounces for every cock to be shown i. e. if there are to be seventeen shown, subtract twenty-four ounces from his 6.08 and name 5.00. If you have two extra fine cocks that would fight at say 4.14, you might name that weight. Yet the habit of making mains to fit one or two extra cocks is a very unwise practice. The main ought always be made on the general merits of the entire coop.

Third, the *time*. Ample time should always be allowed from the day the articles are signed for getting the coops ready together with all things needed for the feeder; for picking the cocks up from their walks; and for putting the cocks in fix. These details should be attended to under orders from the feeder. Each professional feeder has his own peculiar ways and own hobbies. As a usual thing three weeks in Southern and four in Northern rules will suffice.

Fourth, the *place*. This should be accessible to all; suitable for the purpose, and free from interruptions of any kind. It is rarely possible for parties to agree upon a place equally convenient to both sides; so it is customary for the man who has the advantage in distance to allow the other party expenses. Thus, if a cocker in Charleston, S. C., makes a main with one from Atlanta, Ga., to fight in Charleston, he would have to allow the Georgia party a fair amount to defray his additional expenses. This is a well established rule among cockers and is based on justice: *Give expenses and he comes to you; take expenses and go to him; or meet him at some place about equally convenient.* It has been held for a century among cock fighters that traveling conditioned cocks throws them back. For this reason it is wise to move the cocks to the battle ground, if the conditions justify it, the day before the main. For this reason also the man who travels his cocks farthest is at a disadvantage, and the opposite party can afford to allow expenses.

Fifth, the *stakes, stakeholder* and *forfeit*. The articles of agreement should always state clearly the amount fought for—how much for each battle and how much on the odd:

Thus, $50 each battle and $500 on the odd, which means that the parties are fighting for fifty dollars on each battle, and the man that first gets the majority of the fights wins. If, therefore, they were fighting for $500 on the odd, and there were fifteen matches to be fought, as soon as one party won eight battles he would win the $500. A *forfeit* should always be put into the hands of a responsible party named in the contract, who may be designated as referee and final stakeholder. This forfeit is to guarantee good intention and secure an innocent party against encurring useless expenses. The sum named in the articles ought, therefore, to be enough to cover all damages, in the event one of the parties defaults.

Sixth, *receipts from tickets* for admission. The parties in most cases fight in licensed cock pits where an admission fee is charged. The articles should state what is to be done about the money so collected, which is often a considerable sum. Sometimes this is divided, sometimes it is agreed in the contract that all should go to the winner. This point is determined according to the confidence one feels in his ability to win.

Seventh, *the rules* to govern the main. No cocking main can be properly conducted without rules, hence the contracting parties should never omit naming the rules to controll the main. This ought never be deferred till the fight is on. This "let the best cock win" is alright if you can always tell which is the best cock. The rules do away with all such disputes if the judges are qualified and honest.

FORM OF ARTICLES OF AGREEMENT FOR A COCKING MAIN.

These articles drawn the thirteenth of March, 1903, between John Doe and Richard Roe bind the said parties to fight a cocking main on the following terms:

First, it is agreed that the parties will show twenty-one cocks weighing from 4.04 to 6.00, all to be matched that catch by giving and taking two ounces.

Second, the contract is to fight for $50 each battle and $500 on the odd; but the loser shall have the option of not fighting any more after the odd fight is lost, and the entire receipts at the gate shall go to the winner of the main.

Third, it is agreed that this main shall be in inch-and-a-quarter gaffs and fought under Philadelphia rules. But it is specially agreed that either party may use any kind of packing he chooses.

Fourth, the main shall be fought at Richard Fen's pit in the city of Philadelphia, but if from any cause it become impossible to fight at the pit of said Fen, then at such place as can be secured for the purpose in fifty miles of Philadelphia, by three persons selected by the parties to this contract.

Fifth, this main shall be fought May 1st, 1903, the first pair of cocks to be in the pit promptly at 8 o'clock P. M. There shall be no more than fifteen minutes between fights, and wrangling or disputing shall not be taken out of the time except at the voluntary request of the judges for the purpose of looking up and settling doubtful points.

Sixth, there shall be two judges selected by the parties to this contract and the judges shall select a referee who will decide such points as the judges cannot agree upon. No man shall act as judge or referee, who is betting in the main unless he announces that fact before he is chosen and before the fighting begins.

Seventh, a forfeit of $100 shall be placed in the hands of John Den within twenty-four hours after these articles are signed, which amount shall be promptly paid over upon the failure of either party to this contract to meet his obligations, to the party who is entitled to the same.

       JOHN DOE. (L. S.)
       RICHARD ROE. (L. S.)

Witnessed by:
  WILLIAM GILLIVER.
  ALEXANDER DODSON.

It is impossible to give forms to cover every kind of contracts for cocking mains but the above form can be modified to suit any ordinary case.

PICKING UP COCKS FOR A MAIN.

After the main is a settled fact, in a suitable time, the cocks must be taken from their walks. The cocks ought to be brought in as fresh as possible, so that none should be picked up more than two days before they go into the feeding coops. Of course if the feeder requires only nine days, as is true in some sections of the South, the one who is to gather in the birds had better begin to do so at least eleven days before the main; if the feed is two or three weeks as is true in the North, allow time accordingly. Procrastination is a dangerous vice; if you put off till the last day you may not find cocks you count on, in proper form and others may be miles away, so that a day or two is lost and your cocks as well as your friends are put at a disadvantage.

Certain particulars must be closely observed in picking the cocks up. They must be in perfect *health*. This can be determined by the cocks movements, by his appetite, by the gloss on his plumage, by the ruddiness of his complexion and by his feeling in the hand. Always carry along a little corn: if when the corn is dropped on the ground the cock tumbles about over the hens in a desperate struggle for victuals, it is a bad sign. There should be a brilliancy about the feathers, that only appear on healthy fowls, the skin of the head and throat must be of a rich almost cherry red, smooth, and shiney. The cock must also be carefully examined in the hand. You should take along an old or torn cock to catch with, as you cannot always wait to take them off the roost. Hold the old cock in your hand and push him toward the cock to be caught just closely enough to tempt the cock to strike; the instant the cock on the ground strikes, pull the cock in your hands back so as to avoid the blow. Keep this up till you can lay hold of the cock to be caught.

With the bird in hand, you can discover whether he is in proper flesh and feather, to be taken up for a main. The best of the Southern feeders would condemn him if he is very fat and the feed is to be less than fourteen days; the Northern feeders do not care how fat he is if in perfect health and fit otherwise. Medium flesh and perfect health go best together. Now examine his plumage. The cock must have enough tail to balance himself and support him in falling backward. There must be ample wing feathers, so pull the wings out to full length and observe closely how many quills are broken. A cock cannot fight without wings; if the primaries in the wings are broken close to the flesh or shorter than they would be cut for battle, the cock is not number one though he might pass. A bird is not hurt at all if his feathers are only broken where they would be cut off for battle. Hence a hen-pecked cock is not necessarily hurt.

One extremely injurious practice I must condemn, namely, this catching of cocks in any sort of way and sending "niggers" after them. Some of the best cocks in the world have been ruined by rough handling. A cock learns to look upon his handler as a tyrant and unfriendly, so he either becomes "man-shy" or entirely hacked. A "man-shy" cock never gets over it; a "hacked" cock never recovers his former spirit, and a "run-down" cock is ruined forever. A cock that is caught by being run down may come in and stand the feed—he may not hack, but is liable to surprise his breeder by suddenly quitting in a long, hard battle; the majority of them will hack, or become unpromisingly bashful in the coops. Wild cocks raised and walked in woods suffer most from this cause, and in most cases, they are the very best a breeder has. The man who will take up a cock that has been "walking under," for a main, either is a beginner or never can learn anything.

Next, examine the cock for such defects as render him unfit for the training coops. Sometimes they develop crooked breast bone, gouty feet, toes frozen off, eyes injured, beak broken. Sometimes a crooked breast should not rule an extra bird out if he has redeeming qualities. If the feet are badly gouted the cock will not do, but a slight defect of the kind is not fatal while corns amount to but little if the cocks go into the hands of a good feeder. The slightest defect about the eye is fatal; there is no compromise. If a cock's beak is not so badly broken that he cannot get a good firm bill-hold, he is not necessarily debarred. A cock must have feet to stand on and if his toes are badly frosted he will not do to go into a main. A nail or two off does no serious injury, though I prefer to see good nails on the two middle toes.

Supposing the cock passes inspection, put him head first into a clean, dry croacus sack. Under no circumstances put a game cock into a damp bag, nor into one that has contained diseased fowls.

In making the rounds of your walks, observing each time these rules, pick up always a few more cocks than will be actually needed. Some may go lame or show defects you overlooked. If you are to make a show of twenty-one you might pick up thirty cocks. Some pick up twenty-five cocks for a show of thirteen.. This is really foolish if the cocks are properly selected in the first place. In the end, it pays the feeder to pick up the cocks, for he may not have to do extra work on a surplus of cocks to pick out what will be required for the show. For an eleven-cock main fifteen ought to be enough; of course when a man has to pick up cocks not in perfect shape, he must pick up a greater number than if every bird is perfect.

ON FEEDING COOPS.

Too much care cannot *be exercised* in the construction and care of coops used for conditioning a main of cocks. I have heard of coops too large, but have never seen them. The fact is; the more room a cock has to move about and exercise himself in is by far the better. If they are even large enough for a roost so much the better. The only evil to avoid connected with building large coops is having them so deep that the cocks cannot easily be reached from the door. If space could be allowed for a front of three feet a depth of two, and a heighth of two feet six inches, the cock will have ample room to flop his wings, scratch, and move about. The roosts can be taken out during the day. Things about a cock house should be so ordered that a cock can live just as naturally as possible. The doors to coops should be large enough to get the bird in and out without any trouble, and as an additional precaution, every door should close automatically, and be provided with a latch. Every feeder has his own pet ideas, but experience has taught me that cocks fight more eagerly if they are not allowed to see each other often. I would, therefore, prefer to have coops so arranged that all feeding can be done in cups suspended inside; and I would never allow the cocks to stick their heads out of holes in the doors, as most do, and gaze at one another all day.

The coops must be entirely protected against currents, which readily cause roup and distemper. Cocks at some stages of the feed, especially just after physicing and exercise, catch cold easily. For this reason, no cock ought to be put into a "walking coop" just after he is flirted or pysiced, nor at any time when it is damp or windy.

Coops should be perfectly dry, and, if new, made of well seasoned timber. If old they should be thoroughly whitewashed inside and out before they are used, and if old coops or feed boxes are used they should be thoroughly cleansed with vinegar, inside and out. Modern science has discovered that many diseases in men and in the lower animals are due to microbes, or animal organisms so small as to be imperceptible to the naked eye. It is against these we must disinfect to prevent disease. Carbolic acid diluted with water destroys these germs, as also do lime and vinegar. All parts of the coops that might be contaminated should be washed with some disinfectant. Cups ought to be of iron so that they can be baked; wood cups are not safe for two mains, unless they have been used solely with dry feed.

Cleanliness cannot be over appreciated about feeding coops. Besides disinfection, ample preparation must be made to keep things clean. No successful feeder keeps a dirty cock house. A bountiful supply of clean, dry wheat straw should be on hand to give the cocks new beds whenever they need it. Pine straw is used by many good breeders at the South. They claim that the droppings give less trouble than in wheat straw. Oat straw may be used as well as pine leaves but baled wheat straw is the best.

Dust created by walking about and by sweeping is injurious and can easily be avoided by covering the entire floor heavily with perfectly dry straw.

MATCHING FOR BATTLE.

Matching for battle preliminary to a main of cocks is quite an easy task if the purpose of the contestants is to act honorably and fight their fowl squarely on their merits. A few simple observations in this connection are all that is necessary if honest cock fighting is the object in view. Indeed the rules cover the ground in large part, certainly for Southern or long heel fighting. However, there is this to be remembered in matching under Turner's or what are sometimes called Virginia and North Carolina Rules: Since matching is done by description and the scales are not used after the match list is complete, it behooves those who conduct these preliminaries to guard carefully against any possible error, for it must not be forgotten at any time that those who manage the important affairs in a main of cocks are not only looking out for their own interests but for the interest of confiding friends, who are usually about a pit in numbers, ready to bet their money, and in many cases from great distances. I have witnessed mains attended by men from ten states some of them having traveled over a thousand miles with rolls of bills big enough to carpet a house—who expressed more interest as far as money can talk, than the principals themselves. Therefore, he who conducts a main is the custodian of the general good and in honor is bound to see to it that his friends have an equal chance and a square deal. In Turner's Rules the cocks are weighed and matched by colors and marks the first day, and while the scales talk the first day they are dumb thereafter, and if a man is mean enough to do such a thing, it is easy for him to produce the wrong cock in a match and fight a larger cock or even a better one than the one that was actually matched. Some feeders have been known to "spring" a cock nine ounces by the third day of a main under Southern Rules, and many strains of cocks are so much alike in color and markings that an unfair advantage is too strong temptation for some men in their eagerness to win. This similarity in color and weight under the rules to spring a cock, makes it possible for a trickster to sin repeatedly in the same main. The only safeguard against such people is either never to fight mains with them or be extermely careful in taking descriptions. A close observer can always discover some odd mark on every cock. Do not depend too much on plumage: watch the legs, toe-nails, eyes, style of trim of comb and gills, and never depend on any one mark, no matter how peculiar. There are no two things in the world exactly alike. Look for the difference and patiently record that difference. When the cocks are brought to the pit, always have the match list written in a legible hand and require the judges to compare every cock minutely with his description. It is always best to object firmly but politely to fighting the battle until your opponent produces the right bird. The writer was party to one big main that he lost by underestimating the importance of this rule.

Northern Rules generally provide for mains of only one day, and they are usually fought at night. No description of any cock is taken, and the parties are allowed to change as often as they think proper; they are only required to produce a cock to a certain weight. The principals or either representative get together in some quiet place, each with a list of the weights of the cocks which he intends to show. In other words, in Southern Rules there is an actual show of cocks. In Northern Rules there is a "show" only in name. Only the weights of the cocks are produced. Neither party knows what kind of a cock the other is going to produce until they are in the pit. From the two lists all cocks that weigh the same are said to "check," and are matched of course. Then all that are in one ounce or under three, in two ounces or under give and take. But the matching should be done cautiously when it comes to giving ounces. Some hold the opinion that a six pound cock is big enough to fight anything. Hence, they willingly give three and even more ounces. This is a serious mistake. I fought a 6.14 Whitehackle cock once that had a 6 lb. cock as much at his mercy as a 4.14 would have had a 4 lb. cock. Some agrue it rarely occurs. How can one tell when it may occur and is it fair to your friends to assume the risk? I confidently believe all things being equal, that odds are in favor of a 6.10 against a 6.7. Therefore be very charry of giving heavy odds because the cocks are large. A smaller cock may win in a rapid shuffle and has a better chance in long heels. In short heels, his chances diminish.

As to smaller cocks the reasoning is even more forcible, and when it comes to 4 lb. cocks, two ounces amounts almost to a handicap. It is preferable, by way of comparison, to give three ounces against a 5.7 rather than to give two ounces against a 4.4 It is not unfair, therefore, in matching to give ounces against your big cock and take your ounces in favor of your small cocks. It is possible to give a total of six ounces and receive a total of six, and yet have a decided advantage in the matches. Thus suppose you get two ounces on a 4.4, two on a 4.5 and two on a 4.6, for which you give two ounces on a 5.7, two on a 5.8, and two on a 5.9. You will fight your 4.6 against his 4.4. your 4.7 against his 4.5, your 4.8 against his 4.6. In equal condition you should win all three, chances being much better, however, in short than in long heels, because a quick cock has less chance to win in the go off. This point is well illustrated by reference to matching among the Spaniards where their natural heel fighters are very small. With them its no match unless the cocks weigh exactly the same. It is astonishing to see how much larger a 3.4 Spanish cock ready for battle looks than a 3.2. However, when it comes to slashers, the Spanish cockers do not hesitate to fight a 5.14 against a 6 lb. cock. The logic of this reasoning is easily observed by reducing the cocks until one weighs only an ounce. If two ounces were allowed, the match would be with a cock weighing just three times as much as his antagonist. It follows then that the larger the cocks the less the odds in giving weight to make matches, and the smaller the cock the greater are the odds against him. Of course there are rare exceptions. I bred a little Whitehackle cock known as Monte Carlo that fought at 4.4. I matched him against a very fine 4.9 Warhorse in long heels and won easily. I afterwards whipped a favorite Ginger Muff with him allowing seven ounces. My friends always claimed that he could whip any cock regardless of size. These cases are rare and the rule laid down is the safest to follow.

In Northern Rules the cocks must be weighed at the pit side immediately before the fight, and the judges may require them to be weighed after the fight. If there is anything wrong, the fight will be given against the sinner. Balances are used and they should be carefully tested. Some weigh heavier on one side than the other, and by dishonest tinkering a rascal can "doctor" the weights. In the interest of friends, it is best to take men as they are. Such things are sometimes done. Honest men often make mains and dishonest men fight them. These things are touched upon because this work is intended as a guide for that host of rising cockers who deserve the protection such information might secure to them. Let us hope that these as well as all sharp practices that tend to degrade this form of sport, may very soon so completely die out that coming generations of cockers will read of them with that feeling of utter disgust, which overcomes the student of history when he reads of the decay of Roman morals under Nero and Caligula!

COCK HOUSE AND EQUIPMENT.

No breeder can hope to be successful if he has not a suitable place to "keep" his birds. I have seen in my own experience heavy mains lost by the best feeders in the union for the lack of suitable accommodations. Especially at the North houses must be warm and protected against the severities of winter. All northern feeders physic their cocks in the feed and, therefore, must have a house that can be kept near one temperature. Some of the best of the short heel feeders avoid fire or artificial heat in their cockhouses as long as it is wise, but with a sudden drop in temperature, they require a house that can be warmed at least for the time.

Light and *sunshine* have much to do with keeping cocks in health and spirits; hence the house should be not only properly ventilated, but there cannot be too much light. If the bright sunshine can come directly in, so much the better. If the main is to be fought at night the house must be so arranged that the cocks can be handled by artificial light. There must never be any smoke of any kind about the cockhouse, so lanterns, candles, and smoky lamps are to be avoided. A good lamp is the next best thing to electricity.

The furniture of a cock house consists of two "flirting tables," two "running boards," a pair of scales, at least one big basket for taking soiled straw from the coops, and a half-dozen "walking coops."

The best kind of flirting table is made simply by putting the mattress of a baby cradle on any ordinary table of proper size. If this is too expensive, straw can be put on a large goods box and crocus tacked over it, making a cushion to avoid injury to the bird's feet in taking his exercise. Only one of these will be needed if a few cocks are in training, but two are necessary in handling as many as twenty-five cocks, one for the feeder and one for his assistant.

A "walking board" is made by padding an eight foot plank, twelve inches broad, as was done with the flirting table. This should be attached to the wall of the room so as to stand out slightly and about three feet from the floor. This is for developing the cock's leg muscles and two will be needed if there are many to be trained.

I don't care who he is, that man is foolish who does not use *scales* in his feeding coops. The cocks ought to be carefully weighed every morning before exercise and *feeding;* and the weight recorded on the door. Thus an exact record of the cock's progress is before the eye all the time. These should be the old fashioned balances using weights as small as a half ounce.

Miscellaneous machinery may be required, such as a kettle for water on the stove, a spur saw, a pair of muffs, some chalk, a pair of strong, sharp scissors, some "hoods" for vicious cocks, and perhaps, to suit the whim of your feeder, a swing and a punching bag, and a pair of roller skates.

"Walking coops" should be made of light slats and so built that they can be knocked down and folded up like an umbrella. They ought to be about four feet and a half long, two feet broad, and two feet high.

ON FEEDING COCKS FOR THE PIT.

SOME GENERAL OBSERVATIONS.

While this work is not written for the instruction or reformation of professional breeders, it is intended to a certain degree at least as a text book for amateurs and beginners. Certain truths are of supreme importance to any man who fights cocks, and these are within the scope of my labors.

There are certain fundamental principles that cannot any more be ignored in this science than in mathematics, and while the *minutiae* of feeding for the pit are not in the book of an ordinary cocker's knowledge, yet there are some things that every man who stakes his money and judgment ought to know, in self defense.

In the first place there is no earthly safety in the confidence of a dishonest feeder. If he has sufficient inducement, no matter how watchful you may be, he will "throw" you when he discovers that he can make more money by being a traitor than by feeding an honest main; all the detectives in America can't save you. Therefore the first thing in feeding is *honesty*. I like, too, to see a feeder ambitious, energetic, untiring, watchful, intelligent and cleanly. All these things bear seriously on the result of a main, being half of the battle in cock fighting. No matter how well your birds may be bred and walked they cannot win against even common stock in better fix. A main of "strainers" (part game) in good fix and properly handled will win against a coop of the finest game fowl in the world out of fix. Indeed, I have rarely seen it fail yet, if two well bred strains fall against one another, the one in fine condition, the other in poor fix, that there were not some runaways. Bad fix is ruinous! Of course all feeders are caught "off" at times, but as a general thing this is because they have been ignorant and happy-go-lucky in their feed, or careless and lukewarm, if not dishonest. Some things are obvious to anyone, and long experience is not necessary to profit by certain observations. Cocks ought always to be lively after they are over the physicing, and willing to eat; when the house is visited in the morning everything ought to be crowing, scratching, and chatting; a big noise is a good sign. After the first five days a cock ought to hold up well in hand and work his feet energetically or draw them tightly under himself. A cock that looks sleepy, takes little notice, hangs his legs full length when handled is not doing well. Singing cocks are rarely in the best of health and cannot be considered battle worthy. Cocks are generally doing well if they are "tight-fisted," that is, feel stiff and hard in the hand, work their feet well, have a bright red face, a lustrous eye, and a brightness of health about the plumage. If you have not a "good finger" to determine whether the cock is in proper flesh, your only safe guide is the scales. The marks on the door from day to day speak volumes.

Southern feeders do not reduce cocks so much as those at the North. In Southern Rules the object is to secure swiftness, which requires that the cock be shown with enough flesh to make him feel full of dash and animal spirits, so that he may go off as he were shot from a cannon. The Northern men anticipate a long, persistent, bloody fight, and they show their cocks as corky as is expedient. They like a cock to look a "pound bigger than he really is." The fact is, all cocks should look when brought to the pit, to weigh less than they appear to weigh in any length of heels. I have known feeders to reduce big cocks over a pound in Turner's Rules, and win. Therefore, if the principal in a main upon inspecting the cocks just before the main, discovers that the birds have not reduced sufficiently, he will be fighting his *fat,* and in short heels, the chances are he shall be whipped. Fat cocks meet in a long fight and get where the old devotees say "They can't knock a hole in a pound of butter." In long heels they stand a better chance but are not in the pink of condition. I always question the intelligence or the honesty of a feeder who receives a cock in good flesh at 5.10 and fights him at 5.07 in a twenty-one day feed, as his favorite. I have paid for this information.

EXERCISE.

This is of as much importance as the diet of a coop of cocks. The fowl should never be exercised on a full craw; his flirting, running and rubbing should always be given while empty.

There is a variety of forms for exercising cocks, but the old standard methods are flirting, running on the board already described, and rubbing well after exercise. There are three ways of flirting a cock, first by placing the right hand under the breast, the left at the root of the tail, and suddenly but gently throwing the cock backward to make him flutter his wings and kick his feet out in front. Always do this in such ways as to avoid bruising the craw. This is the most beneficial form of exercise. The second way is to run the hand between the cock's legs from behind, hold him up and drop him off as if to let him fall on his breast. To recover himself he will kick his feet out behind and flutter, which is good exercise. This should alternate with the first. It helps to make a cock steady on his feet and exercises muscles that the first might not reach. The third is to catch the cock between the hands over the wings from behind and pitch him up with a twist as if to throw him on his side, first right then left. This will help to make him sure footed in battle and may reach muscles the other two plans neglect. However, some feeders flirt cocks differently from any of these plans. They stand the cock on the table with his tail towards the handler. They then seize the bird between the hands, the thumbs being over his wings and the fingers under the breast in front of the thighs. The cock is tossed into the air about two to three feet so as to make him throw his feet to the front. Just as he lands, he is tossed again until he begins to show fatigue, at which time exercise should always cease. The amount of exercise must be determined by the feeder's knowledge of the cock in hand. Cocks just from the walks are rarely given more than twenty flirts three times the first day. They cannot stand much running at first, either. A good plan is to add about five flirts and a little more running on the board each day. Of course if the cock stands it well, more may be added, but no bird is benefited by exercise after he begins to pant. There is no choice between too much and too little exercise. After the cock has had his exercise he should be "rubbed" with the hand over the thighs, sides, and back, giving a little more pressure over the back from day to day till after a time, he can stand heavy pressure without squatting.

There are other devices for training cocks, among them, a system somewhat peculiar, formerly in use about Albany, New York. A cock is put into deep straw and followed around with a paper on the end of a buggy whip to make him tug away and help himself along by his feet and wings at the same time. Some at the South use the almost obsolete race-course. A cock is put into a narrow kind of lane with hurdles here and there and the cock is pursued around this circular lane by small boys hired for the purpose. I question the utility of such a plan though it has been used by one of the most successful feeders in the Southern States. There are many who have faith in the "swing." A cock is simply put on the bar of a swing and swung back and forth. He is exercised by trying to steady himself with both legs and wings.

The cock should, in all forms of exercise, be handled gently and in such way as to make him glad to see you. Impatience is inexcusable. A man who will fly into a passion because a cock bites or kicks him is unfit to feed a main, and demonstrations of passion in a cock house are as much out of place as showing favoritism—giving some cocks more attention than others. Perhaps the best cock suffers from neglect at the hands of a man who picks out two or three birds because of some personal whim, to lavish his work upon. The writer has seen as many favorites whipped as any others. In a main Feb. 16, 1900, it so happened that the favorite on each side was whipped, and easily.

"Pointing" cocks is a decidely difficult undertaking. The cocks on the day of the main should be at their best and exactly right for battle both in mettle and in strength. In order to tone them up to buoyancy and eagerness for fight, it is customary to omit exercise the day before the main, though unquestionably this plan is a dangerous one and often brings more injury than good. Moderate exercise, just a few flirts and a little rubbing, is decidedly safest. In three-day mains under Turner's Rules, unquestionably the exercise ought to be kept up, though just enough should be given to keep him at the climax of activity and strength. More feeders ruin cocks by attempts to point than are successful.

The use of *drugs* in preparing cocks for a main deserves most careful examination. It must be remembered in the first place, that feeding human drugs to feathered animals is a very unnatural thing, and it follows that physicing is a fine art. To reduce cocks rapidly our forefathers used much jalap and cream of tartar. Calomel has now come into general use, and while it is very nearly the same chemical as corrosive sublimate, some feeders give a cock as big a dose as would be given to a man with a very torpid liver. This shocks a cock's system and there is serious doubt whether he ever recovers. I watch a feeder very closely if he gives my cocks over 3-4 grain of calomel. All physicing is artificial and of course can be done only by those who have had the benefit of experience or of observation. As to feeding for Southern Rules I agree fully with Col. Grist that physicing is entirely out of place. The feed is short and even in nine days the cock's system can scarcely be restored to its normal state after medicines have been used. With better reason would a nine-day feed not justify artificial means of any kind.

From long experience and close observation, I have arrived at the conclusion that wet feed is not the thing; if kept up the cocks are likely to be soft and it will be hard to keep down flesh. Cocks fed too much soft or wet feed will prove difficult to keep well in hand; when it is desired to "spring" them an ounce or two it may be found impossible. Dry feed certainly brings the best results after the first four days. If the birds are kept in health and their appetites are right they can easily be put on the rise, which should always be done the last two days. Cocks that spring two ounces the day before a main are more likely to win than those that lose two ounces. Cocks must be fought to reach best results, "on the rise."

There has been much said about the use of water: unquestionably a few sips of water three times a day is far better than too much or too little once a day; and while it is unwise to give cocks water and feed during the main, if they are to fight soon, they are greatly benefited and will fight with more heart if given a few sips of weak beef tea. A couple of picks into an apple after heeling is an excellent idea. Bear this in mind, too, that stags cannot stand starvation like cocks. Twenty-four hours of hunger will ruin a main of stags. I paid several hundred dollars for this information; the other fellow went away with $460.

Sparring in the feed is very much overdone. Two sparrings is a plenty; one first after the birds have been given their soft mess to work off their dose. This helps to discover defects both in body and in spirit. At this stage, for instance, it may be found that a certain cock is lame or that another "wheels" in battle, another "ducks," all of which should be "thrown out." The cocks must never be sparred without "muffs," and their heads must be carefully examined to see that there are no wounds left unhealed. If they are bit about the face, canker may set in. To avoid this, sponge the face and head off well with brandy and water.

The second spar should amount to only a few passes. It is best to let the cocks go together then promptly pick them up and let them rush together once more, then examine for wounds and put away. This should be about two days before the fight.

Each cock should have his bath every day. This consists of sponging the face with clean tepid water and wiping, then washing the feet and legs and drying well before putting away. A little whiskey added to the water is good, as it toughens the skin and renders the birl less susceptible to cold. The water used should be just luke warm.

PREPARING COCKS FOR BATTLE.

Cocks as they are, just from their walks, are not *battle worthy;* it is necessary to put them through a course of preparation for battle, which requires good judgment, untiring energy, and time ranging from nine days to three weeks. All that is necessary to be kept in mind as to fitness of cocks for mains, when they should be taken from their walks, in short, everything of importance to the time the cocks are delivered to the feeder, has been discussed in detail elsewhere. It is our present purpose to give a method of feeding and exercise that will be found satisfactory in the different lengths of heel and rules under which mains are fought in this day and generation.

CONDITIONING FOR LONG HEELS.

AS USED BY THE AUTHOR.

From nine to twelve days is long enough for the proper preparation for a good cock for long heel fighting. In so short a time the feeder cannot hope to practice medicine on cocks. He must be provided with perfectly healthy, wide-awake fellows, neither very fat nor very lean. Cocks are not expected to fight so light in long heels as in short, and should not be put through such severe treatment. I am convinced beyond all doubt that physic is more injurious than beneficial for long heel feeding. The most successful long heel fighters in modern times hoot at the idea of using jalap, calomel, soft soap, &c., on cocks, and justly because such things are extremely unnatural and the time a cock is cooped is too short to restore system to its normal condition after so violent a shock. The wisdom of simple feeding may be seen in the record of Col. F. E. Grist on his celebrated campaign in Georgia, when he met and defeated such pastmasters as Chas. F. Brown, "chiefest of ten thousand," in those days; and Sledge and Hanna, the great Arkansas Traveler combination. No physic was used on the cocks, and so simple was their feed that they were kept in perfect condition for an indefinite time. Had the artificial methods of feeding been pursued the cocks would have had to be "pointed" for battles, from which time they would have gone back. Major Bacon, of South Carolina, it is true, used an extremely artificial method, but it is also notoriously true that the Major sometimes showed a very weak main of cocks. Dick Lee in his palmy days had the best success in long heels of all the physicing feeders in my knowledge, but his feed was two weeks. The following will be found easy to follow and if the feeder is faithful and intelligent it will bring the best results in Turner's or Southern rules.

FIRST DAY.

The cocks are supposed to have been brought from their walks as directed heretofore, and put into the feeding coops, the evening or night previous to the morning the first feeding begins. Cocks should be handled and fed every six hours. Beginning at 6 A. M. the first day, saw off each cock's spurs, leaving enough to come well through the socket of a gaff. Weigh the cocks carefully, and record their exact weight on a card suspended from their coops for the purpose. Examine carefully for any defects, including the eyes. Clean each cock of vermin, by using a little grease at the root of the tail, just below the anus, under wings, and just behind the comb, on the head. Some of the best feeders trim every feather clean from the head of each cock, from the top of the head to the base of the neck. Then dust each cock lavishly with a good quality of insect powder, not allowing him to flutter. Now cut the feathers off around the anus and the belly, same as for battle. Return cocks to their coops, being all the time patient and gentle. Give each cock a small tea-cup full of stale bread soaked in boiled milk. Let the cocks remain quiet in their coops until 12 M., when they should be matched by the weights already suspended on their doors, then carefully muffed and sparred, but not long enough to tire or be badly pecked. Cocks are always pecked some in the first spar, and the wounds must be treated. These are easily controlled by rubbing the parts thoroughly with a good quality of brandy in water that has been sterilized by boiling. Return to their coops, noting any defects or imperfections. Should any cock show lameness, turn blue in the face, or prove to be weak in legs or back, such cock is useless and should be thrown out without further loss of time, and, if necessary, a fresh cock put into his place at once. Give the cocks a feed of a tablespoonful of cold corn mush without salt, and let them be quiet till

5 P. M., when they should have twenty flirts, as directed elsewhere in this book. It is necessary to be extremely careful in exercising cocks, until they are accustomed to their new surroundings. Feed for the night, giving a tablespoonful of crumbled soft cornbread, made by cooking a good quality of cornmeal with nothing but water. Close up the house and let all be quiet till the

SECOND DAY.

Remembering all precautions given under "First Day," at 6 A. M., weigh each cock and record his weight; hand-flirt him about twenty times altogther, the three ways described on another page, but not too fast. Rub the cock steadily and gently, on the thighs, down the back and sides a few times. *Never exercise a cock till he pants or shows weariness.* The feeder must use his judgment as to the amount of exercise each cock should have. Wash each cock's feet, legs and face, and dry them thoroughly; then rub a little of the brandy and water on the face and head. Clean out the coops and put in clean, sweet, fresh baled *wheat* straw if possible. Some feeders in the South prefer "pine straw" fresh from the forest, but dry. In handling the straw, dust must be avoided, as should smoking in a cock house be absolutely prohibited. Return each cock to his coop. He can now be fed with a heaping tablespoonful of cracked corn and first quality of clipped oats—equal parts. From the time hard feed is given keep the cock supplied with nice clean gravel—not dirt. Give the cocks three sips of water that has been boiled. Boil clear freestone water three times during the feed and keep it on hand bottled and corked. Offer three sips after each feed. This is better than giving nitre to allay fever. Put the cocks away and let them rest until 12 M., when they should all be exercised again and rubbed as before, but let that part of the rubbing be done down the back from this time out *while the cock stands on his feet.* Feed as before, but not quite so much. At 6 P. M. go through the same order of exercise and feeding, not forgetting the water and supply of clean, big gravel—not dirt. Close the cock house as before, and see that there are no currents of wind, unless it be hot weather, till the morning of the

THIRD DAY.

Commencing at 6 A. M., weigh each cock carefully and compare his weight with his weight the first morning. If he has lost very rapidly, he may need an increase of food, or he may not be well. These are things that must be left to the judgment of the feeder. Large cocks in good flesh will lose several ounces by the third day, smaller ones in proportion. Cocks cooped in good flesh, that lose nothing by the third day are not doing well, and need more exercise or less food, perhaps both. What is called a "good finger" among old English feeders is the ability to tell how a cock is taking his feed, by handling him. This is a gift few possess, and it is safest to *depend on the scales,* which must be used every day. By careful feeding, mostly on *clipped* oats, decreasing the corn, I have taken twelve ounces off a 6.08 cock and fought him hard, quick, and strong in ten days. Here is the point for feeders to determine, whether they prefer liberal feeding and hard work, or less feed and less work. The more a cock is fed in this system the harder he must be worked. Very hard work makes a cock rather sluggish for long heels. Rather light feeding with moderate exercise three times a day is best for long heels. By this plan it will be found that cocks can take severe punishment, yet come up strong, and they will be fast. Let the feeder begin with the idea of taking about seven ounces off a 5.10 cock as he comes from a good walk in winter, and other cocks in that proportion. The larger the more; the smaller the less. After this 5.10 has been reduced by feeding and exercise to 5.03, he should be "sprung" slightly the day before he is to fight, say one-half ounce, by almost no exercise and more feed. But to continue the third day's work. Give each cock about twenty-five flirts in different forms, as heretofore described, not depending too much on one style. Rub him gently as directed above; then put him on the "running board," making him walk up and down the board by catching him gently at the root of the tail and pushing him along with the palm of the hand against the rump, not too fast at first, increasing the speed as the cock learns his business on the board. Give a gentle rubbing, wipe the feet with a cloth dipped in tepid water and return cock to his coop, having put in fresh straw, after cleaning thoroughly. Have an assistant to begin feeding each cock about ten minutes after he has been returned to his coop; same feed as before. Do not wait till the last cock is exercised before feeding. This will not put all cocks on a par. Repeat noon and evening.

FOURTH DAY.

Weigh and record weight as before, noting the progress of your work, as directed under "Third Day." Exercise as before, except add about five flirts and run more, not forgetting that too much exercise is worse than none. As soon as the cock pants or sets down on the board, the feeder will know he is giving too much work. Let up a little if the cocks do not take more satisfactorily. However, it is a bad sign if a cock cannot take thirty deliberate flirts the fourth day. From half-after ten to half-after eleven the cocks should all be walked in walking coops already described. However, coop walking on gusty, damp days is worse than no walking. Hot sunshine is very injurious, and the cocks must not be allowed to eat dirt. If the coops be placed over straw and a few grains of oats, very few, strewn on the straw, the cocks will work hard for the grain and gain much benefit from the open air and sunlight. Cocks should be taken in by 12 M., given their regular exercise and fed as before at noon feed. Do not place them in walking coops just after feeding. It is better for them to be quiet until 2.15, when they may be walked in the coops again for one hour, if the weather be suitable. Be extremely careful to avoid colds in your cocks. If the cock catches cold it becomes necessary to open his bowels with some purgative, which causes him to lose never less than one day, generally two. This cannot be recovered in so short a feed as nine to twelve days. Feed and exercise at 6 P. M., as before.

FIFTH DAY.

Do everything exactly as on the fourth day, but add to the feed at night one-fourth of the white of a hard-boiled egg, chopped fine. Add five flirts to the exercise, and run more.

SIXTH DAY.

Repeat feed and work and walking of the fifth day, but add about five more flirts and run longer on the board.

SEVENTH DAY.

Just as fifth and sixth days in feed and exercise, but give about forty-five flirts and run about twenty times back and forth, rubbing as before.

EIGHTH DAY.

Repeat seventh day, raising the flirts to about fifty for each cock and about twenty-five times back and forth on the running board. The cocks ought to be feeling pretty good, rather corky and hard in flesh. They should seem to enjoy their work and do a good deal of chatting while the exercise is in progress.

The cocks may be sparred today, if the feeder has not already learned all that is needed about each cock. By no means let the cocks spar long enough to tire or lose power. Just long enough to make them eager for more, without having a scratch, is the best rule. Don't forget the brandy and water.

NINTH DAY.

If it is desired to feed the cocks ten, eleven, or twelve days, repeat everything as on the eighth day, adding from three to five flirts, but no more running. But if his is the *last* feed day and the battles will begin tomorrow, "point" the cocks in the following manner: Weigh as before, compare weights; flirt the cock about ten times; run him a few times on the board; rub but little; wash feet and face as before; return to coop; feed two-thirds clipped oats to one-third pop-corn, if possible, one heaping tablespoonful; coop-walk as before. Noon: Same exercise as morning, but give a tablespoonful of oats only, with the three sips of water that has been boiled, as has been directed to be given after each feed throughout the whole time. Evening: take each cock out, handle him a little, place him back, and feed oats and pop-corn, half and half, with one-fourth of the white of a hard-boiled egg; water and let the cock rest without any interruption.

Throughout the feed if friends want to see the cocks they must do so during the hours for exercise and feeding. Absolutely no handling of cocks must be allowed, except as directed in these instructions. Tack the following notice on the cock house if necessary:

Notice—Friends may see the cocks during exercise hours only. John Doe, Feeder.

TENTH DAY.

This is the day for battle, and after weighing and matching has been done according to Turner, or Southern Rules, which it is not necessary to repeat here, cocks may be sprung as much as the feeder may desire, but he must not forget that his labor has been to get rid of useless fat.

While, then, he is at perfect liberty under Southern Rules to feed his cocks and push them up in weight, he must not overlook the fact that weight may be gained at the expense of speed, strength and wind. Feed, therefore, after matching, so as to keep the cock in tip-top fighting trim. If the main is to be fought three days, a gentle rise of a half ounce a day for the *last* cocks to be fought is sufficient. Nor should the cocks be permitted to *rust,* so to speak. It is best to feed and handle the third day cocks just as in the ninth day of the feed. Handle the second day cocks the same way, and coop walk all the cocks when possible.

COCK BREAD AND ITS USE.

Under direction for short heel feeding, by Jakey Magruder, will be found the best recipe for making cock bread published. This bread is the best for all feeders. The feeder must make his bread as there directed, have the same on hand, and feed to his cocks in small quantities, in place of a part of the regular feed, for the sake of variety; and those cocks that do not appear to feed well should be allowed more. The basis of this feed is oats. Nothing bears any comparison with oats in this respect, but cocks very often do not care for them. These can be brought to the oat feed by degrees, which should be done; for the finest food in the world for increasing the wind power and endurance of any animal is oats.

FEEDING FOR SHORT HEELS.

I am giving below the famous system that gave Baltimore its reputation as a cocking center. This system was used by the most successful of the old time feeders, Jakey Magruder, and was afterwards kept as a great secret and improved by a man that has had very few equals in the recollection of men now living—Pat Spellman. It was received by me from intimate friends in Baltimore, who had the confidence of Spellman. I copied the original myself, with the solemn promise that I would not give the secret away. This agreement was entered into with gentlemen even then advanced in years, but all of whom have crossed the great divide. I deem it excusable, if not my duty, under the circumstances to give this feed to the present generation and preserve it from oblivion. However, as it was dictated by a man of few words, it would be well to read the feed already given for long heels, for incidental instructions. As to exercise, the feed is not sufficiently explicit. By increasing the flirts daily as the cocks seem to bear the work well, cocks in this feed should be able to take from about 75 to 125 flirts on the thirteenth day without fatigue. The recipe for cock bread has no equal, and is no small part of the Spellman secret. This feed is given the public for the first time with confidence and pleasure in the thought that it will be an agreeable and welcome surprise, especially to the host of Baltimoreans themselves, who will never forget the success of that famous feeder.

JAKEY MAGRUDER'S RECEIPT.

IMPROVED BY SPELLMAN.

Fourteen days order for short or long combat: When empty, give each cock a pill made of 30 grains cream of tartar, 2 grains sal. purnell, or 3 grains nitre, ¾ grains calomel (the calomel may be left out if thought best), mix together with common rosin soap and molasses. Spar the cocks after giving the medicine. Then give all a common bread toast mixed with warm water, with the water well squeezed out. Then a good drink of the warm water (never give them cold water). Then feed with bread

THE GAME FOWL. 135

mixed with water and milk, three times daily for two days. Then give corn mush and milk one day. Fourth day give each fowl cock-bread (see receipt) three times, and three sips of warm water after feeding. Fifth day, give each cock yellow hominy, barley and oats, and at night one-fourth of the white of a hard boiled egg. Sixth day, hominy, oats and bread and give them three pecks into an apple. Seventh day, barley, oats and hominy; water as usual. Eighth day, hominy, bread and oats, and at night give each one a teaspoonful of chopped beef. Ninth day, hominy, bread oats and barley, and at night one-fourth white of a hard boiled egg. Tenth day, bread, oats and hominy. Spar with muffs each pair of fowls, or do so the next (eleventh) morning before feeding. Eleventh day, hominy, bread, barley. Twelfth day, bread, hominy and oats, and one-fourth the white of a hard boiled egg at night. Thirteenth day, hominy and oats. Fourteenth day, hominy, oats and bread, and at night (this has reference to fighting in daylight, say about 10 in the morning) the whites of half a dozen hard boiled eggs chopped fine as hominy, and bread, oats and hominy enough for a double feed. Pour over this half a pint of ale or porter. Then take one quart of sweet milk (boiling) and pour over it, stir until it becomes a thick mush, and give each cock all he will eat, warm. Keep cocks warm with plenty of straw under them. Fifteenth day, before the fight give each cock one dozen grains of hominy.

If fowls must be traveled after being fed, be sure they are kept warm (not hot). During treatment, keep fowls warm, but never hot. The legs should be washed every morning in lukewarm water, and the heads washed thoroughly with a wash composed of one teaspoonful of cider vinegar, and two of whiskey or brandy, in a pint of water. Should the fowls be quite thin, all the water given them should be iron water procured by pouring fresh water into a pan containing two or three pounds of tenpenny nails. It should stand twenty-four hours before using aad should be made fresh two or three times while feeding.

Cock bread:—Take 7 lbs. best bolted oatmeal. 2 1-2 lbs. best yellow corn dough, ten cents worth purest rock candy, the white only of fifteen fresh eggs, a bottle of the best Scotch ale, a bottle best Dublin porter; powder and put the rock candy into a large bread pan, pour the ale over it, stirring well till thoroughly dissolved, then after having stirred thoroughly (not heat up) put in the whites of eggs (fifteen), stir these all well together, then add the porter, gradually sift the corn and oatmeal into the mixture, until a stiff dough is produced, bake an inch thick or more by a slow fire until done (not burnt).

EXTENDING THE FEED.

If it be required, the feed I have given for long heels may be prolonged by adding as many days as may be necessary *just like the eighth*, simply putting off "pointing" until the day before the main. In a feed so natural and simple, it is possible to keep cocks in fix for battle several weeks.

For short heels, some claim that three weeks is necessary; some, even four. If the feeder holds to this opinion, he should insert as many days as he chooses just after the 13th and with the same treatment, when work may be increased or not to suit the feeder; but cocks must be "pointed" as directed, on the last feed day.

HEELS OR GAFFS, AND HEELING.

To be successful in the pit, a cocker must arm his cocks with suitable weapons. It would be absurd for the United States Government to spend millions of dollars training soldiers and then send them against the enemy, with old rifles—match locks. There is not so much to be lost in short heels, as in long; good long heels on a very poor cock will whip a first-class cock poorly heeled.

No wonder then that cockers from time out of mind have, valued at fabulous prices, certain favorite old gaffs; but the difficulty of getting a first-class pair is not nearly so great now as formerly. However, once the heeler finds by actual trial that he has the right thing, he should cease to experiment.

There is no question that America leads the world in gaff making. A number of gaff-makers have excelled and by their fidelity to an ambitious purpose, have won universal praise. Conspicuous among these are the veteran W. J. Helwig, of North Carolina, whose New York Regulations (1 1-4 inch) have no equal; and Geo. Huff, of Kentucky, whose long gaffs are the most perfect steel spurs ever manufactured in any country. On another page will be found pictures of the New York Regulation gaffs tied on as it would be done by the skillful artists of York and Jersey; and of the style gaff used in Southern or Turner's Rules, tied on as it would be done by many leading cockers of the South. These cuts represent heels kept in stock by The Gleezen Supply Co., of Lawrence, Mass., at the head of which is the distinguished founder of the National Cockers' Association, H. B. Gleezen, popularly known as "Dad" Gleezen. This company represents the wonderful development of cock fighting in the United States; so great has the demand for cocking supplies become in recent times, that here we have a large concern devoted entirely to meeting the demand for cockers' goods from gape medicine to steel spurs.

Two things—good gaffs, and properly tied on—are essential to success in the pit. No gaff is safe if made of steel too hard in temper, or too soft. The former will break, leaving the cock at the mercy of his foe; while the latter will twist up in the course of a battle and perhaps kill the wearer. The best quality of steel for a gaff is that which will bear great pressure before it gives way, but will under too much strain *bend* and not break. Some heel makers will insist on making gaffs of steel too hard for the purpose. I have seen two pairs from one maker snap off in one short main. Heels should be as light as possible consistent with strength. Nearly all the heels manufactured up to this time have had too much metal in the socket. It is hard to imagine how heavy and unwieldy a pair of 2¾ inch gaffs become in a long dragging battle, to a weary, wounded cock. I have not the slightest hesitancy in claiming that skeleton gaffs (i. e., those made with a large opening and a narrow ring in the place of the regular heavy socket) are the best. But such gaffs can be properly tied on only by a professional heeler, and cannot be recommended to amateurs. A well made "skeleton" gaff may be tied on by the proper use of washers and packing in any position the most expert heeler may desire, which is impossible with gas-pipe heels.

The most ordinary kinds of heels are: (1) New York Regulation inch and a quarter, which are blunt and big in the blade—the most severe heel in use at the present day. (2) Inch and a half for Maryland Rules, which differs little from any New York Regulation, except in being a quarter of an inch longer. (3) Cincinnati Drop Socket, which is a heel of any length so made by projecting the metal in the socket downward as to throw the blade near the "prop toe" of the cock. (4) Half Drops, heels that have the blade lower on the leg than regulation, but not (5) Full Drop Sockets, which have the blade as near the "prop toe" as it can be gotten, when tied on for battle. (6) Singletons, which are made practically "half drops" by making a bend downward in the blade near the socket, then raising the blade to a suitable height by a graceful curve in the blade. But it is not the purpose of this book to go more fully into shapes of gaffs. The curious reader may find all he desires in such matters in the various handsome illustrated catalogues of gaff makers who are advertisers in such publications as "Grit and Steel," published at Gaffney, S. C., "Game Fowl Monthly," published at Sayre, Pa., and "Southern Pit Games," published at Blakely, Ga., and others.

The *choice* of heels is a matter almost entirely dependent upon a cocker's experience and his ability to pick spurs adapted to the cocks he fights. I cannot in this connection come to believe that "full drops" are the proper style of gaff for shanky cocks, and I prefer them for cocks set low to the ground. Note well one fact in this connection: A long-legged cock will be found bloody *above the spur* after a long battle; a short-legged cock, on the other hand, will be found bloody about the natural heel and near the foot. Any breeder has observed this fact in the combats among his stags before they are walked. The average marksman must have his rifle to his shoulder, so the cock should have that gaff tied on which points from the part of his leg with which he strikes his antagonist. If the reader has been a close observer, he will recall the fact that after those sanguinary combats that have occurred in his yard, his very high stationed stags are often found bloodiest just below the knee, and frequently there are no signs of the leg below the spurs having hit the bloody neck and head of the other stag. These things speak volumes to the thoughtful heeler.

One thing more in this connection: Avoid all unusual styles of gaffs. The general shape of a natural spur was considered by Providence a dangerous one; and it is a well known fact that, although the natural spur of a cock is blunt and hard to force in beyond the point, yet the Spaniards fight their small breed of cocks in no other weapon, and with all the artful side-stepping and wheeling characteristics of that famous stock, death frequently ensues in a few seconds. Spaniards who frequented the pits far South a few years ago were always ready to match their three and a half pound cocks with natural spurs against the largest American cocks armed with steel gaffs, if allowed odds. It is also true that fights in parts of Scotland and in Belgium at the present time, where cocks are still fought with natural spurs, do not last any longer than those in England and in this country in the same length of spur. Hence, it follows that nature knew what she was doing when she put the spur where she did on a cock's leg, and also knew what was the most effective shape for that spur.

As to the contention seldom heard that one steel gaff is as effective as another; such a contention is absurd. An extra fine cock armed with inch-and-a-quarter gaffs may whip an ordinary cock in 2½, but all things being equal, the odds are three to one in favor of the long heels.

HEELING.

With a little practice, heeling is by no means difficult in short heels. The ambitious man has only to be faithful in the observation of a few essentials, and the cock on which he ties a gaff will have an equal show.

First. Your strings, or "wax-ends," for tying on the gaffs should be made of the best flax shoe thread, at least four strands, twisted together and well waxed with first-grade beeswax. The *wax-end* should be neither too large nor too small—never over six strands. These should be about two feet and a half long, and should be made before the fighting begins, and in sufficient numbers to meet any emergency.

Second. "Packing" is necessary to make the gaff fit tight enough over the leg. The substances in common use are: Paper dampened, which is required by Philadelphia

Rules; kid, in general use for all other rules. This is gotten by cutting an old kid glove into strips of different lengths and about one-quarter of an inch broad, some slightly less, some slightly more; Chamois, which is thicker and softer than kid and can be utilized to greater advantage. This should be cut into strips as directed for kid, and a few washers added, to be put over the natural spur and pressed smoothly against the cock's legs. I am forced to believe that Chamois thus handled is far more comfortable to the cock, and a smooth fit can be gotten. Chamois seems to combine the virtues of paper and kid.

Third. These things, with gaffs, shears, and a knife with pointed blade for cutting off the gaffs after each fight, complete what is often called a "cocker's kit." The *kit* should be kept in good order so as to avoid all confusion and loss of time.

Fourth. "Trimming," or "cutting out." This is the method by which cocks are stripped for battle. The cock should be gently but firmly held so as to avoid all struggling and fluttering, and the feathers that remain about the belly and rump neatly cut off close to the hide. Then, lift the end of the cock's wings over the root of the tail and cut off the heavy shield of feathers over the thigh. Then trim all feathers from the thighs. Turn the cock over and cut out other side same way. Hold the cock squarely upon the palm of the hand—if possible use an assistant—then place the shears under the saddle feathers; beginning at the root of the tail cut every feather neatly off, working from the tail toward the head. Cut other side same way, then trim off all fluffy or loose feathers at gall bladder. If the cock has a perfect tail, cut off every king or sickle feather down to the skin. Push the fan forward and cut out the loose feathers under it. Then take the fan in the left hand and cut it off so as to leave it sufficiently long to prop the cock if he should fall backwards, and to give him a graceful gamey look in the pit. If the cock has a defective tail, utilize all the feathers he has to give him enough tail for battle. Next, stretch out the wing with the left hand, or have the assistant to do so with his right hand if trimming the cock's left wing; with his left hand if trimming the cock's right wing. Commencing at the short, stiff flight feathers, cut them off very short. Take each flight feather, or primary, between the fingers and thumb, and cut it off, not straight across, but slanting, so as to leave the sharp points towards the cock's breast. Not much can be cut from cocks that have very short wings, but cocks with long, full wings should be trimmed so that the end of the flight feathers after cutting should be about on a line with the cock's rump. After cutting each primary, close up the secondary part of the wing and cut all at one stroke to suit the length of the trimmed primaries. Here trimming for battle often ends in Southern and Western Rules, but never in New York, Maryland and Philadelphia Rules. In these rules the trimming out is completed by running the hand under the entire shawl at the shoulders, placing the thumb and fingers around the neck. In this position push the whole shawl forward towards the head, as if the cock were angry and preparing to spring upon another cock. Place the shears close to the skin on the left side of the cock's neck, at the throat, and with a firm grip and steady hand cut down all the way around the cock's neck, as closely to the hand as possible. This will leave only a few straggling shawl feathers. Trim these off neatly and then trim all loose feathers from the cock's head and face. If a muff or tassel, take these ornaments off clean, and the fowl is then stripped for action.

N. B.—The cock house should be supplied with a barrel over which the cock is held while being cut out, and into which all feathers should be deposited and kept from floating around.

Fifth. "Holding" is an art. The assistant should seat himself upon a stool or armless chair facing the heeler. Press the cock gently against the person, if the left heel is to be tied on, having the cock so pressed against the body with the left hand, with his head to the left and his back against the assistant, the right leg firmly between thumb and finger of the left hand; with the right hand stretch out the cock's left leg almost straight, holding securely though softly with the flat inner surface of the leg level, the thumb resting on same, just above the spur. The holder may rest his hand on his knee, which will make his position steadier. As the heeler places packing around the spur to make the gaff socket fit the spur stub, the holder should slip his thumb up and place same on the loose ends until the heeler proceeds with the work. The holder should also place the ball of the thumb on the single knot when tied in the wax-end until the heeler doubles the knot. When the left heel has been tied on, the heeler sshould give the cock a few seconds' rest by placing him on his feet and letting him stretch. Then, placing the cock in his left hand, head to the right, the holder should press him gently but securely with back to his person as before, holding the leg that has been heeled safely as directed before, but between the thumb and finger of the *right* hand, stretching the cock's right leg out with the left hand, and assisting the heeler with the ball of the thumb in placing his packing and turning his wax-ends, as directed before. After the heeling is done, the holder stands the bird on his feet as before, and then delivers him to the heeler, who in turn hands the cock over to the pitter. The principle is to hold firmly, gently, securely, and conveniently for the heeler.

Sixth. Heeling, or tying on the gaff requires a good eye

and a steady hand. The less experienced but ambitious heeler will find much assistance in certain points often overlooked. We shall assume he has a pair of heels properly made and leathered. This being true, the form of the heel socket and leathers should be carefully noted. Setting on a stool facing the holder, who stretches out the left leg as before directed, the heeler places his "packing" around the base of the spur in such a way as to make the base of the socket fit nicely against the cock's leg; taking the longer pieces of kid (if kid is used), cup the stub of the spur by placing as many pieces of the dampened kid across same as may be necessary to make the gaff socket fit, being sure to have the ends of the kid go down low enough to be caught and pressed against the leg, when the gaff is forced on over the packing. The packing is usually dampened by running it through the mouth. Never have packing very wet, nor can the work be well done if it is too dry. The packing in place, take the left gaff, point toward the eye, holding the same by the leathers between the thumb and fingers of each hand, thumbs close to the socket; press gaff on but *do not twist* in doing so, or the stub may be shelled, giving the cock much unnecessary pain. Now note well whether packing is necessary above or below the socket in order to raise or lower the point of the gaff to the right position. If the point should be raised, put more below the spur; if the point is too high, put more above the spur. But do not forget that if the rules call for heeling *flat on the leg,* nothing will be allowed between the gaff and the leg except what is absolutely necessary. The more put between the leg and the socket of the gaff the longer the gaff becomes; so that what often is done happens, namely, that an inch and a quarter heel may be made virtually an inch and a half heel. This is a great advantage over fair heeling flat on the leg, and unless the rules be modified beforehand, a fight won by a cock so heeled with too much packing would be forfeited. But as a general thing, more *bolstering* is needed *above* than below the spur, because there is serious danger of having the point of the gaff too high. If the gaff is properly made it is easy to locate the exact elevation of the point by line of socket; that is, the gaff should be on the leg as if *tied to the side of a man's first finger held perpendicularly*. Another test: The point of a gaff is at the proper elevation when the gaff is tied to a perpendicular rod that fits the naked socket. Try this test experimentally. It will also serve as a good test of the gaff maker's work. Therefore, applying this principle, bolstering must be resorted to until the same relative position of the point is secured on the cock's leg. The same principle applies to front and back, and the gaff should be so tied on as to have the leather *straight around the leg,* not twisted. This is another test of good gaffs. If they are not properly leathered, they must be twisted to put the gaff on right. But an equally important secret in successful heeling is the position of the point relative to the leader in the leg. By working a cock's hind, or prop, toe, the leader may be seen working up near the knee inside the leg. The great weight of authority in heeling for short heels favors putting the point of one gaff just on the inner edge of this leader, the other on the outer edge. A cock heeled inside of that leader is said to be "heeled in," or "heeled close." When cocks become weary they nearly always cut themselves if heeled close, though they do more execution while fresh. In setting long heels some heelers follow the leader the same way, but many of the best heelers in the South at the present time heel much "wider," going so far as to set both points entirely outside the line of the back of the leg. One old time South Carolinian who fought cocks between those two cities, used to say to his young friends on this point, "Boys, set one in Greenville and the other in Columbia." When a cock is clipping, single-striking, and sparring, no doubt close heeling in long heels is best; but when it comes to a mix-up, desperate body fighting and shuffling, there can be little question that "heeling wide," as this old cocker advised, is preferable. In the same way, a whole strain of shuffling cocks would require wide heeling, while high-flying, sparring, single-blow strains would do better heeled close. However, any cock heeled very close is liable to cut himself in any heels. Some prefer to put the left in, others the right in. I have never seen any difference, though the Mexicans verily believe that cocks do most execution in slashers, with the left leg. The point of the gaff having been fixed and the gaff securely set, carry the ends of the leathers around the legs so as to make them fit smoothly and closely, lapping so as to leave the outer end pointing to the rear, when possible. The holder having placed the ball of his finger on the ends of the leather, the heeler takes the wax-ends in hand, places the string against the leather just below the blade of the gaff as close up as possible, keeping the ends of the string about equal. He then carries the string around and brings it back, drawing it tight enough to hold the point of the gaff securely in position where it has already been set. He then makes a knot by running the ends through the loop twice instead of once. Now the two ends of the string are carried around the socket of the gaff above the spur, there tied in a hard knot exactly even above the spur, when the ends are carried around the leg and brought back, where they are drawn close but not too tight, and tied in a hard knot as before. In heeling, every knot should be a hard knot. Cut the ends of the string off, but not too close. Press them down with the ball of the thumb. Work the prop toe to see if the leader moves freely, and pull the toes of the cock, allowing him then to stand upon his feet. It has been said that the string must be tied very carefully above the spur but cannot be drawn too tightly below. This is a dangerous rule, and will lead to cramping the cock. Nine out of ten of the men I have seen heel cocks draw the strings too tightly, and I have seen many a fine game cock murdered by just such foolishness. Tie the string firmly but not any tighter than is needed to effect the purpose for which the string is used, whether that be above or below the gaff, but always tie below first. This is a safe and satisfactory way of using wax-ends, but by no means the only way. By studying the picture on another page it may readily be seen that the string has not been carried around the socket as recommended. Some good men prefer the plan in the picture, but my preference is the system I have described. With it I have gotten the best results. The pitter will next walk the cock up and down two or three times, holding him by the tail, then lick his face well with the tongue and lips, after which he should be given two or three pecks of an apple, carried to the pit side and delivered to the pitter. Here end the duties of the "handler" and the "heeler." However, the heeler should be on hand to take charge of the cock after each battle, cut off the heels and return him to his coop if alive, for the heeler is responsible for the heels throughout the main.

RING TACTICS.

The general in ring tactics is the pitter. On him rests the whole responsibility after the heeler delivers a cock to him trimmed out and heeled for battle.

A man who is cut out for the business becomes a good pitter by knowing the rules, being quick to think and act, a good nurse, cool, quiet, courteous and faithful to his friends. Some of these things any man may possess, but others come from careful study and long experience. This is what a pitter ought to be.

The biggest ass in the whole range of sport is a quarrelsome pitter who gazes right and left while the cocks are fighting, and engages in a war of words with critics always at a cock fight. An intelligent pitter never talks, except when he must. He acts just as if there were no one in the house but him and the other pitter. The fellow who shoots off his mouth at every half-tight ignoramus who ventures to make some unfavorable observation, is too shallow ever to become a successful pitter. At best the task is such a difficult one that I have never known any man to excel as a handler in more than one set of rules. Watson, of Philadelphia, and Chas. Eslin, of Washington, D. C., stand preeminent when in Philadelphia Rules alone; "Toney" Billingham and Cass, of New York, made their reputation entirely in New York Rules; Steve Moore and Henry Flock owe their reputation to their victories in long heels. Good "Kirk," of Baltimore, surpassed all men in Maryland Rules, though he was *among the best in* Philadelphia Rules.

A pitter that knows his business will stick to the rules every time. He is a man that is thoroughly acquainted with rascality in every form without being a rascal himself. A thief has never thriven to the end, as a pitter. The model of a pitter worthy of emulation was Kirk, already mentiond. He pitted thousands of cocks in his lifetime and won many a close main just by his cool head, good nursing and knowledge of the rules. He had no equal in Maryland Rules and was the peer of any man for years in Philadelphia Rules. Yet no man can say that he ever in his life saw Kirk, after pitting cocks for fifty years, do a single mean or unfair thing.

Pitters of low instinct and given to dirty methods lose the confidence of all their acquaintances, and degrade the sport.

Such men must be condemned and suppressed if the genteel class of cockers expect to raise this amusement to the plane of bird hunting and the chase.

It is impossible to name the many unfair advantages a dishonest pitter can take of greenhorns. In New York, for instance, nothing can be done to make a cock fight. No nursing, nor pulling of feathers from the eye, yet sharpers do these things in the slyest possible fashion. I have seen them rub the floor of the pit with the sole of a shoe when it became necessary to make a cock bite, or take the count. Other rules prohibited the doing of anything to make a cock fight, yet unfair pitters find a way. They often prick a cock, or slyly pluck feathers from his rump. A blind bird if game is always the best claimer, thus when it comes to the simple question of taking the count in Philadelphia Rules, the pitter who can outwit his opponent will pluck a soft feather and stick it over his cock's eye, as if it had gotten there accidentally.

If honorable men are fighting a main on the square, and the agreement, no matter in what rules, is, "the best cock to win," there is rarely any trouble. I am perfectly free to say that cockers around New York and Philadelphia are entirely too technical, and such a demand is made on pitters by disorderly rabble the fraternity find it impossible to slough off in those cities, that it is often more than a man can resist; while the methods of the Baltimore pits, especially as run by Pat Garvey and his successor, O'Conner, are of the highest order, and crooked dealings are unknown. At the South as a rule, cocks are fought for amusement, and the best class do not care to win with a dunghill cock or a runaway, or by tricks of any kind.

A wide-awake pitter will see that none of these tricks is resorted to and he will see that his opponent observes the rules, which contain provisions against most of the common errors and tricks of ignorant and dishonest handlers.

Some things, however, the rules do not contain, yet are perfectly fair and should be done by a pitter: A cock that has been blinked should be "delivered" with his good eye to the other cock, unless he has the count and does not care to stir his foe to action. Never press the fight when a cock needs nursing and will improve if he gets it. If a cock has received a death blow, pit as quickly as possible; he may make one more desperate effort and kill his antagonist. In New York and Philadelphia Rules, never urge a cock to fight if he has the count, nor force him upon his foe. Stay away as much as possible. It is by virtue of this practice that a dead or a quitting cock sometimes wins in these rules. Until the rules have been changed, such things will be possible. In the last main (1903) Geo. Wilson pitted against Casey, of Boston, a Grade Aseel *runaway* won and perfectly fair under Philadelphia Rules. Just as soon as the cocks were brought to a breast, before the Casey cock could bite the Aseel having the count, turned tail and ran away. Wilson counted the game cock out with a rank quitter. It was also seen in this fight how important it is to take the count, for had Casey taken the count, Wlison's runaway could not have won.

A great trick is unfair breasting. A dead cock having taken the count, upon an unfair breast, may win, by being slipped under the other cock, or laid down on the blind side of a blnker, so that the other cock cannot see him, while the pitter of the down cock takes the last count and counts out a live game cock. This is an impossibility, however, if the pitter attends to his business and insists on the rules.

A man-fighting cock should be carefully delivered, so as to avoid his turning on the pitter, giving his foe a chance to strike him from behind. A blind cock is by no means whipped, and if game is more desperate and kicks harder than a cock that can see. But a blind cock ought always to be handled so as to keep him facing the enemy, and an expert pitter will avoid every pitting he can by counting his cock up as quickly as possible, so as to let his blind cock never meet his foe except upon a breast. Keep the count with a blind cock, if possible.

Whatever is to be done in the pit, do quickly, though the advantage is not always with the first man to handle. I saved the life of a very fine cock once by snapping him up as quick as a flash just as the other cock, both outside the pit limits, struck a vicious blow with long heels. I also won against one of the greatest fighters in the South by letting the other pitter handle first. The cocks had fought beyond the limits of the pit, and it was optional whether we handled or not. My cock struck the last blow and killed a great cock, by his handler's interrupting.

Nursing an injured cock in the pit is allowed under some rules. When permissible the breeder should exert his utmost energy and skill to relieve the sick cock. Often a cock that has been struck in the back and coupled or "knocked down," may be put on his feet again, by counting him up as quickly as possible, and rubbing him freely, hard down the back, and by pulling the cock's legs down at full length with the bird resting on the palm of the hand. Kirk of Baltimore was a famous nurser and won with many cocks after odds were twenty to one against him. He nursed deliberately and always *gently*—he was never nervous and hasty. Force the fight when your cock has a death rattle; do not push matters if your cock has a light rattle. He will soon recover if not forced to exert himself. A little rubbing of the knee joints is good for a weary cock and is easily done with the thumb. Ordinarily, nothing is gained by an incessant pulling at and pinching of a wounded, weary cock; but at times, badly hurt cocks become very drowsy. Such must be aroused in time for each pitting, sometimes by clucking like a cock and pinching the bird's face; at other times by slightly biting the comb. However, a cock should always be so handled as to keep him in heart, and lead him to think the pitter his friend.

By kind permission of Col. F. E. Grist, we herewith present his Keep which has been for forty years a success:

GRIST'S KEEP.

In this section (the South) cocks will be found in good fighting condition in January. While they may apparently be in plumage as early as November, only a very few will be found with that hardness of feather necessary for a cock to be at *his best* before January, yet more cocks are fought in November and December than in the other months and many make hard stubborn fights.

To properly condition a cock to make his fight for life, it is necessary that the feeder should be provided with proper stalls, sun coops, exercise board, muffs, and pit in which to train his cocks.

From my experience of over forty years I find that a stall 40 inches long, 30 inches high, 24 inches deep, with roost pole so made as to be left in place or taken out will be found the most convenient. My door to this stall is hung with hinges and fastened with a hook; this door is in a neat frame and the size is 12x16 inches. Four inches from bottom of door is a small bracket shelf upon which to set the feed cup, which is held in place by a piece of hoop iron. The opening of this coop should be covered with clean straw, which should be changed every third day.

The sun coop that I use is flat on top with slide door and is 40 inches long, 26 inches wide, and 24 inches high. In our Southern country these coops are indispensable for the purpose of allowing a cock to exercise himself and should be placed on such ground as he can roll and dust himself in. If the weather be cold he should be placed where not exposed too long in the sun, but should be allowed to remain much longer in sun coop in Summer than in the Fall or Spring.

FLIRTING AND TOSSING.

Having your stalls and coops, you will next need an exercise board. Mine is 31 inches from the floor, cushioned on top to prevent hurting the cock's feet during his flirting or tossing exercise. My exercise board is 10 feet long and 2 feet wide. A cock should be tossed first day not over 25 times. This is increased each day until he will show no fatigue when tossed 100 times. You must not toss your cock high in commencing this exercise, but gradually increase the height you toss him, changing the position of cock. An experienced cocker can tell very much about the fighting qualities of a cock by observing how he acts in being tossed. While exercising a cock, as soon as you find he is fatigued, do not wait until he is unable to stand, but stop his work and put him back in his coop. A cock is not tossed more than 4 or 5 feet above the cushion and usually not so high.

EXERCISING A VICIOUS COCK.

Another method of training a cock is to get in the pit, holding another cock in your hand, and by tossing the cock you are conditioning, you can get him to fly all over the pit after you, and he will learn to strike the cock in your hand, hold him as high as you will. It may be necessary, in commencing, to hold your cock with his head towards the cock in training, but he will soon learn to strike the cock, you holding him in such position as to motion his tail at him. This is not only one of the finest exercises possible, but it trains a cock to strike his opponent during actual battle in any part of the body, and not wait to find the head, which has cost thousands of cocks their lives. Many a cock, untrained, will not strike an opponent if his tail be towards him, but will wait until he can see his opponent's head. Training will correct this. You cannot over-estimate this plan of exercise, and with a very vicious cock it is one of the few plans that can be adopted, and by this method you can give him exercise. Very often a vicious cock is damaged more by being handled than benefited.

MUFFS.

No description is necessary as all are acquainted with this important article. They are usually made of chamois skin stuffed with wool. Cheaper ones are made of thick homespun cloth, cut in a circle, 3½ inches in diameter, gathered up and stuffed with wool. Tape for strings will answer every purpose.

While I'm aware that many cockers do not use muffs, I know that it is as impossible for cockers to train a cock without them as it would be to train a standard-bred horse to trot without a sulkey. It is only by sparring a cock that you can know his speed or his style of fighting, and it is only by sparring that you can possibly know that he is sound in legs and wings, and this is the best method by which to judge his strength and killing power.

I prefer my pit to be dug up till the ground is soft, but when you have no ground floor straw can be used, the object being to prevent cocks from bruising themselves against any hard substance.

It is by the use of muffs that cocks can be trained to fly from the score the moment they are loosed; and why I urge so strongly the importance of muffs is that so many have used them without knowing how and condemn their use. I dwell upon this at length. A cock that is muffed too much and allowed to get tired, will acquire the habit of dodging. If fresh from his walk and muffed (sparred) too long, he will be sore two or three days, and no matter how fast when first sparred, will be found comparatively slow until over his soreness. This is charged up against the muffs. It must be remembered that the harder you work (exercise) your cock, whether flirting or muffing, the slower he becomes.

My plan for muffing is, the first time I spar my cocks I let them spar until I see they are becoming tired; after this I never allow them to strike but three or four blows. In pitting my cocks when muffed, I first let them bill until very mad. They are then set within two feet of each other, and this trains them to commence fighting as soon as they are turned loose. By this training your cock is apt to get in the first blow, which frequently settles the fight. If for no other good, it prevents a cock from walking all over the pit before commencing his fight, as untrained cocks will frequently do. In training cocks I spar every other day. I find no advantage in using weight, on cock's legs, to make him strike higher. A cock to be a good fighter must get up high, and with your muffs in sparring you can tell whether he is worth training, or should be discarded.

RACE TRACK.

I have found only a few cocks that training would not cure of their savageness. These I could best exercise by having a small boy chase them around a track I have for that purpose—one so constructed that they can not fly out, though he has hurdles over which he must fly. This cock running is good exercise, but the cock must not be frightened and made wild. Remember you cannot have a cock too tame.

SWING.

I have not used a swing in several years. This, too, is fine exercise, and one who has never witnessed it would hardly believe that a cock could be made to swing himself, very much like a school boy when he "pumps" to make himself go backward and forward.

FEED.

Oats of all grain is the best to make muscle, and is the least heating, which makes it an ideal food. Corn is the most heating and is the greatest fat-producing grain we have. But a moment's thought, and it will be seen that the few days in which the feeder has to condition a cock, food will have but little part in making muscle, and that food which the cock is most accustomed to and relishes most is the best.

The time to have fed him on oats to develop his muscle was when he was growing up and on his walk. Now no better food can be found than our common corn. This I have cracked into very coarse hominy or grits, and is the principal food when fed dry; the meal to be sifted out through a coarse sieve. When fed damp the meal can be washed out. With this damp grit is mixed an equal part of clean oats. This dry grits, when eggs are used, is mixed with an equal quantity of the white of hard boiled eggs, no portion of the yellow being used.

A good bread is made of finely-sifted oat meal, stirred into 1 quart of sweet milk with the beaten whites of 12 eggs and one gill of good grape wine. This mixture is to be of same consistency as you would have it for cake. Bake in shallow pan until done; then cut into small pieces—small enough to be easily swallowed by cocks. Beef, when fed, whether cooked or raw, is to be lean—no fat used.

It will be seen that the above food is substantial and easily digested.

Cocks should be selected from their walks at night, and after being carefully examined for any defect in health, if satisfactory, should be examined for lice. I clip the tail about proper length for fighting; clip the feathers from behind at vent, and dust him with some reliable insect powder. If he is from a good walk his crop will be full and not until the afternoon will he be sufficiently empty to commence your work. His spurs are sawed off—leaving about one-half inch. Now you give a hard sparring. When finished, if worth conditioning, wash his head, feet and legs with equal parts of whiskey and water; dry with cloth and put him in stall. Now give his first feed, since he has been up—a heaping teaspoonful of cracked corn, slightly dampened. As soon as you can see, feed the next morning. This cock is to be taken from the stall and handled carefully, so he will not hurt himself in a struggle to escape. I now grasp each of his legs at the knee (not tight), his head and breast being towards me. With little practice you can teach a cock to flap his wings until he exhausts himself. There is no better plan for testing his wind. This I always do preparatory to flirting. I now flirt him about twenty-five times, and then wash his feet, legs and head, dry him and put him in stall. I again give him a heaping tablespoonful of damp grits and oats, and when he has eaten this I take him out and drop him in sun coop for at least half an hour. He is then put in his stall. If he is empty at 12 o'clock you can feed him bread and lean beef, chopped fine. He wants now, and during the balance of keep, all the food he will eat up eagerly, the object being to keep his appetite sharp so as to make him eat all that it is possible for him to digest between feeds.

You can soon regulate his feed, keeping him a little hungry. I give what water and food a cock wants. About four dips of water after each feed is enough.

Just before dark your cock should be flirted again, say twenty-five times, and then given a good feed of cracked corn (grits) dry.

REDUCING COCKS.

Only by experience can a man tell about the fatness of his cock. It is seldom that a cock, found on a good walk up to January, will require to lose on day of fight more than 4 ounces. This I mean for 5½ and 6-pound cocks; smaller ones about half that much. In January if I take up a cock from his walk in fine order, say 6 pounds, the third day he will be reduced about 8 ounces, but by the ninth day he will have gained back 2 or 3 ounces. Resting him on the ninth he will gain one or two more, making him fight within 3 or 4 ounces of his weight on walk. This resting a cock on the ninth day is called pointing him. The exercise and work you have given him has tended to make him slow, but the one day's rest will bring him out of the stall full of fire and dash. He will be like a pampered horse. You have gotten all of the surplus inside fat out of him; you have developed his muscles and wings and put new life into him. He feels good—*feels like a fighting cock!*

For fear I may be misunderstood about reducing, let me say that I sometimes find a cock in January so fat that I have no take off over a pound. These are either those lazy, indolent cocks that have small room in which to exercise, or had some favored stable walk. I find that, after I get the lice off and regulate the feed, I more often have to add to the weight than reduce it. Cockers whom I have defeated in winter have stated to me they doubted my keep for summer fighting. They had fought cocks in January weighing say 6 pounds, and in hot weather the same cocks had done well at 5½ pounds, and they imagined they had done this. But this is nature. The cock on his walk in January and July would show the same difference, or more. I have never seen a cock from the walk, when he had plenty of exercise, in the fall of the year up to December, but what needed more flesh. Plenty of feed with plenty of exercise is the secret.

I have given the kind I deem best; the quantity you must regulate so as to keep the cock with a keen appetite. The change of food is only necessary to prevent your cock from getting surfeited on one kind. The lean beef is commenced the first day, and if it does not disagree with him (making his bowels too loose), can be fed in the morning every other day. The cracked corn and oats is your main food, and if no other is convenient, is good enough alone.

You must always exercise your cock, morning and evening, about the same time of day, before feeding, and if doing well his crop should be comparatively empty. Feed early in the morning, at noon and late in the afternoon. I feed all damp food the first two feeds, giving dry food the last time.

I like to give a cock at least one feed of white of egg and grits the night before he is to fight the next day. The cock's droppings should not be allowed to get too hard—should be a little moist. If too hard, a feed of the beef will correct it; if too loose, a feed of soda crackers will check same. In five days from commencing your cock should, if handled nicely, be over his soreness. This work has reduced him, and he will now gain by the ninth day. You should have him so well *in hand*, that by not exercising he would gain, in twenty-four hours, from 3 to 4 ounces. He should be able to stand the most active tossing—at least one hundred flirts—without show of fatigue; but if his fight is to take place on the tenth day, I do not on this, the ninth day, give him the hundred flirts, but instead about twenty-five, morning and afternoon. Feeding goes on as usual. I also let him take his usual exercise in sun coop. Next morning (day of fight) I give no exercise. If to be fought in the morning, about half feed for breakfast; but if to be fought in the afternoon, full feed.

It takes about nine days to exercise your cock sufficiently to give him wind and develop muscle. In this condition you can with use of judgment keep him with advantage for fifteen or twenty days, remembering to rest him the day before his fight. I recommend no medicine. If a cock needs doctoring he is not fit to fight. I am sometimes obliged to order one of these over fat cocks and to these, when time is short, I give a small dose of calomel, or a teaspoonful of Epsom salts and butter mixed half and half, or pills of half dozen grains of cream o' tartar and half dozen grains of rhubarb, mixed with unsalted butter and lard. Any one of these is good to work him out. Follow these instructions and you will have your cock in good fix.

SOUTHERN RULES.

NOTE. On the morning the main is to commence the parties decide by lot who shows first. It is to be remembered that the party obtaining choice generally chooses to weigh first and consequently obliges the adverse party to show first, as the party showing first weighs last. When the show is made by the party, the door of the cock house is to be locked and the key given to the other party, who immediately repairs to his cock house and prepares for weighing. There ought to be provided a pair of good scales and weights as low down as half an ounce. One or two judges to be appointed to weigh the cocks. Each party by weighing the cocks intended for the show a day or two beforehand and having all their respective weights, would greatly facilitate the business of the judges. There ought to be no feathers cut or plucked from the cocks before they are brought to the scale, except a few from behind to keep them clean, and their wings and tails clipped a little.

2. As soon as the cocks are all weighed, the judge, the writers and the principals of each party and as many besides as the parties may agree upon, are to retire for the purpose of matching. They are to make all even matches first, then within two ounces; but if more matches can be made by breaking an even or one ounce match, it is to be done.

3. On the day of the showing, only one battle is to be fought. It is to be remembered that the party winning the show gains also the choice of fighting this first battle with any particular cocks in the match. Afterwards they begin with the lightest pair first and so on up to the heaviest, fighting them in rotation as they increase in weight. The first battle, too, will fix the mode of trimming.

RULE 1. When the cocks are in the pit, the judges are to examine whether they are fairly trimmed and have fair heels. If all be right and fair, the pitters are to deliver their cocks six feet apart (or thereabouts) and retire a step or two back; but if a wrong cock should be produced, the party so offending forfeits that battle.

2. All heels that are round from the socket to the point are allowed to be fair; any pitter bringing a cock into the pit with any other kind of heels, except by particular agreement, forfeits the battle.

3. If either cock should be trimmed with a close, unfair hackle, the judge shall direct the other to be cut in the same manner, and at the time shall observe to the pitter that if he brings another cock in the like situation, unless he shall have been previously trimmed, he shall forfeit the battle.

4. A pitter when he delivers his cock shall retire two paces back, and not advance or walk around his cock until a blow has passed.

5. An interval of ten minutes shall be allowed between the termination of one battle and the commencement of another.

6. No pitter shall pull a feather out of a cock's mouth or from over his eyes or head, or pluck him by the breast to make him fight, or pinch him for the like purpose, under penalty of forfeiting the battle.

7. The pitters are to give the cocks room to fight, and are not to hover and press on them so as to retard their striking.

8. The greasing, peppering, muffling and soaping a cock, or any other external application, are unfair practices, and by no means admissible in this amusement.

9. The judges, when required, may suffer a pitter to call in some of his friends to assist in catching the cock, who are to retire immediately when the cock is caught, and in no other instance is the judge to suffer the pit to be broken.

10. All cocks on their backs are to be immediately turned on their bellies by their respective pitters at all times.

11. A cock when down is to have a wing given him if he needs it, unless his adversary is on it, but his pitter is to place the wing gently in its proper position, and not to lift the cock; and no wing is to be given unless absolutely necessary.

12. If either cock should be hanged in himself, in the pit, or canvas, he is to be loosened by his pitter; but if in his adversary, both pitters are to immediately lay hold of their respective cocks, and the pitter whose cock is hung shall hold him steady while the adverse party draws out the

heel, and then they shall take their cocks asunder a sufficient distance for them fairly to renew the combat.

13. Should the cocks separate and the judge be unable to decide which fought last, he shall at his discretion direct the pitters to carry their cocks to the middle of the pit and deliver them beak to beak, unless either of them is blind; in that case they are to be shouldered; that is, delivered with their breasts touching, each pitter taking care to deliver his cock at this, as well as at all other times, with one hand.

14. When both cocks cease fighting, it is then in the power of the pitter of the last fighting-cock, unless they touch each other, to demand a count of the judges, who shall count forty deliberately, which, when counted out, is not to be counted again during the battle. Then the pitters shall catch their cocks and carry them to the middle of the pit and deliver them beak to beak; but to be shouldered if either is blind as before. Then if either cock refuses or neglects to fight, the judge shall count ten, and shall call out "Once refused" and shall direct the pitters to bring their cocks again to the middle of the pit and pit as before; and if the same cock in like manner refuses, he shall count ten again and call out "Twice refused," and so proceed until one cock thus refuses six times successively. The judge shall then determine the battle against such cock.

15. If either cock dies before the judge can finish the counting of the law, the battle is to be given to the living cock, and if both die, the longest liver wins the battle.

16. The pitters are not to touch their cocks while the judge is in the act of counting.

17. No pitter is ever to lay hold of his adversary's cock, unless to draw out the heel, and then he must take him below the knee. Then there shall be no second delivery, that is, after he is once delivered he shall not be touched until a blow is struck, unless ordered.

18. No pitter shall touch his cock unless at the time mentioned in the foregoing rules.

19. If any pitter acts contrary to these rules, the judge, if called upon at the time, shall give the battle against him.

PHILADELPHIA RULES.

Art. 1. The pit must be a ground floor, unless otherwise agreed to.

Art. 2. The cock or stag must be weighed enclosed in a small bag, and then two ounces deducted for the weight of the bag and feathers. A stag fighting a cock has an allowance of four ounces in weight, a blinker cock fighting a two-eyed one has four ounces; a blinker cock and stag of one weight are a match.

Art. 3. The cocks being weighed and matched, you will cut them out; you must cut the hackle with all the shiners off; you can use your own pleasure about cutting out other parts of your cock.

Art. 4. Your cock now being cut out you will heel him; you can heel him with paper and water, and nothing but that; if you do you will lose the battle if the opposite party finds it out.

Art. 5. Your cock being heeled, you will bring him in the pit for battle; you will bill the cocks one minute, and then put them down behind your scores for their battle.

Art. 6. In fighting a battle, according to Philadelphia rules, when you deliver your cock on his score, you must stand back of him and not lean over him to hide him from the other cock.

Art. 7. A cock breaking with another cock is fight, and a cock picking at any time when on the ground is fight; but picking while in your arms is not fight; he must fight after you deliver him out of your hands.

Art. 8. When the cocks are fast, you must handle by drawing your spur out of your cock; you then have thirty seconds to nurse your cock. The judge will call, "Down cocks;" then you must strictly obey and put your cock down to renew the battle. In case one of the cocks gets disabled, you can count him out; you can lay your cock down on his wing on his score, and count ten without the other cock making fight; you can handle him again, and so on until you count five tens; then you can get ready to breast your cocks. You must put them down on their feet and breast to breast, and if the crippled cock refuses to fight while the opposite handler counts twenty more, he has lost the battle.

Art. 9. You are not bound to lay your cock on his wing: you can use your pleasure whether to lay him on his wings or on his feet; if it is to your advantage for your cock to fight, put him down on his feet and let him fight.

Art. 10. In counting a cock out, after you breast the cocks and you are counting twenty, if the cock should get in the disabled cock, you dare not put your hand on them unless the disabled cock makes fight; and if he does make fight, you handle, and by his making fight it will renew all the counting from the first, and if the disabled cock makes fight last it is his count.

Art. 11. The judges cut the heels off, and if all is right you must get ready for the next battle; you are allowed twenty minutes to be in the pit with the next cock. The judges are to keep the time.

Art. 12. All outside bets go as the main stakes.

Art. 13. Any man not paying bets that he has lost will not be allowed in any pit in Philadelphia thereafter.

NEW YORK RULES.

1. The pit shall be circular in shape, at least eighteen feet in diameter and not less than sixteen inches in height.

The floor shall be covered with carpet or some other suitable material. There shall be a chalk or some other mark made as near to the center of the pit as possible. There shall also be two outer marks which shall be one foot each way from the center mark.

2. The pitters shall each select one judge who shall choose a referee. Said judges shall decide all matters in dispute during the pendency of the fight, but in case of their inability to agree, then it shall be the duty of the referee to decide and his decision shall be final.

3. Chickens shall take their age from the first day of March and shall be chickens during the fighting season.

4. It shall be deemed foul for any of the respective pitters to pit a cock or chicken with what is termed a foul hackle, that is, any of the feathers left whole on the mane or neck.

5. The pitters shall let the cocks bill each other three or more times, but this is not to be construed that the pitter of a cock has a right to bill with his opponent's cock for the purpose of fatiguing him.

6. No person shall be permitted to handle his fowl after he is fairly delivered in the pit unless he counts ten clear and distinct, without either cock making fight; or shall be fast in his adversary, or fast in the carpet, or hung in the web of the pit or in himself.

7. Any cock that may get on his back shall be righted again by the pitter, but not taken off the ground he is lying on.

8. Whenever a cock is fast in his adversary the pitter of the cock the spurs are fast in shall draw them out, but the pitter of the cock has no right to draw out his own spurs except when fast in himself or in the carpet, or in the web of the pit.

9. When either pitter shall have counted ten tens successively, without the cock refusing fight, making fight,

again breasting them fair on their feet, breast to breast and beak to beak, on the centre score or mark, on the fifth ten being told, and also on the ninth ten being told, shall have won the fight. The pitters are bound to tell each ten as they count them, as follows: Once, twice, etc.

10. No pitter after the cocks have been delivered in the pit shall be permitted to clean his cock's beak or eyes by blowing or otherwise, nor be permitted to squeeze him or press him against the floor during the pendency of the fight.

11. When a cock is pounded and no person takes it until the pitter counts twenty twice, and calls three times, "Who takes it?" and no person takes it, it is a battle to the cock the odds are on; but the pitter of the pounded cock has the right to have the pound put up, that is twenty dollars against one dollar. If this is not complied with, the pitter shall go on as though there was no poundage.

12. If a cock is pounded and the poundage is taken, and if the cock the odds are laid against should get up and knock down his adversary, then if the other cock is pounded and the other poundage not taken before the pitter counts twenty twice, and calls out, "Who takes it?" three times, he wins, although there was a poundage before.

13. It shall be the duty of the respective pitters to deliver their cocks fair on their feet on the outer score or mark, facing each other, and in a standing position, except on the fifth ten being told, and also on the ninth ten being told, when they, the two cocks, shall be placed on the center score, breast to breast and beak to beak in like manner. Any pitter being guilty of shoving his fowl across the score, or of pinching him, or using any other unfair means for the purpose of making his cock fight, shall lose the fight.

14. If both cocks fight together, and then both should refuse until they are counted out, in such cases a fresh cock is to be hoveled and brought into the pit, and the pitters

are to toss for which cock is to set-to first. He that wins has the choice. Then the one which is to set-to last is to be taken up but not carried out of the pit. The hoveled cock is then to be put down to the other and allowed to fight while the judges, or one of them, shall count twenty. The same operation shall be gone through with the other cock and if one fight and the other refuse, it is a battle to the fighting cock; but if both fight, or both refuse, it is a drawn battle.

15. If both cocks refuse fighting until four, five or more or less tens are counted, the pitters shall continue their count until one cock has refused ten times, for when a pitter begins to count, he counts for both cocks.

16. If a cock should die before they are counted out, he wins the battle if he fights last. This, however, is not to apply when his adversary is running away.

17. The crowing or raising of the hackle of a cock is not fight, nor is fighting at the pitter's hands.

18. A breaking cock is a fighting cock, but a cock breaking from his adversary is not fight.

19. If any dispute arises between the pitters on the result of a fight, the cocks are not to be taken out of the pit, nor the gaffs taken off until a decision has been made by the judges or referee.

20. Each cock within two ounces of the other shall be a match, except blinkers when they are fighting against two-eyed cocks, in which case an allowance of from three to five ounces shall be made. When blinkers are matched against each other, the same rule to apply as to two-eyed cocks.

21. All matches must be fought with heels, round from the socket to the point, not exceeding one and a quarter inches in length unless otherwise agreed upon. Drop Sockets, Slashers and twisted heels shall be considered foul.

22. Previous to heeling the cocks in fighting mains, the four spurs of same pattern and size shall be placed together and the pitters shall toss for choice of them.

23. In all mains, at the end of each battle the judges shall order the spurs to be changed, i. e., the spurs of the winning cock must be placed on the loser's next fowl and changed at the end of every battle.

24. Any person fighting a cock heavier than he is represented on the match list, shall lose the fight, although he may have won.

25. In all cases of appeal, fighting ceases until the judges or the referee give their decision, which shall be final and strictly to the question before them.

26. When a bet is made, it cannot be declared off unless by consent of both parties; all outside bets to go according to the main bet.

27. Each pitter when delivering his cock on the score shall take his hands off him as quickly as possible.

28. Any person violating any of the above rules, shall be deemed to have lost the match.

WESTERN RULES.

1. The two pitters shall choose a time-keeper and a referee. It shall be the duty of the former to keep time between rounds, and notify the handlers to "get ready" at twenty-five seconds, then call "Time" at thirty seconds. The referee shall pay close attention to the handlers and birds, and see that the following rules are strictly adhered to:

2. All birds under 6-4, weighing within two ounces of each other, are matched, except stags and broken-bill and blinker cocks, which shall be allowed four ounces against sound cocks. Sound cocks weighing 6-4 and upwards shall be fought as shakebags and matched regardless of weight.

3. All gaffs shall be round from socket to point; no others will be allowed.

4. After the birds are heeled they shall be weighed by the referee, who will call out their respective weights. He shall also examine the birds' gaffs.

5. Upon entering the pit the handlers shall let the cocks peck each other three or four times; they shall step to their respective scores (which scores shall be four feet each way from the center), set their birds squarely on their feet and instantly release them.

6. It is no fight unless a blow is struck while both cocks show.

7. It shall be unfair for a handler to touch either cock except as directed by the referee.

8. The referee shall order a handler to give his cock a wing when necessary, or turn a bird that is on its back. These directions may be given only when the cocks are not touching each other.

9. The referee shall call "handle" whenever a cock is fast in his antagonist, in himself or in the pit, (except during a count, in which case the birds are not to be handled until the end of the count), also at the end of "counts" and "minutes," and at other times when necessary.

10. The handler of the gaffed cock shall draw the heels, catching the leg of his opponent's bird below the hock joint. The birds must not be raised from the pit floor until after the gaffs have been drawn.

11. Thirty seconds is the time allowed in all handlings, time to commence as soon as the cocks are lifted off the floor of the pit.

12. Between pittings it shall be fair for the handlers to wash their birds' heads, give refreshments, and help their cocks in any other way possible, but they must be ready to pit promptly on call of time.

13. As soon as one cock ceases fighting, the referee shall call to the handler of the fighting cock, "Mr. A., count;" whereupon that handler shall count ten in an audible tone. After being handled the cocks shall be pitted again and so continue until three tens in all have been counted. After the third count and handle, the cocks are to be placed breast to breast on center score, when pitter having count shall count twenty and the fight is ended in his favor.

14. The count can be broken only by a peck or blow from the cock which is being counted out, or by the death of the cock having the count, or by that cock showing unmistakable evidence of wanting to run away, in which cases the referee shall call "Count broken."

15. If the cocks should both cease fighting at the same time, or should refuse to meet at the beginning of a round, the referee shall call for one minute's time, at the expiration of which the cocks are to be handled and again pitted. If they refuse to meet after the second minute, they are to be handled and pitted again, until the expiration of the third minute, and then they are to be handled and breasted and put on the center score. And if they still refuse to fight at the expiration of one minute, a fresh cock is to be brought to the pit. If one combatant shows fight and the other does not, the battle is given to the fighting cock. If both fight or both refuse, it is a drawn battle.

16. If both cocks die, neither having the count, the longest liver wins. If the cock having the count is dying and the other cock wanting to run, the former wins the battle even though he dies before the expiration of the count.

17. The referee shall watch all movements of the fight and confine the handlers strictly to the above rules. He may overlook what he believes to be an unintentional error, but must decide the battle against any handler who plainly and willfully violates the rules.

BALTIMORE RULES.

Rule 1.—All birds shall be weighed. Give or take two ounces shall be a match or otherwise, if parties see fit to make it so.

Rule 2.—When a stag is matched against a cock the stag will be entitled to four ounces advance in weight. Blinkers are allowed four ounces when fighting against two-eyed cocks.

Rule 3.—The handlers shall each choose one judge, who shall choose a referee. Said judges shall decide all matter in dispute during the pendency of the fight, but in case of their inability to agree, then it shall be the duty of the referee to decide, and his decision shall be final.

Rule 4.—Thirty seconds or a count of fifteen by the judge (or referee, as the handlers may agree) shall be allowed between each and every round.

Rule 5.—It shall be the duty of the referee to keep time between the rounds, and notify the handlers to get ready at twenty-five seconds. On time being called at thirty seconds, the handlers must be prompt in pitting their cocks, and if either handler refuses to do so, he shall lose the fight.

Rule 6.—It shall be fair for handlers to pull feathers and sling blood or any other thing to help the bird between handlings.

Rule 7.—It shall be foul for A or B to touch their birds while fighting, unless one is fast to the other, but if a bird should unfortunately fasten himself with his own heel, it shall be fair to handle, but on no other consideration, and either handler violating or deviating from the above rules shall lose the fight.

Rule 8.—In counting, the bird showing fight last shall be entitled to the count.

Rule 9.—The handlers shall pit their birds in their respective places when time is called, and the handler having the count shall count ten, then handle two more successive times and count ten each time. When time is called again the birds shall be placed in the centre of the pit, breast to breast and beak to beak, and twenty more counted; and if the bird not having the count refuse to fight, the one having it shall be declared the winner.

Rule 10.—It shall be the duty of the respective handlers to deliver their birds fair on their feet at each pitting on the mark or score, facing each other and in a standing position.

Rule 11.—A peck or blow at the opponent's head and not at his handler will be considered fighting.

Rule 12.—When time is called the handlers must let go their birds from their respective places fair and square, for it shall be foul for either handler to pitch or toss his bird upon his opponent's, and either one violating the above rule shall lose his fight.

Rule 13.—If both birds fight together, and then if both refuse they are to be pitted at the outer score twice and then breasted on the center score breast to breast and beak to beak in a standing position. In this case the birds are to lay in the pit thirty seconds at each pitting and at the last pitting if both should refuse it is a drawn battle.

Rule 14.—In the case of a bird that dies, if he fights last and his handler has the count, he wins the battle.

Rule 15.—Whenever a bird is fast in his adversary the handler of the bird the spurs are fast in shall draw them out, but the handler of a bird has no right to draw out his own spur except when fast in himself or in the floor or in the web of the pit.

Rule 16.—Greasing, peppering or soaping, or any other external applications made to a cock are unfair practices and by no means admissible in this amusement.

Rule 17.—The handlers are to give the birds room to

fight and not to hover and press on them so as to retard their striking.

Rule 18.—Any person fighting a bird heavier than he is represented to be on the match list shall lose the fight, although he may have won.

Rule 19.—In all cases of appeal, fighing ceases until the judges or the referee give their decision, which shall be final and strictly to the question before them.

Rule 20.—Each handler when delivering his bird on the score shall take his hands off him as quickly as possible.

Rule 21.—No handler shall touch the bird except at the times mentioned in the foregoing rules.

Rule 22.—If any dispute arises between the handlers on the result of the fight, the birds are not to be taken out of the pit, nor the gaffs taken off until it is decided by the judges or referee.

Rule 23.—It shall be the duty of the judges and referee to watch all movements of the fight and judge according to the above rules.

Rule 24.—When a bet is made it cannot be declared off unless by consent of both parties. All outside bets to go according to the main bet.

Rule 25.—Any person violating any of the above rules shall be deemed to have lost the match.

DISEASES OF GAME FOWL.

An attempt has been made in the first part of this work to impress the breeder and cocker with the positive necessity of perfect constitution in game cocks. Delicate men are not cut out for the prize ring. No pugilist ever won great battles on a diet of pills and plasters. It is therefore without the province of a book like this to catalogue all the ills to which chickens are subject. We wish to lay down the plain truth that the only safe cure for most diseases if they appear in *game* chickens is "the axe at the woodpile." Impaired constitution and inherited tendencies will ruin any breeder eventually. One of the safest rules to follow in the difficult task of perpetuating first-class game fighting cocks is never bred from any fowl that is not in perfect health.

What this book will contain, for the above reason, will be very little on the science of medicine, for the design is to include only those diseases that a *game* chicken may have without permanent injury. *Prevention* is the whole art of game chicken medical science. If game fowl are allowed their own way where they can get enough to eat by working for it; where they find fresh running water; where there is plenty of shade as well as sunlight; they will take care of themselves and now and then a hen will live to be twenty years old. Common fowl die of old age when game chickens are at their prime if the latter are right in constitution. The nearer a game fowl can live as the birds of the air, the finer, stronger, healthier and gamer they will be. No man not so fixed as to raise cocks according to this plan is prepared to raise the best specimens of fighting fowl; and it must not be forgotten that the health of a chicken begins *in the egg*. Eggs from breeders that are in close confinement and badly cared for never hatch the right kind for fighting. I have known the gamest kind of fowl to throw quitters, so bred.

The following diseases are fatal in *game* chickens:; they render the fowl useless, and their treatment is only a loss of time: *Cholera, Indigestion, Asthma, Melancholy or Moping, Consumption, Rheumatism, Apoplexy, Giddiness, Roup in the advanced stages, Chronic Diarrhoea.*

Prevention is the only remedy for this group of troubles.

Confinement, bad ventilation, over feeding, too much soft and sloppy food, and filthy water are the main causes of these diseases. Consumption, Cholera and Roup are contageous, and will quickly spread unless the sick birds are at once removed and the premises disinfected. Whitewash in liberal quantities is the best chicken disinfectant. Geese and ducks are bad companions and play-mates for game fowl. They evacuate with great complacency in the drinking water, and appear to thrive on their own faeces.

Beware of slop barrels; these are the game chicken barrooms, and they soon become persistent "booze-fighter," with all the aspect and demeanor of a confirmed drunkard. A game cock walked in an enclosure with an open slop-barrel could not whip a Pekin duck.

Curable diseases and such as it is worth while to treat are:

1. *Roup* in the early stages. This disease is found everywhere, and is the game kind's greatest enemy. It begins with a running at the nose and resembles a cold in the head, at this stage. The face begins to swell behind the nose, a froth boils from the eye, the eyes are gradually closed, the nostrils entirely closed, a yellow substance forms therein. The fowl suffers from a high fever, and is very thirsty. This is a statement of symptoms just as they develop.

Treatment. Isolate the fowl at once; give water sparingly, and never allow other fowls to drink from the same vessel. Often the disease will disappear in a few days if the patient is fed nothing but *dry bread*. But when the disease has advanced, or refuses to yield to such simple treatment, try some of the best Roup cures according to directions. Many of the finest breeders in America endorse Bisdee's Roup Cure and it is generally considered almost a sure cure. None of the old specifics are safe.

2. *"Gaps"* is a disease peculiar to game chickens. About

the time they begin to feed well, sometimes sooner, the chicks begin to gasp; to stretch up the neck, open the mouth and, press the tongue far forward in the painful attempt to get enough air into their lungs for breathing. If not attended to, the chicks will die of gradual, torturing suffocation. This disease is due to red worms that form in the wind-pipe. Take one affected chick in hand, open its beak, stretch the neck turned to a strong light and look down the wind-pipe. The worms may be seen distinctly, adhering to the surface of the wind-pipe, sometimes near the larynx, often down near the bronchial tubes. The last is severest, and will soon smother the chick. It is astonishing how large the worms are in some cases. They are evidently hatched from the eggs of the hen louse, which the young bird inhales while nestling in its mother's feathers, and grow to be as large as a darning needle, and about an inch long. They are as red as blood, until they become old.

Treatment. Prevent if possible, by keeping the fowl all perfectly free from lice. Some high authorities claim that there are gap *larvae* deposited in the soil of some places, and the chicks peck them up in their food. I have noticed that perfectly clean hens rarely have gaps among their chicks. On the same yard, I have had one hen's young all to die, while another hen with a larger brood raised every chick and none had the gaps. I examined the two hens, and found one covered with large lice, while the other was perfectly clean. However, there can be no question that gaps is a very troublesome disease on old places, while it is hardly ever seen on a perfectly new yard. This may be because the theory is correct that *larvae* of some kind are in the soil, but it may also be due to the fact that old places are infested with lice, while new yards have none.

The cure of "gaps" is purely mechanical and no medicine taken internally will do any good; boxing the birds and dusting them with different *sneezing powders* is simply brutal as it would be impossible for the tortured chick gasping for breath, to sneeze strongly enough to break all the worms loose from the wind-pipe and "cough them up," as the farmers call it. The only remedy is a direct removal of the worms. This can easily be done by using a gap extractor advertised by Montgomery Ward & Co., of Chicago, or the Gleezen Supply Co., of Lawrence, Mass. This extractor is a small tube of brass cut across one end diagonally, in which end there is a small hole. Two horse hairs are run entirely through this tube, a loop made in them, the ends being passed through the small hole in the end and then carried back through the tube. By pulling the loose ends at one end of this tube, the loop at the lower end can be made long or short. To operate, the chick is firmly held, while the neck is stretched at full length, the beak held wide open. The operator should watch carefully the opening and closing of the wind-pipe, and holding the loop end of the "extractor" with the hairs drawn up as far as they can be in the tube; he should insert the loop end of the extractor just as the wind-pipe is opened in breathing—still holding the chick firmly, also the head between the thumb and fingers, press the "extractor" into the wind-pipe about a quarter of an inch, more if necessary, then taking the hairs by the loose ends, push them down to form a large loop inside the wind-pipe. Now twist the "extractor" between the fingers about three times around, withdraw it, holding the hairs just as they are in the tube, and worms will be found tangled up in the loop of the hairs. It is easy to see how the work progresses by taking an occasional peep into the wind-pipe as directed. But to make a perfect job, an *operating box* should be used. This is made by taking a box just large enough to hold the largest birds to be operated on. In one end on top, cut a round hole large enough for the chick's head to come through. Place the chick in this box, packing enough paper behind to keep it well pressed up in position with the head projecting through the hole in the end of the box, tie something around the box to keep the lid on. Place this box on a shelf with the chick's head downwards. In this position it will be "upside down," so to speak, and the operator will operate *upward* instead of downward; and when the worms are dislocated in the chick's wind-pipe, they will fall out if not caught by the hairs when withdrawn, or the slightest effort by the chick will throw them out. The advantages of this operating box are that no assistant is necessary, the bird is more securely held, and the worms cannot when dislodged clog the wind-pipe and smother the chick, as often happens in the old way. To hold the box steady wherever placed put a weight upon the top.

The "extractor" costs about twenty-five cents and the box must be made by the operator. It is an invention of my own and I have never gotten a patent. After a few operations almost anyone may become quite successful.

3. *Gout* is entirely due to dirty, sloppy, surroundings, and is aggravated by roosting in houses with plank floors. If the affected fowls are removed to a clean place where their diet will be what they can find in fields and woods, together with a feed of wheat and oats or such, the disease will disappear; though in very old fowl, it sometimes lingers till death. By all means change the fowl's food if it has been eating soft feed, and force it to roost low and over the ground. Very persistent cases will disappear in young fowl, with one moult, if treated as here directed. Slop-barrel cocks are often gouty.

4. *Corns* are all incident to bad roosting. No henhouse with a *hard floor* is suitable for game chickens. Corns in the feet are caused by flying down on the hard

floor. It comes from the constant bruising of the ball of the foot. Large fowl that roost high, even over the ground, will have corns.

Treatment. Force the fowl to roost in a suitable place. Bind the foot in flannel, having rubbed the place thoroughly with cedar-berry salve, and covered it with the salve before trying on the flannel. Repeat the operation twice and when the third bandage is taken off, the corn may easily be cut out with a knife. After operating, bind the part with cotton cloth until all bleeding has ceased and the place has healed.

But there is another kind of corn that I consider incurable. This forms on the rear part of the leg between the spur and the foot. These are common in heavy cocks that are allowed to roost on poles too large for the comfortable grasp of the foot, causing the cock to rest his weight upon that portion of his leg. Prevention is the only cure: force the bird to roost on a small pole, so that no part of the leg will touch it. Nearly all roost poles are too large, and many fowls if not ruined by these hard corns, become "duck footed," that is, the proptoe turns under, which hurts the cock for fighting and spoils his looks.

5. *Diarrhoea* is often caused by too much soft or sloppy food—most often, it is a swill-tub disorder. In coops, old rye, rarely wheat, will cause a looseness of the bowels. *Oats* is almost what might be called a specific. Change of feed and surrounding will cure simple diarrhoea that is not chronic. If the disease has been of long duration, take the fowl to the wood pile, not forgetting the axe.

6. *Scaly, Limed, Rough or Scruffy* legs are caused by mites that breed in great numbers under the ends of the scales on a chicken's legs. They lodge in the fleshy place just between the edge of each scale. A hen with scaly legs will give the trouble to her brood. It cannot be treated

while the hen is setting, safely, because the oil that must be used will destroy the eggs.

Treatment. Any kind of oil or grease will distroy these mites if persistently rubbed in while warm, not hot. The fowl's legs should be kept well greased with a mixture of cne-half oil of tar, one-half sweet oil; but before treating, wash the fowl's legs well with soap and tepid water. Take a sharpened stick and stir under the edge of each scale, getting out all the scruffy, white stuff that can be removed. Then rub in the mixture while tepid. Repeat until a cure is effected. Stamp the trouble out with no delay. It will spread and spoil your nicest fowls.

7. *Chicken Pox* or simply *Pox* starts with pimples which ripen into yellow pustules on the fowl's head and face. This comes without any apparent cause sometimes, but more frequently follows a fight. Where the bird has been picked, it seems to be poisoned. Pox is a painful chicken disease, which unless carefully treated, renders the fowl totally blind.

Treatment. Isolate the fowl and keep its head, throat and face well rubbed with a mixture two-thirds sweet oil, one-third spirits turpentine. Besides roup cure has been found useful in treating the disease. The fowl should be well fed all the time, on wholesome good food. Some scrape the scales off till the places bleed before treating as directed.

8. *Moulting.* This is a natural change in the fowl's system, which will result in serious disorder, unless it is sufficiently fed and kept in proper surroundings. Fowls that run in grain fields and roost in trees never suffer from the disorders of the moult. It has been discovered that greasy food—such as corn bread "made up" with a large amount of lard—hastens and increases the moult. The plucking of feathers to assist moulting is unwise. Let nature take her course; and by no means handle fowl, or allow them to fight or set while moulting. It is also ruinous

to an old hen to allow her to set as late as dog days. Cocks are very sore while moulting, and must be gently handled, or not at all. Many game cocks easily become "man-shy" in moult.

9. *Lice* must be fought from start to finish. They destroy young chicks and enfeeble the constitution of even adult fowls. If fowls roost in a house, whitewash the house every month, and grease every roost pole. A large piece of bacon skin is very good for the purpose though many prefer kerosene. When a hen begins to set, she should be thoroughly dusted with insect powder and some of the powder thrown over the eggs in the nest. Some advocate placing a handful or ordinary fertilizer, or guano, in the nest, though the odor may prove injurious to the eggs. The hen should have another thorough examination and dusting, on the *eighteenth day* of her setting, and the day she is taken off she should be dusted again and greased on top of the head—what is better, cut every feather off of her head as if she had been shaved, to a quarter of an inch behind her comb. Also, grease her under each wing and around the anus. Start the little fellows clean and if the hen is allowed her way, she will probably keep them clean in the earlier part of the year.

10. *Hard Craw or Crop Bound.* In this trouble the fowl has a full craw, and that organ seems to fail in the performance of its duty. This sometimes occurs in the feeding coops. It is not a good sign and should perhaps be put in the first order of diseases, or such as are fatal to the usefulness of a fowl. However, if the attack yields readily to simple treatment, fears may not be well grounded. As a general thing, a hard craw should pass off if the fowl is confined and deprived of food and given the privilege of picking an apple twice a day until the craw is free. The fowl can be allowed water as much as it may wish. Some

go so far as to give a teaspoonful of castor oil, but I class these as suspicious cases, for reasons already given.

11. *Wounds.* Stags and hens often give much trouble by fighting until severely hurt. The best treatment for birds that have their heads badly bruised by fighting, is to wash the parts thoroughly in luke warm water that has been boiled. Then make a mixture of whiskey, or brandy, and sweet oil, equal parts; and paint the parts with a feather dipped into the mixture. If possible, let the wounded bird run at large, and feed plenty of wholesome food. As soon as a main is over, all cocks that are to be saved should be treated the same way and then fed a good feed of milk and bread. If the weather permits, walk them as soon as possible.

12. *Canker* often follows neglected wounds, but will appear rarely without any apparent cause. This is an offensive yellow, cheesy substance that forms in the mouth, sometimes extending down into the throat. *Treatment*— I am not aware of any safe specific for this trouble, unless it be to scrape out the cheesy formation and rub on the "Bisdee's Specific" before mentioned. Some use salt with good results in simple cases.

13. *Limberneck* is a new name given to an old disease. The fowl is rendered deathly sick by gorging itself on maggots, which are intensely rich diet in the first place and such as are not deposited in the crop dead, commence to eat in the crop. It is said that they will eat their way through the wall of the craw. A few drops of spirits of turpentine in a teaspoonful of water will kill the maggots that are working in the fowl's craw and assist the digesting of the dead ones. The disease takes its name from the fowl's not being able to hold up its head.

14. *Feather Pulling* is a great nuisance common among game fowl that are confined. Hens usually pluck the plu-

mage from a handsome cock, seemingly for pastime. This habit is sometimes called feather eating, but it will be noticed that the feather plucked is dropped, unless it be a pin-feather. These any fowl will eat under any circumstances. It is true, however, that females often pull each other's feathers. The harm is usually done to the shawl and breast. A cock that has been thus robbed of his beauty by pretended affection is said to be "hen-pecked," from which arises the same expression as applied to a patient husband. Feather-pulling is beyond question a vice incident to confinement, and only illustrates the adage, "Idleness is the devil's workshop." *Treatment.* While the same fowls are kept confined together it is next to impossible to break them, though some claim it may be done by painting the breast and neck feathers with red pepper and sweet oil. This will injure the fowl's feathers, however, and others try cutting the offender's beak off to the quick, thus giving her pain when she tries to pull a feather. This will do good a short time. Just as soon as a female begins plucking a cock's plumage, find another stall for him, and allow him in the pen only long enough to tread, if possible.

GAME FOWL LITERATURE.

In no line of literary pursuit has there been greater progress in the past fifty years than in the art of composition on the subject of game fowl. There have been few formal contributions to the book shelf, but the number of those that have given study to this subject and contributed to the press has increased beyond all comparison.

Papers devoted entirely to game fowl were unknown fifty years ago; a handsome monthly magazine exclusively on that subject was unheard of. In recent times, on the other hand, there have been numbers of well edited, newsy, bright papers exclusively set apart to the amusement of breeders and cockers, such as "The Game Fanciers Journal," published in Michigan; "The Dixie Game Fowl," published in Tennessee; "American Game Keeper," a weekly paper published in New Jersey; "Southern Pit Games," published in Georgia. There have been other papers published, but discontinued from time to time.

Of the magazines, the eldest is "The Game Fowl Monthly" established in 1885. The pioneer and educatinal work of this popular old publication cannot be too highly commended. It has been edited with skill and conspicuous learning. Every country where cock fighting is practiced has contributed to the columns of The Game Fowl Monthly, and accomplished linguists on its staff have translated the foreign languages into the vernacular with a facility that would do credit to any college professor. Dr. H. P. Clark has edited the foreign department, and it was he who has done more than any other man to "join hands across the sea." The doctor was the first importer of pure Aseels, and it was through him that oriental grading became almost as popular a fad as bob-tail horses in Boston. A complete file of "The Game Fowl Monthly" published at Sayre, Pa., would be a history of breeders, strains and cock fighting for the past nineteen years (1885-1904).

The "Game Breeder" published by P. W. Carew, the veteran breeder of Indiana, went into the hands of a wildly enthusiastic young man who astounded the country by sudden conversion under the convicting eloquence of some evangelist, and the fraternity woke up one fine morning to discover that The Game Breeder had sold out to the Salvation Army, and instead of accounts of mains and hack fights from California to New York, the columns were filled with quotations from Genesis to Revelations. The jar was very sudden, and "the blow almost killed father" (Carew) who supplied the place of his favorite child by "Chanticleer," a magazine still published by him with as much energy and fidelity to his purpose of suppressing "dunkies" as when he got out the first issue of Game Breeder. However, this translation of Game Breeder to the realms of church literature was even more marvelous than that of Elijah lifted from earth in the flesh, to glory; and the reader may faintly imagine the surprise of game chicken cranks that morning after the translation, when upon opening The Breeder, their eyes feel upon—"Peace, good will among men," "Love them that despitefully use you," "Woe unto you, scribes and Pharisees!" where they had expected an account of the last main between Eslin and Kearney.

"The Derby Game Bird" has been published for many years, in Indiana, and enjoys the distinction of having more "ads" than any game fowl organ ever published.

"Grit and Steel" published at Gaffney, South Carolina, was founded in 1898 by J. L. Sherrill, an enthusiastic fancier. The publication fell into the hands of Ed. H. DeCamp who had financed it from its inception. Under the management of the latter, it has grown to be the largest and most popular game fowl organ that was ever published. Its subscribers are numbered by thousands and it can truly be said that "the sun never sets" on its subscription list; for it has subscribers on every continent on earth. The contributors to "Grit and Steel" are of the highest order, including men whose writings appear in the best papers and magazines in the world, and this illustrated magazine, of about 60 to 75 pages, is published after the most approved models, in the neatest style, on good paper. Nothing but energy and talent of a very high order could have effected such results, and any line of sport would be honored as well as benefited and elevated by such an exponent.

Books and Pamphlets. The nearest approach to a consecutive history of cocking to our own times may be gotten by reading Wm. Sketchley's work of Game Fowls, a book of some hundred and fifty pages, published in 1816. This book was written by a practical cocker, a successful breeder, and a man of learning. It extends back to about the year 1760, containing information the writer has been gleaning to the time he published his book, from that date.

After reading Sketchley, take up the largest book ever published exclusively on game chickens—Dr. J. W. Cooper's "Game Fowls." This volume was published in 1869, by one of the most extensive breeders in the United States. It is a large 12 mo. and contains 304 pages. Dr. Cooper tells us in the last part of his book that he assisted in a main in Westmoreland county, Pa., in 1819, and was at that time sixteen years old. Hence, he was born in 1803. It will be observed that Sketchley's work was published when Dr. Cooper was thirteen years old. So that the latter may be said to take the subject up in America where Sketchley put it down in England.

Dr. Cooper's work is an irregular collection of chapters on different topics on the subject of game fowls; and while utterly without system, must have been intensely interesting to fanciers of that day and generation. However, it may be of interest to men of these times to know that none of the famous strains of our day are mentioned. *Shawlnecks, Warhorses, Grists, Yellow and White Legs, Reds or Whitehackles, Blackhackles, Redquills, Redhorses, O'Neil and Minton Dominiques, Huddlestons*—were all unheard of in Dr. Cooper's day. But the following strains were known to the doctor, and are discussed in his volume published in 1869—just thirty-five years ago (1904):

Thompson Whites. These fowl were said to come from a white cock imported from China by a Virginian, and sold for $50 to Bradford Thompson, of Georgia, who bred him to his favorite hens producing by selection a strain of pure white fowl equal to any color in the South.

Claibornes. Dr. Cooper claims that these fowls are from a cross of Spanish and English stock. He describes them as yellow and white-legged light-reds, that were fought into distinction by a Mr. Claiborne, from whom they took their name. The doctor further states that he received a trio from a gentleman in Georgia, in 1859—45 years ago. He says they showed at that day a subcross, perhaps Baltimore Topknot.

Arrington Fowl. Old Nicks are mentioned and the Arrington family as breeders and cockers from Nash and Halifax counties, North Carolina. From these men come the modern "Stone Fences."

Baltimore Topknots. These are ascribed to old man Goss, of Baltimore county, Md., and are found now only in crosses. They then (1869) ran as high as 7 1-2 lbs. in weight.

Earl Derby. This old strain is described exactly as they are at this day—white-legged, black-breasted, light-reds with white beaks. Quotations are taken from "The Illustrated Book of Domestic Poultry" edited by Martin Doyle and published in London in 1854—just fifty years ago, to prove the standard markings of Derbys.

The Eslin Stock. This strain must have resembled very closely the fowl bred by the Eslins in recent times, for Dr. Cooper describes the cock he got through Jonathan Dorward, as a "7 3-4 lb. brown-red with green legs." The Eslins, even in those days, were living in Washington, D. C.

Gee Dominiques are credited to Georgia, and are the breed described as of a peculiar hawk-like color. It will be remembered that the famous Dr. Gee, originator of this strain, died in Alabama. It was from his daughter, Miss Sue, that the writer secured a trio. Dr. Gee Oakey, a nephew, preserved the strain for years, and it is still being bred in different degrees of purity throughout the country.

Nubcombs and Pea Combs are spoken of. It is well to note that this is long before the Japs and Aseels were imported to this country.

Goss Fowl. Goss, of Maryland, is credited with reproducing the "Counterfeits," besides the Topknots. The Counterfeits were *rose comb* fowl. Goss also in later years, bred a first-class strain of Pyles.

Hennies are condemned as worthless under the name, "Hen Tail Mexican." He gives a list of "Worthless Games," including all from "Sumatra," "Malacca," Java, "Wild Indians," "Chineses Albine." However, he does not condemn what are "known in the South" as "Hen-Feather," but says these do not look at all similar to a hen, having only short sickle feathers in tail.

WRITING AND REPORTING.

The success of our game journals all depends upon good, fair, honest contributions on subjects of interest and importance, as well as upon disinterested reports of mains and hack fights. Not for an instant is it true that nobody but accomplished scholars should write for the "game papers," on the other hand, rugged, fair, common-sense pieces by an honest, practical cocker are of greater value than the wordy fustian of bookish men. These may contain slips in grammar and rhetoric, but the editor will attend to such minor matters so as to give to the fraternity the solid part of such compositions as come from the pen of experienced cockers, whether they be scholars or not.

Knowledge acquired by years of experience and observation ought to be published for the instruction of younger men. However, there is room for patience and charity on the part of both contributor and reader. The reader may become hypercritical and blind; while the writer is equally unreasonable in a morbid sensitiveness that will not brook the slightest objection to his views.

There is nothing today in the line of game cock literature that hinders the harmonious co-operation and united sympathy of game fowl breeders throughout the land more than harsh criticism, to which nearly all the game journals have surrendered. It can profit the breeder, who is struggling to reach an exalted standard in his fowl, nothing to learn that some poor, well-meaning fellow who volunteers to write a piece advocating "the everlasting influence of a previous sire," has himself a glass eye or a cork leg. All such attempts at personal abuse are "off the subject," and prove nothing. Hence, the sparring matches of ink-slingers are much like the music of bagpipes, far more entertaining to the performer than to the listener. When some of our even best writers begin, for instance, to give opposite views on the gameness of cocks in long and in short heels and proceed to lay down their propositions and make all the formal preparation for a logical determination of a most important problem, in an instant, one suggests that the other is a *rectangular parallelopipedon,* and all argument vanishes in the air, reminding one forcibly of his boyhood days, when the proverbial chip was so easily unbalanced on the shoulder of ambitious scrappers to be found everywhere with their coat tails dragging so far behind that it was impossible to keep from treading on the same. The reader will pardon one example with a personal reference. Before the writer had reached his teens, he was so unfortunate as to enter into a hot discussion with a sturdy, game cousin, on the advantages of being able to write. He discovers that that said cousin had not yet acquired the "art preservative of all arts," so digressing from the legitimate lines of the debate, suggested that that said cousin was an ignoramus. That cousin thereupon drew a line in the sand, depositing the usual saliva of a complete challenge thereon, with these words: "I may not be able to write, but you just step in that line, and I will lick the stuffin' out of you." Your writer "toed the mark" and at it the two boys went till one had his face scratched into the striking semblance of a checker board and the other had all the hair chewed from the top of his head. They ended the controversy looking like two Kilkenny cats and further from the solution of the problem than ever.

Disputation that relies upon personalities in the stead of argument, is exactly the same as a resort to arms when international arbitration fails. Germany and France debated the abstract question of title to Alsace and Lorraine for years; logic gave place to bullets. The Franco-German war was fought and Germany won. France and the world at large are just as much in doubt as to the real question of right, as they were before the first gun was fired. The Breckenridge and Douglas men did not adjust their differences at the Charleston convention. The Douglas men withdrew in a fit of temper, and thus was divided the Democratic party which rendered the election of Abraham Lincoln possible, resulting in the secession of South Carolina from the Union. Thus was precipitated the most disastrous fratricidal war in the history of mankind. Had the cool heads of the nation under the leadership of such men as Henry Clay found by logical, patient discussion and compromise, a way to steer around the rock which threatened to wreck the ship of State, the Union would today be fifty years in advance of what it is. Constitutional differences have been settled and no question has been forever answered except by "the heaviest battalion." The "Yankee" as well as the "Rebel," with his empty sleeve, after forty years of reflection, knows he was right. No man is convinced by coercion. The demand for courtesy and moderation is just as imperative in game fowl literature as in any other line of composition, and unless the demand is met, papers and magazines on the subject can be nothing more than media of mud-slinging and gymnasia for third class verbal acrobats.

years, and are rapidly increasing in numbers. Among those

Distinguished Writers have been many in the past fifteen that have had the public ear to an unusual degree are *Dr. H. P. Clarke,* of Indianoplis, Ind., a physician, scholar and chief among the advocates of Oriental crossing. *Chas. Judd,* of New York, and New Jersey, who wrote under the *nom de plume* of "Old Grey." His contributions were almost entirely to Game Fowl Monthly and were never surpassed in popularity.

"*More Anon*," was the pseudonym of another distinguished writer for "Game Fowl Monthly." He opposed with great energy, the crossing of "Caucasian" game fowl with those from the far East—Japs, Aseels, Malays, etc., which he, we believe, was the first to style "Orientals."

"*Kicker*" was the pen name of *A. M. Trask,* the veteran breeder of Brocton, Mass., who perpetuated the "Jack Saunders Brown-reds," and who was the first breeder of the Irish fowl John Dolan, the young Irishman brought over to John Stone, afterwards spread all over the country in crosses known as "Warhorses." Frask numbered among his friends and admirers such men as Geo. A. Fletcher, the Whitehackle breeder of Mass., Jack Morrell, sport and humorist, W. L. Morgan, of New Jersey, breeder of the famous Morgan Whithackles, and the writer of this book. He was generous and true to a friend, he never forgot a favor.

"*Dal*" *Johnson* sprang into popularity by a series of articles in Game Fowl Monthly under the title, "Secrets of

The Brood Yard," wich were afterward published in pamphlet form and generally circulated among his friends. Johnson is the originator of a popular strain of game fowl called "Swamp Foxes." He is a wealthy lawyer and planter in South Carolina, and is one of that vast number of Southern gentlemen of means and culture, who fairly revel in the pleasures of cocking.

"New Jersey" has written a number of interesting articles for the various leading game fowl maganizes, chiefly "Grit and Steel." His contributions after returning from a tour of "the old country," including a visit to William Gilliver, the veteran feeder at Polesworth, are among the most interesting of recent times. "New Jersey" (*Mr. Pierce,* of N. Y)., is a gentleman of unlimited means for the gratification of his fancy, he is enthusiastic, and generous. He not only writes for the journals, but breeds and fights cocks with success.

John Mackin, of Chicago, has been a liberal contributor of first-class main reports and, at times, he has expressed himself in vigorous English on subjects that called for discussion. Mr. Mackin is also a practical cocker, having fought a number of the largest mains in recent times. He whipped such men as McWhorter, of Chicago, Casey, of Mass., and Winston, of Virginia. Mr. Mackin is a multimillionaire and bars nobody, either with the pen or the gaff.

F. H. Graves, has for many years contributed to nearly all the game journals. He yields to no one in point or fervor. He breeds and fights his cocks. Mr. Graves is a firm believer in Aseel crosses. He is the perpetuator of a strain of fowl known as "Gypsies."

Nearly all of the breeders and advertisers of game fowl, as well as those that fight mains, are good writers and have done their share to make the game papers interesting. It is impossible to name all of them, but conspicuous in the number are: *Hery Flock, D. H. Pierce, C. A. Kenney, Hugh McLucas, C. E .King, S. A. Ginn,* famous breeder of the "Ginn Cocks," *Alfred Aldrich, F. E. Grist, W. L. Allen, Anthony Greene, Homer Davenport,* famous cartoonist and the greatest pheasant breeder of the world, *J. H. Hammond,* breeder of "The Gordons," *Jeff Flemming,* editor of Southern Pit Games," *Dr. H. C. Paine,* extensive importer of English game fowl, *A. P. O'Connor, M. Garrigan,* of "Fardown" fame, *S. D. Harris,* perpetuator of "Stone Irish" or "Irish Gilders," *P. W. Carew,* founder of "Game Breeder" of "Chanticleer," *F. A. Clarke* (Inchand A Quarter)," originator of "Shawnees," *Jno. C. Davis,* breeder of the "John Davis Tassels," *"Felix,"* who may justly be termed one of the founders of "Grit and Steel," in which organ all of his articles have appeared, *J. M. Hillsman,* breeder of "Whitehackles" and "Gilders," one of the most successful cockers Virginia has ever produced, *W. Aiken Rhett,* member of the famous Rhett family of South Carolina, orginators of the "Rhett Fowl" known wherever cocking is practiced, *A. L. Shampanore,* founder of the only weekly paper devoted to game fowl ever published, *Ed. F. Burke,* main-mate of J. H. Madigan, originator of the "Texas Rangers," *J. A. Monroe,* originator of "White Hornets" and "Black Warriors," one of the oldest and most accomplished writers of this generation and second to none in enthusiasm, *H. B. Gleezen,* perhaps the most useful man to the fraternity of his time—"Dad," as he is popularly known—is president of "The National Game Fanciers Association" and of the "Gleezen Supply Co., of Lawrence, Mass. *H. C. Benseman,* a veteran in both war and cock fighting, author of a valuable work entitled "The Management of Game Fowls," *E. H. Macoy,* the wealthy importer of "Jungle Fowl" direct from India through the famous Hagenback.

T. E. Lipscomb, editor of "Dixie Game Fowl," one of

the most thrifty and satisfactory game papers of the day, *W. H. Rightmyer,* who has become one of the most liberal breeders of "Spanish Fowl," *J. C. Sturzel,* famous for his crayons of game cocks and as the breeder of "Sturzel's Hurricanes," a strain of well-known, and successful fighters; *H. E. Estes,* originator of the "999 Greys," a cherished friend of many of the first cockers of our time, *J. H. Rathbun, Gwynn,* and *Y. D. Plumley*—the last named is author of a series of "Reminiscences" contributed to "Chanticleer" unsurpassed for interest, candor, honesty and manly good feeling, *"Game Cock,"* whose contribution on "Cock Fighting," to The London Fancier's Gazette in 1875 deserves to stand among the very best ever written, and no less instructive than the lengthy contribution of "Outing" for December 1902, and a host of others, many of them equally as deserving of commendation as a number of those I have named.

I consider *Mr. Mackin,* of Chicago, already mentioned, and *Mr Dudley H. Pierce,* of Wisconsin, two of the best *main reporters* that contribute to the game journals. It would be well for those that wish to excel in this line of literature, to follow the models these gentlemen have given the fraternity. Although they write of mains in which they are principals, they are always fair and truthful—they report in a truly sportsman-like spirit. In good main reporting the basis of success is truth and fairness. There is always a disagreeable something about main reports that are written for free advertising, and the general reader can detect the real purpose so easily between the lines, that there is serious doubt if such advertising accomplishes the end in view.

The time was when a main report was such a curiosity that it was necessary to give a form to be followed by the reporter. But reports are so numerous now, that it is no longer necessary. Models may be gotten from such organs as those we have named, and special mention should not be withheld from "Southern Pit Games," in which many of the finest specimens in existence of main reports have appeared.

Some points, however, should always be included, among which are: 1. Weight of each pair. 2. Colors. 3. Strains and breeder. 4. If an extra specimen, include the fact; if a dunghill, "cry aloud and spar not."

FAMOUS STRAINS AND THEIR BREEDERS

OF RECENT TIMES.

Each generation produces a new race of men, and with them, a new race of cocks. In rare instances a strain of game fowl has passed from one generation to another, and while it has been claimed that certain fowls in Ireland, England and America have not had an outcross for a half century, to get anyone to accept the statement is next to impossible. Some Hennies weighing seven pounds were imported to this country by the famous cartoonist, Davenport, in 1899, from the yards of Lord Lonsdale, in England, said not to have had an out-cross for forty years. The writer imported fowl from Ireland in 1893 represented as having been kept pure in a certain Irish family for one hundred years. Nevertheless, as a rules, twenty-five years will completely revolutionize the strain of the average breeder. Hence, any work on cocks that fought twenty-five years ago is ancient history. For a rather extended description of fowl fought in the past generation, though by no means complete, reference must be had to Dr. Cooper's work; while, should the inquirer be still more curious as to cocks and cockers of still more distant times, Wm. Sketchley's English work will be found instructive. This writer takes his reader back to 1760. But our purpose is to write of cockers and breeds of game fowl bred and fought in the present generation

Beyond a doubt the most famous fighting cocks of this generation are the following, whose reputation is established on every continent under the sun:

Whitehackles, Warhorses, Shawlnecks, Mugwumps, Grist Champions, Grist Henry Gradys, Red Horses, Red Quills, Cubans, Shenandoahs, Roundheads, Huddlestons, Dominiques, Pyles, Gordons, Gulls, Irish, Tassels or Toppies, Muffs, Hennies, Ginn cocks, Pierce cocks, Orientals.

WHITE HACKLES.

These fowls are light reds with white or yellow legs. They often show a greenish tinge in the leg. They are generally duckwing reds, but, only a few show clear black breasts. They vary from a few streaks of brown to a solid brown breast, or rather what may be more accurately described as a robin breast. They are heavily feathered, very graceful and handsome on the walk. No better bred cocks ever lived. The kicking instinct has been bred into these fowl to perfection. They produce fewer wing fighters than any other strain. They are never over medium in station, showing a powerful thigh of good length, but a very short shank. They are very broad in the shoulder, have good backs, nearly always carry their tails well off, never "squirrelled." They have daw and red eyes. All breeds of the Whitehackles are desperately game and have a wonderful capacity for taking and administering punishment. As claimers in New York and Philadelphia Rules, they have no equals.

The *Morgan Whitehackles* take their name from Wm. L. Morgan, the famous veteran cocker of New Jersey. There is no breeder of game fowl in the Union that can show more mains to his credit and fewer losses than this gifted past-master of the pit. He has been "caught off" now and then, but victory is usually perched on his banner, which has inscribed on it a list of honors that would stir the pride of Lord Derby in his palmiest days. And be it remembered that hundreds of mains are fought from Maryland to Canada in the stillness and quiet of secrecy necessitated by the bitterest blue laws in America, enforced by the meanest officials in the world. Hence, that publicity which is given to Southern mains would be ruinous to the interest of cockers in the North. For this reason, let our Southern friends not presume that the sport is not progressing. Just as the laws became bluer the cockers became smarter, and the said laws, if effective at all, have served only to close public pits and force the fraternity to do their fighting in clubs or at their homes. Here, they can never be molested except by measures as obnoxious to the American sense of liberty as were the general search warrants reprobated in the Declaration of Independence.

Mr. Morgan's Whitehackles descended from fowl he got from an Englishman by the name of Gilkerson, who brought them from the Northern part of the island, hence, they were often called "North Britons." They are, therefore, distinctly of English origin and there seems to be a strong probability of their having descended from the famous Duckwing Reds of Lord Derby, though there must have been other blood in them, since they have as often yellow as white legs. These fowls trim as white as cotton in the neck, and fight from 4.4 to 6 lbs.

The *Kearney Whitehackles* differ widely from the Morgan, being of Irish origin. Mike Kearney is a native of the Green Sod, and brought these fowls directly over about thirty years ago. Kearney is one of the most successful feeders in the world. He is always open to fight any man for any amount. Like most of the product of Ireland, he will risk the entire earnings of a lifetime on the fighting of a main of his Whitehackles fed by himself, with as much confidence and complacency as if he were sitting down to dinner at Delmonico's, with a big appetite and strong digestion. No man has been in better position to perfect a strain of fighting cocks than Mike Kearney, for he brought to this country the best in Ireland, he has no superior as a feeder, and he has run a pit for twenty years. These facts alone are a strong indication of the excellence of the Whitehackles, as it is reasonable to suppose that a professional of the most finished school would hardly perpetuate a strain of fowl that he did not believe to be the best fighters in the country. Kearney ran a pit on Long Island for a number of years, where some of the largest monied mains ever fought in the history of cock fighting were pulled off. It was here that he defeated the veteran Tom O'Neal and his Kentuckey Dominiques at the height of his glory, for $5,000, the Whitehackles winning nearly every fight.

Kearney's Whitehackles frequently come gingers as well as streaky-breasted light-reds with white and yellow legs. They do not all trim out perfectly white. They have very tough, long plumage and show the result of in-breeding by their uniform quality and style of fighting. They are very quiet cocks in hand but upon being pitted seem propelled by electricity. They are savage, desperate, persevering, bloody-heeled cocks that never stop till dead. Kearney wins many a fight with these fowls after all hopes seem to have vanished. These fowls are specially valuable for one quality rarely possessed by a strain. They are not man-fighters, and have but little disposition to fight turkeys. The hens are prolific layers and splendid mothers. Kearney cocks fight from 4.4 to 6.4. They run rather smaller than formerly. I have owned cocks of this breed that weighed 7.8 on the walk. Kearney's Whitehackles are medium in station, long, big, strong thigh, short shank, very broad shoulders, and can come as near winning with no eyes, legs or wings as any cocks that ever lived. Their vitality is simply wonderful, and they are very easy fowl to condition for a main, taking to the feed most kindly. They have no disposition to coop-hack or man-hack, a valuable characteristic, and I have never seen one that would not show fight the next day after the most severe cutting in a main, no matter how badly hurt.

Davis Whitehackles take their name from Mr. R. C. Davis, of Mars Bluff, S. C., whose march to the front is the most rapid in the history of American breeders; while not so old a breeder as Morgan and Kearney, his fowls have done more fighting in different parts of the world. From California to New York, from thence by way of Philadelphia, Maryland, District of Columbia, South Carolina, to the City of Mexico—in the shortest to the longest gaffs and slashers—in the loosest handling of amateurs and the most skillful handling of the world's best ring masters and under the most technical rules—they have been uniformly successful. When they did not win, which was extremely rare, they acquitted themselves nobly. No wonder, then, Mr. Davis came so promptly to the front. He has the goods. Mr. Davis is a retiring man, indisposed to boast; he has not the *cocoethes loquendi* nor *scribendi,* hence his Whitehackles have had to do all the talking in the pit, and win distinction for their breeder against the sky-splitting declamation and soul-stirring petitions of the greatest generation of game cock paper fighters in the history of mankind. They have "cried so loud that all the hollow deep of hill resounded:" without the eloquence of the quill, these Davis Whitehackles have risen to the first place in popular favor.

"The name that dwells on every tongue
No minstrel needs."—*Manrique.*

The Davis Whitehackles descend from a Kearney cock fought in New York in a main ten years ago. This cock was about 6 lbs. running weight. He was a white-legged red one year, a yellow-legged the next. While a duckwing, he showed streaks of red in his breast. He won a battle that lasted one hour and a half with a wing broken, one eye out, and his bill off. He was bred to sisters of the famous main of Redhorse cocks known as the "Elevator cocks"—that whipped the New York people eight out of eleven—no finer main of fowls was ever seen in this or any country. The writer remembers these cocks well. They were a grand show of straight brown-red Redhorse fowls of the old Eslin blood. The old Whitehackle cock was then bred over his own daughters, making them 3-4 Kearney 1-4 Eslin Redhorse. Two of these hens were bred under a famous old blinker Derby cock—a winner of a hard battle in Baltimore. This cock was of the Derby blood imported by a well-known New Jersey breeder. He was a 6 lb. cock with very long, heavy plumage trimmed white, and was a perfectly marked duckwing red with white beak and legs. The pullets from this cross were bred to a brother of the two hens—that is to their uncle on their mother's side. More Kearney blood was infused two years later by placing a 6 lb. stag over the yard, from one of the two old hens by a cock that Kearney bred and used as a getter. He was also a six pound cock, a streaky-breasted red with yellow legs, five times a winner—in long heels, inch and a half, and inch and a quarter. Mr. Davis has a successful plan of breeding an early blooming stag back to the oldest hens, that he has in perfect health, and he is another example of the value of judicious in-breeding. On a recent visit to that section of Carolina, I saw thirty or forty of Mr. Davis' Whitehackles on their walks. They, like the Kearney's and Morgan's, are uniform in build, extremely handsome and gamey in appearance. They will fight from 4.4 to 6.2. All are about the same in station, big thighs, big shoulders, short, broad backs, and short in shank.

In color the Davis fowls are the same as Mike Kearney's. They run from streaky or dotted-breasted reds to gingers and even a yellow jacket appears at times. They trim different shades of white in hackle.

Mr. Davis is a prosperous planter, owns a fine plantation, and dispenses hospitality with an open hand.

James Dugrey, of Albany, the well known racehorse man, has bred a cross of Kearney's Whitehackles with signal success. It is said that Dugrey furnished Kearney with twenty-one of these cocks with the understanding that every survivor was to be returned. Kearney returned the twenty-one cocks, every one a winner. *Wm. Oyster,* of Washington, got some of these fowls from Dugrey and had fine success with the feed of Dick Lee, the veteran cocker of Washington. He won a number of mains and was never defeated until he came against Butler, Goodhart and Felix, the early spring of 1902.

WARHORSES.

This is a strain of very dark-reds with dark legs. They should come with good plumage and of medium station. They fight from 4 lbs. to 6.8. The hens are often solid black.

These fowls are more extensively bred, certainly in the crosses, than any other in the world. There is scarcely a breeder of game fowl in America that has not owned a Warhorse, or bred crosses of the blood. There are not a dozen breeders in the Southern States that do not breed these fowls—said to be pure or in crosses. The popularity of the feather is unparalleled even by the famous Shawlnecks. We have only to look over the "ads" in any game chicken paper to discover this fact. It is safe, therefore, to conclude that "wherever there is so much smoke there must be some fire"—that the Warhorse fowl must have possessed decided merit to win such wide spread popularity and confidence. They are to the South what the Whitehackles are to the North.

It would be an endless task to follow the blood into its multitudinous crosses, and we must confine ourselves to the origin of these fowls and to the breeders that have made a specialty of breeding them "in their great purity."

Before the war between the States, about the year 1854, Mr. John Stone, of Marblehead, Mass., who was an enthusiastic cocker of that day, was engaged in feeding a main of stags. An Irishman, recently over, in his employ, looking at the stags in the spar, remarked to Mr. Stone, "I have seen one stag in the ould conthrie that could lick the whole main of 'em." Upon investigation it was discovered that the Irishman's brother was gamekeeper for a certain Irish lord who had a strain of fowl known all over Ireland. Mr. Stone paid this Irishman's expenses to Ireland and back with instructions not to return without some of these fowls. In due time he came back with the fowl—dark-reds, with dark eyes. These fowls were carefully bred by an old veteran, who died in 1904, and a personal friend of the writer, for Mr. Stone. They were great game fighters, far superior to anything even the best cockers in New England had seen. After defeating all comers, Mr. Stone, like Alexander the Great, sought other worlds to conquer. He made a tour of the South, winning everywhere. During this trip a friendship sprang up between him and Major Thomas Bacon, of South Carolina, the most successful breeder and cocker in the South. Thus Major Bacon secured the blood, and Mrs. Bacon, his widow, is still breeding it in South Carolina. Her cocks are fought yearly in the Charleston pits. They are uniform winners and always command a high price. Major Thomas Bacon has been dead many years; so has Mr. John Stone. Let us hope that by some decree, the wisdom of which we cannot understand with these brains of flesh, those noble spirits bask together in the eternal sunshine of Elysium, among the scenes that gave them so much joy on earth.

Walter Hopkinson, the most famous breeder of Warhorses in recent times, secured his start from Major Bacon, and it was, perhaps, through him that these fowls got the name of "Warhorses," which had been known as "John Stone Irish." It is said they were first nicknamed "Warhorses" in Charleston, S. C., by an Irishman, who remarked upon seeing them fight with uniform success against all comers, "Ah! but ain't they war horses?"

Walter Hopkinson got the blood straight. He bred it straight for several years and from him the present generation of Southern breeders were supplied with brood stock. Mr. Hopkinson, now advancing towards seventy, lives near Augusta, Ga., and still breeds his favorites, though he does not hesitate to try crosses. He has a strain of dark-greys that have proved a hit on his old Warhorse blood. These Grays have won great popularity, and are being bred in many parts of the Union. They generally come black-greys, with dark eyes and legs, and are game, persevering fighters.

R. C. McGinty, a well known breeder of Warhorses, gave Hopkinson $20 and a demijohn of fine whiskey for a young stag and an old hen of the Warhorse blood, about twelve years ago. From these "Bob" got his start. He has been a persistent in-breeder of the old stock, but he has not hesitated to make crosses. His Brown-Reds and Dandies are happy crosses on the old Hopkinson stock. McGinty Warhorses are known in almost every State. Among the greatest fighters in short heels the writer has ever seen were a lot of cocks got by a McGinty cock over two old hens from Geo. S. Smith, of Washington, D. C. The McGinty Warhorses have been successful in long heels, and they have an instinct for claiming that makes them valuable as short heel fighters.

Felix Rood, of Alabama, is also a breeder of the old fashioned Warhorse. Mr. Rood owns a handsome estate not far from Eufaula, where his fowl roam in broad fields, scratch in leafy woods, and drink at never-failing streams. The *Rood Warhorses,* for all their not being so well known abroad, are the terror of local cockers, and when mains are fought in Georgia or Alabama it does not increase the composure of those interested on the other side in a main to learn that "Felix Rood is on hand with a coop of his Brown-Reds and Warhorses." These fowls are among the gamest in America, and are fit to fight for any man's money.

James Norwood, of North Carolina, has won an enviable reputation as a breeder of Warhorses. He, like McGinty, got his start from Walter Hopkinson. Norwood Warhorses have been shipped to almost every State in the Union, and not a few think them the best of all the Warhorses. Mr. Norwood is well fixed for breeding and walking cocks. While he has made a specialty of Warhorses for years, yet he has not confined his breeding to them alone. He has a strain of Murtishaw Blues, Dominiques and White Pyles that enjoy wide-spread popularity. The Studwick Whites, of Georgia, Alabama and Virginia, are from Norwood's White Pyles.

Besides these there are several breeders of good game Warhorses that are less extensive in their operations. C. M. Shackelford, W. M. Bigger, Jeffcoat, Mabry and others.

SHAWLNECKS.

In general popularity, these fowls stand second only to the Warhorses. They have been bred by every successful game chicken man in the South, and the blood runs in the veins of nearly all the Southern cocks of this generation. The

"Shawls" are unquestionably a cross of the old Claibornes, which were a yellow or white-legged breed that came from crossing a Derby cock over a Spanish hen. The Derby cock gave the progeny white legs while the Spanish hen gave them yellow legs. There was a later infusion of Baltimore Top Knot, a famous strain in Dr. Cooper's day, in the Claibornes. This gave them the tassel often seen in the old time Claiborne fowl. Shawlnecks to this day show the white and the yellow leg as well as the tassel of their Claiborne ancestors. Of the pure blood Charlie Brown, of Columbus, Ga., was the most successful breeder. However, in later years, after Mr. Brown's health failed, he could not give his fowls the attention game fowl must have, and there was a decided degeneration from that pristine merit which won their reputation in the "better days."

Shawlnecks are yellow or white-legged, black-breasted reds. At their best they fought from 4.8 to 6.8. They nearly always had long plumage and very heavy hackles that came down full on the shoulder, whence they were named "Shawlnecks." And in this connection let us say it is quite a mystery why there should be a tendency to short feathers among many strains of Southern cocks of our day. Some of them are becoming more leggy and shorter in feather every year and are rapidly approaching the "points of perfection" (that win in the show pen). Such fowl were never seen on the yards of reputable breeders "in the good old summer time." Men that ought to know better have no excuse for the perpetuation of a breed of chickens that look like sand-hill cranes dipped in grease.

The Shawlneck hens, if without the sprig so often seen among them, can scarcely be distinguished from White Hackles. They run from a partridge red to light buff, are good mothers and attack any foe to the brood with all the fire and fury of she devils.

GRIST GAMES.

In this connection, it becomes our pleasure to pay a well merited tribute to that prince of cockers, Col. F. E. Grist, of Georgia. It was he who dignified the business of breeding game fowl for sale and first opened the eyes of game chicken people to the important fact that game cocks are in the same class with racehorses and all other high-bred stock, that one is just as much a legitimate object of sale and exchange as the other. Since the Colonel began breeding his Shawlneck-Stampers for sale and shocked the fraternity about twenty years ago by publishing a catalogue of his pit games, he has bred more game fowl than any other man that ever lived in America. It is no exaggeration to say he has bred 250,000 game fowls in that time, and his sales have netted him such an income as to necessitate his closing out a large, lucrative mercantile business and resigning the office of mayor of his town. It is due Colonel Grist to say that no one living man has furnished so many brood yards as he, and there is not a nook or corner in the game chicken world where *Grist* is not as familiar a word as air and water. Genial, courtly, generous, extremely liberal towards the faults of others, and appreciative of their virtues, not one man can say that Grist has invited controversy or sought to humiliate his fellow-breeders by public arraignment of their mistakes and misfortunes. He has good fowls, they suit him and his patrons, he makes due allowances for the narrow-minded criticisms of envious competitors, whose rant creates as little commotion as a tempest in a teapot and is just about as oppressive as that gnat on the bull's horn in Aesop's fable. The cocking fraternity of this generation cannot overestimate the benign influence of such men as F. E. Grist. Without this slight tribute this book would fall far short of its purpose as a faithful "history of our own times." Col. Grist has bred his Stamper-Shawlnecks in different colors, but the great majority of his fowls are what he calls *Champions* and *Henry Gradys*. The Champions are dark-reds with dark legs, many coming the old-fashioned green-legged duckwing reds with red eyes. They are also brown-reds and rarely a gray. These fowls show the result of intelligent inbreeding. Although "bred together" for twenty-five years, they fight from 4.8 to 7 lbs. These Champions run on the walk from 5 lbs. to 8 lbs. As a rule they are of medium station and have plenty of plumage. The Champion hens correspond with the cocks in color. They run from brown-red to partridge with green, black and blue legs, and red eyes. But Champions also show very dark colors from a cross on a Bacon Irish Gilder made in 1875.

The Henry Gradys were named in honor of the brilliant editor and orator, Henry W. Grady, of the Atlanta Constitution. These are light reds showing more of the Shawlneck or Claiborne blood; except being shorter in feather and rather higher in station, they are similar in color to the Whitehackles. They are yellow or white-legged reds with red eyes, and most of them trim perfectly white in the hackle. They are fowl of fine size like the Champions although "bred together" for years. However, in years gone by, the Gradys did show a brindle or a blue now and then, which makes it quite possible that a cock of that feather may crop out even at this day, from a blue Irish cock crossed into the strain nearly twenty years ago. This is true of the Dugrey fowl of N. Y., that is, though this cross of Kearney are yellow-legged reds, yet, one in a hundred perhaps may be a dull black with brass wings and yellow legs. The Gradys run on the walk from five to seven pounds and eight ounces. They are made right and are heavy in bone.

Col. Grist gives the origin of his fowl in his catalogue in fuller detail than our limited space will allow. The Stamper blood he got when a young man from the well known racehorse man by that name, from whom the colonel learned much of that information which has brought him to the front as one of the most successful breeders in the history of cock fighting. The Shawlneck blood came from Charles Brown when at their best. Two victories alone would entitle Col. Grist's cocks to undying fame. He beat the "Shawls" in Brown's hands after the latter had defeated such men as Col. Bacon, of South Carolina. He afterward defeated the world renowned Arkansas Travelers in the hands of Sledge & Hanna. In the season (1902-1903) the Grist cocks won a victory in short heels in New York that netted their backers $15,000.

RED HORSES.

Red Horse is a name given during the war, to a strain of dark brown red cocks originated and bred in great perfection by the Eslin family of the District of Columbia. They are such dark brown-reds that some might call them black-reds. These cocks have black eyes, black or green legs, medium station, they trim black in hackle, have very long tough plumage, and while they favor the Warhorse they show much more red on the wing butts. However, many of the Red Horse come lighter brown-reds and these trim copper in hackle. The Eslins claimed to be the originators of the famous "Tartar Cocks" so highly prized by Dr. Cooper, and the Tartars were of this Redhorse blood. It is peculiarly interesting to know that this famous strain characterized by a very lustrous, black pop eye, derives this distinguished mark from fowl sent to Governor Floyd, of Virginia, by the old Lord Derby, before the Civil war. There was more or less communication between Maryland and Virginia cockers in those days, and prominent politicians like Governor Floyd were naturally found quite often in Washington, especially during the sessions of Congress.

Cock fighting was very popular among the statesmen of that day, and the Eslins—James, William, and Columbus—often furnished the cocks and experience for a private round in the committee rooms of the Capitol, "after office hours." The walls of that grim old structure "could a tale unfold." Dick Lee, the Eslins' feeder, gives an interesting account of those famous committee-room battles, which originated possibly with George Washington, who bred an excellent strain of game fowl at his home—Mount Vernon. And it does not require a great stretch of the imagination to picture old Andrew Jackson off duty, at one of these private entertainments, and even pitting one of his game blind-fighters against a black-eye of Gov. Floyd. However, this origin of the Red Horse would be incomplete were I to omit the blood of a South Carolina cock sent to Mr. James Eslin, which cock was crossed on the old Eslin stock. This was a large cock from a gentleman in Charleston, and in strong probability was of the Lord Sefton blood imported from England by the Rhetts, and known in after years as the Rhett cocks.

From 1869 to 1890 these cocks were fought and bred almost, one might say, in copartnership, by Columbus Eslin, Charles Eslin, Geo. S. Smith and F. W. Maddux. Dick Lee did the feeding; Columbus Eslin, the selecting and heeling—his judgment was never questioned; Charles Eslin did the handling, for which he had a splendid reputation; George S. Smith did much of the walking and picking up, and bred quite a number; F. W. Maddux owned an extensive estate in blue-grass in Virginia where he bred and walked cocks in great numbers, and his money, of which he carried a generous roll, was always in sight. These gentlemen fought all comers from New York to New Orleans, and in that day were the most conspicuous group of professional cock fighters in the Union. They whipped the best both

North and South, but as they never sold fowl, they conducted all their campaigns in the quietest manner. These men whipped Dr. Gee and a strong Southern combination down in Mississippi, bringing home a roll "as big as a flour barrel." They whipped Holt, of North Carolina, the greatest cocker in the old North State, in Richmond and in Norfolk. They whipped Kearney, in New York, Pat Carroll, in Philadelphia, and they whipped the Blackhackles in their palmiest days. It was F. W. Maddux that bred the famous coop of Red Horse fowl known as the "Elevator Cocks" spoken of under the Davis Whitehackles, which whipped Kearney eight out of eleven.

But it was not alone with the Red Horse cocks that the Eslin combination scored their many victories. Another strain of fowls equally as well known, bred by these gentlemen, are the *Redquills*. However, Mr. Columbus Eslin, who has the name of being the best judge of game cocks in America, has often expressed his opinion of the comparative merits of these two strains by saying in the writer's presence, "The Red Horses made the Redquills." Which means that after the Eslins got some of the old Winans fowl from Baltimore, which were the foundation of the Eslin Redquills, they crossed the Red Horses over them, producing the "Quill" of the present day. It may surprise many, too, to learn that the original Winans fowl were duckwing reds with yellow legs and red eyes, showing cherry-red quills. Knowing this, the influence of the Red Horse blood is quite apparent in the black eyes and dark legs of modern Redquills. This cross was Harry Middleton Rusty Reds, the peer of any pit cocks that ever trod the earth. Harry Middleton bred many of these fowls over his saloon in Washington city, and the "Washington Party" were always ready to back them to the last penny. Geo. S. Smith, of Washington, and Duncan Davis, of South Carolina, are the only men that bred this blood as far as the writer is informed, but they only in crosses (1902).

BLACK AND TANS.

Geo. S. Smith, the "Black and Tan Man," may properly be termed successor to the Eslin combination. While the Eslin brothers still breed a few fowl and fight occasionally, they are no longer "wrapped up in it" as of old. Columbus is a man of fortune and is taking his ease. William quit years ago. Charles is a wholesale contractor in the District and gives but little time to the sport. Webb Maddux has entered into a new combination with Western parties and is breeding a number of New York fowl, Minton Dominiques, White Pyles, Irish and Flatheads. Dick Lee is feedding for whoever may need his services, and though advanced in years, continues to have great success. As a feeder of stags he has no equal, and they all had rather tackle somebody else than "Old Dick," in a cocking main.

George Smith's Black and Tans are from the pure old Eslin stock. They are Red Horse fowl with a cross of Redquill. Hence, they come very dark brown-reds, brown-reds and gingers, with black, green or blue legs—all with dark or black eyes. They are, perhaps, the heaviest feathered game fowl in the country. The name "Black and Tan" seems to have been applied to these Smith fowl because they show a rich red on back and shoulders and black elsewhere when trimmed for battle—giving a combination of colors like the Terriers that were so popular some fifteen years ago. All that has been said of the Red Horse and Redquills is equally applicable to the Smith fowl. He was one of the Eslin combination, or "Washington Party," as stated before. He did much of the walking and breeding, hence was in a position to procure the very best, which there is little doubt that he did. It is due Mr. Smith to say that no strain of game fowl has a better record than his, *in the pit*. They are fast, desperate, game, splendid fighters and no fowl are better claimers. You have heard that when Greek meets Greek then comes the tug of war—so it was when Smith made a main in 1898, against Erie, (Pa.) parties who were backed by the Eslins and Maddux. Only eleven pair fell in; the fighting began at 8:30 p. m. and although no time was lost, the main was not fought out until broad day next morning, Smith winning by the odd. The main was decided by a typical Red Horse (Black and Tan). Odds for twenty pittings, were against him—down, cut to ribbons, bleeding from a hundred wounds, after one hour and forty minutes, he rose with the last bit of strength left him, made one heroic effort and killed his opponent, thus landing a main the like of which is not seen in one hundred years. The battles in this main, fought in inch and a quarter heels, averaged almost an hour, and both cocks in each fight were literally cut to pieces.

The Black and Tans as bred by Smith are without a rival in short heels, excepting the Whitehackles. A full main of one against the other would be the feature of this cocking century. The writer calls to mind a number of mains won by the Black and Tans for sums as high as $200 a battle and $2,000 on the odd, but cannot recall where they have ever lost, as bred and fought by Mr. Smith.

Besides the Black and Tans, Mr. Smith breeds a very fine strain of greys imported from Ireland by a gentleman in Virginia, also some very handsome game, Irish Whitehackles imported by the same party. He has also bred for years the Shenandoahs, a strain of blues that were brought over by Tom Sayers, the pugilist, in the good ship Shenandoah, whence thier name. The Shenandoahs are bluereds, with very heavy, tough plumage. There seems little doubt that they are the heaviest feathered blue fowl in the

States. Smith has always bred a few Muffs that were as good as cocks ever get to be.

HANSBOROUGH FOWL.

In his day no man was so successful a breeder of winners in one hundred miles of Washington, as Blucher Hansborough. He lived on a large farm, well watered and wooded, in Culpeper county, Va. He made his reputation on Muffs, Shenandoahs and Red Horse crosses. These fowls he received from George Smith, who sent him brood cocks for years, and used nearly all of his cocks in the various mains fought by the Washington Party. Hansborough had signal success with a strain of Flatheads sent him by Smith, one of which, a grey, is on his knee in the cut on another page. We learn that Hansborough furnished fourteen of his famous Muffs for a main once; all were matched, all fought and all won. Nearly all the Hansborough cocks had a cross of Redquill in them which came from a little Redquill cock bred by Charles Eslin and sent to Hansborough by George Smith. A standing complaint against the old man was that he would never return a cock he used for a stock getter. The reason was discovered to be that he was a "stickler" for gameness and he always chopped his brood cocks out in the severest kind of way. They had to die under the most trying tests to satisfy him.

Other successful breeders of the Eslin stock are *William C. Boteler,* of Maryland, who has a glorious string of victories to his credit with the aid of J. W. Goodhart's feed. The "Doctor" inherits his genius for breeding fine game cocks from his father who is so higly mentioned by Dr. Cooper in his work. He is a bachelor and lives in ease on his fine estate at Brownsville, surrounded night and day by the sweetest music to his ear—the crowing of his game cocks and the singing of his hens.

Charles T. Jones, of Virginia, is known as a breeder of some fine Red Horses and Redquills, and he has many staunch friends in the fraternity who value his generosity and respect his integrity.

KENNEY REDQUILLS.

No one man has exercised more intelligence and deserves more commendation for perpetuating the Eslin Redquills than the distinguished breeder of Kentucky, Charles Kenny. Mr. Kenny obtained these fowls from headquarters, both before and when the Eslins fought a main for him at Paris, Ky. He has exercised rare good judgment in the selection and breeding of the blood, and judging from the high merit both for gameness and fighting qualities, of those the writer has seen fight in mains, the old stock has lost nothing in his hands. They are of fine size, have vigorous constitutions and are game to the core. What is better, they win. Mr. Kenny has shipped these fowls to the four quarters of the earth and they have given entire satisfaction to every customer that knows what a good cock is.

Besides the Redquills, Mr. Kenney has perpetuated the Cincinnati Racehorse, an elegant old strain whose record is unsurpassed in the States "west of the mountanis." These fowls are dark-legged reds with red eyes and more nearly owe their salvation to Mr. Kenney than to any other living man. Mr. Kenney's "Top Knots" are the best and most favorably known strain of tassels in this country. They are fowl of fair size, well built, handsome and just like all other high-bred game fowl, except that they show the top knot, peculiar to that famous old strain everybody was bidding for thirty years ago, known as the "Baltimore Top Knots." The cocks have a few long feathers back of the comb, but the hens show quite a hood. They are valued higly by all by whom they have been bred and fought, and are well worthy of the care they receive at Mr. Kenney's hands. Mr. Kenney's friendship is prized and his honor is unimpeached.

ALDRICH AND THE MUGWUMPS.

Here, dear reader, is the rarest combination in the cocking world! A strain of fine fighters backed by the most gifted writer on cocks and cocking, in our generation. These cocks nearly always win, but it matters little if they lose, for the inspiration of their breeder whose birthright is a divine *efflatus* which lifts him far above the possibility of defection, and all victories over the "Mugs," when painted by this gifted artist, are only Pyrrhic. Whoever wins against the Mugwumps must go back over the field with the Colonel and view the situation from the standpoint of grand strategy and before he has finished, the man who has defeated the Mugwumps is horrified to learn like Pyrrhus, that he has won "a victory worse than a defeat." The Colonel has a literary dragnet which he flings into the ocean of universal literature and from the "catch" he selects figures, quotations and analogies from Holy Writ to Shakespeare, as appropos of a cock fight as they could possibly be in the minute description of St. Peter's of a storm at sea. In the words of Addision, however,

> View the whole scene, with critic judgment scan,
> And then deny him merit, if you can.

There is no question that the contributions of Colonel Aldrich have given a certain classic tone to game chicken literature, which has helped to lift it to a higher plane of excellence and dignify it with a place in the range of English composition. The Mugwumps enjoy a unique and enviable place in the cocking world. They are South Carolina cocks bred by a South Carolinian. The Warhorses are, strictly speaking, acclimated Yankee cocks. They were sent South by John Stone, of Mass. The Davis Whitehackles are from New York, but the Aldrich fowl are the old time Rhett stock crossed with the Morgan blood so successful and popular in Carolina some years ago. The original Rhetts, as far as we are informed, were imported from the yards of Lord Seiton in England, by the distinguished family from which they take their name—a family distinguished for daring and courage from the earliest times, themselves as game as the cocks they bred. One demand the Rhetts made of a cock—that he die game—and they never shed a tear over the heaviest losses if their cocks died as game cocks should. Hence, the Rhetts were famous for their unflinching gameness. They were mostly green legged, black-breasted reds with red eyes, and came of fine size. They were snappy, quick, savage and disposed to be in trouble all the time. The Morgan side of the Mugwumps were darker reds with darker legs and eyes, and were from Major Morgan who stood among the best in those good old times when such men as Major Tom Bacon, Holt, and the Arringtons, of North Carolina, and Charlie Brown, were at their best.

Col. Aldrich has only in the rarest instances made any *permanent* outcross of these fowl. One, however, highly prized and perpetuated is that made by placing Mugwump hens under a black cock from Baltimore—a very fine game cock and winner of a hard battle in Charleston. From this cock come all those solid black and black brass back cocks that crop out in the "Mugs." "Otello," whose picture by Sturzel is on another page, is a member of this family. The writer saw one of these black cocks with brass wings win under the most trying circumstances in Philadelphia—he had offered 5 to 2 against this cock without takers. The fight lasted nearly two hours and the "Mug" finally, after any odds a person might offer would be refused, persevered until he brained his opponent—a very fine Ellis Blackhackle—and won out an unusually game battle. For all the rant about these Mugwumps, they are a fine strain of game cocks and the writer has seen several mains of them fight before forming his opinion. What is more he has never seen one show the slightest signs of quitting. They are strong hard fighters. They are above medium in station and have rather longer shanks than some would like for short heels, but according to the standard set for long heels in our day, they have all the advantage that can be claimed for station.

The Mugwumps come all shades of red, have both dark and light eyes, dark and yellow legs. They run from 5 lbs. to 7.08 on the walk. The unkindest cut of all—to name a good strain of Southern game cocks with the blood of the Rhetts in their veins, by such an uneuphonious and libelous name, is a sin for which Col. Aldrich can never atone. Horace said *de gustibus non disputandum,* but Roman philosophy in these days of sweet dreams and melifluous sounds would be as little in accord with modern thought as Maori ideals of female beauty at a Presidential Ball. Cooper was certainly right when he remarked in The Task:

"Some to the fascination of a name
Surrender judgment hoodwinked."

It can fairly give no one offense to say that the "Mugs" are as extensively sold and fought as any strain of game cocks in the world. It would seem the froth of jealous envy to question the merit of fowl that have won such place in public favor, and hold it. As the Colonel might say, "*Palmam que meruit ferrat.*"

RED CUBANS.

Hon. Geo. W. Means, of North Carolina, successor to

a generation among the most famous breeders of game fowl in the history of America, has sustained the lofty reputation of the Old North State, and in a way peculiar to himself. He has depended upon foreign blood to establish a new breed. Mr. Means has made a number of importations from fighting, game cocks which come from any country where the Spanish gentleman can be found. It cannot be forgotten that the greatest fowl in this country, in an illustrious past generation descended from a Spanish hen—I mean of course the Claibornes. Aware of the possibilities, Mr. Means, in the spirit of modern progress, ventured, experimented, tested, tried and was convinced after many years faithful labor, and has been rewarded. He now has a fast, reliable, hard fighting strain of game cocks that have brought him fame and money. With perhaps two exceptions, these fowl are bred and fought in greater number than any others in the world.

Mr. Means is still comparatively a young man. He, like most of the prominent Southern breeders, is a gentleman of education, culture and prominence. He is an excellent writer, a thorough gentleman, honorable in his business relations, and enjoys the confidence of his own section, having been elected mayor of his town—a flourishing little manufacturing city on the Southern Railway.

The Cubans are of a variety of colors—indeed almost "any old color." However, the dark-reds have come more frequently to our notice than the others. They show from white to black legs and are either "straight combs" or "roundheads." These fowl are a fine size running from 5 lbs. to 8 lbs. on the walk. "Jay Bird" whose picture appears on another page, is one of the many Cubans Mr. Means has sent to Mexican customers. This cock won $10,000 in one battle. It is easy to tell when any man or commodity begins to convince the interested world of their merit, from the avalanche of criticism and even vituperation that invariably follows. Against all this the game chicken world has shut its ear, as far as the Cubans are concerned, and Mr. Means with a dignified reticence reminds us of Pope's epitaph on one who would not be buried in Westminster Abbey:

> "And still care not a pin
> What they said, or may say."

For fuller explanation of the variety in colors seen in the Cubans, it is sufficient to say that they contain the blood of a famous Derby cock which accounts for the white legs that appear in some specimens. There is also a cross of the old Nick Arrington Stone Fence in the Red Cubans, than which there were none better in their day.

ROUNDHEADS, OR FLATHEADS.

These are a kind of game cock rather distinguished from all others by a peculiar feature than by a difference in blood. They have a small excrescence in the place of the high straight comb of the ordinary game cock. This little "pea comb," is sometimes no larger than a field bean, but may grow to the size of the end of the thumb, when it always turns over and may hang to one side of the head. The gills are usually very small. These cocks are known as "Roundheads" at the South and often as "Flatheads" at the North. This marking may be found on the yards of many of the best breeders, and has been in this country ever since it was a country, while it has been in England and Ireland "time whereof the memory of man runneth not to the contrary." Some have been so unreasonable as to claim boldly that all pea comb fowl are descended from Japs or Aseels. They think well enough of their theory to assert it as a fact and, although the "Affirmative of the issue carries the burden of proof," they demand of the opponents to this view to disprove their assertions. Upon the same plan of argument, it would be easy to prove that certain negro tribes in Africa are Caucasians, because they have straight, thin noses. This method of disputation reminds us forcibly of Mark Twain's proof in his "Tramp Abroad," that he stood on the grave of Adam while in the Holy Land— simply because *nobody could prove that he didn't*. Beyond all question Pea Comb game chickens were in Ireland long before the Opium war in 1854, which opened the gates of China to the world, and long before any intercourse between England and Ireland. Japan had little to do with the occidental countries fifty years ago. The probabilities are so strong against the claims of these theorists as to the origin of Pea Combs, we cannot accept their statements without some stronger evidence than mere assertion. A variation in the shape or size of any feature may be so great as not to look like a thing of the same kind. For instance, who has not seen a big broad faced Irishman with a nose too small to cover his nostrils, yet in two minutes walk up against a little Jew with a nose like the cow-catcher of a train? Yet both are noses and both men are Caucasians. It would hardly be fair to say that every man that had a big flat nose and thick lips was a negro! Yet these are distinctive marks of the African. Our friends must admit that cocks may have pea combs and yet be no relation to Japs or Aseels. Because a Hindoo has a black skin, he is not a negro.

Roundheads appear in the "Red Cubans," and many of the "Arkansas Travelers" fought by Sledge and Hanna in their palmiest days were Roundheads. Frank Casey, of Boston, has fought Flatheads for years. Joseph Wingate, of New Hampshire, breeds Roundheads every year. The McCann blood carried from Massachusetts to Pennsyvania has been bred with greatest care about Erie and thence spread into the District of Columbia, Virginia, South Carolina and Alabama. Kirk's Flatheads fought in Baltimore for years were among the gamest and best cocks in the world. Mr. Kirk fought one of these cocks three times one night in one and a half inch heels, winning all three, the last stone blind. He put this cock in a barrel and won a battle with him, still totally blind, the next night, against a fresh, good ordered cock. Moore and Ginn fight Roundhead cocks often. F. W. Maddux, of Virginia, breeds a good hard-fighting strain of them that descend from an old brown-red cock brought to New York from Ireland about fifteen years ago. There are excellent Flatheads around Baltimore now, and have been for years. So it is that these markings are found everywhere and in the best hands, perpetuated by the most reliable men, not that there is any such thing as a pure strain of Roundheads, but many like the marking. The cocks are much easier to trim. They have a very gamey appearance, but their heads are rather small and their beaks are are often too slender.

THE WINGATE FOWL.

Joe Wingate represents the highest type of New England breeders, and there are a number of them deserving of commendation. Wingate belongs properly to the old school of cockers that can never submit patiently to the modern blue law restrictions on cock fighting. He is above sixty, and has been a breeder, feeder and fighter of game fowl for forty-five years. One of the highest authorities in America has to say of this well known breeder of Roundheads and Brown-Reds: "Wingate himself is an honest old-timer A better breeder never lived." Of his fowl the same authority says: "In regard to Joe Wingate's Roundheads, I have used a number and they have the highest grade of gameness and cannot be beat as fighters. They are first-class in every respect, and if I were not united in wedlock to my own fowl I would have them in preference to any fowl I ever saw." These quotations are from a letter to the author, written by Wm. L. Morgan, of White Hackle fame, himself an old-timer.

Joe Wingate is partial to the Ginger; nearly everything he breeds is ginger. Perhaps "Ginger Joe" would not have been bad as a nickname for him. His fowl are Roundhead and Smoothhead Gingers and Brown-Reds. The cock whose picture appears on another page is a favorite Irish Brown-Red Roundhead brood cock, and a good specimen. This cock was a deep ginger in color, with dark legs and hazel eyes. His weight on the walk was 5.04. This cock's head will give the reader a correct idea of the appearance of a cock with the roundhead. These fowl are exactly the same in breeding as Wingate's Irish Brown-Reds, the only difference being that some of the get from the old imported Irish stock show the round head, while some show the straight comb. Mr. Wingate says that while he never liked the marking, especially after the Jap craze struck this country, yet they always won, and he has put away his prejudice and has begun breeding to pea comb instead of trying to breed it out. These Irish fowl of Mr. Wingate's were brought over for him about thirty years ago. He has bred them "together" rather than "in," by breeding two separate yards in different surroundings and crossing back and forth between these yards. He claims that this can be done without trouble for fifty years. Various systems of the kind are called "line breeding." However, the Wingate Brown-Reds include one family that are a cross of that old stock with an importation from England in 1893, which has proved excellent. Nor does Mr. Wingate make any secret of having crossed one yard of his fowl with the son of a cock bought by Holly Chappel, the great Detroit cocker, for $50.00 in Alabama, after winning a brilliant battle. The "Alabama cock" was a brown-red. Holly Chappel was at one time one of the most successful breeders and fighters of cocks in the Union, and became famous as the breeder of a game winning strain of Hennies for which feather Detroit became as noted as Milwaukee is for beer, whether through the climate or the influence of Holly Chappel, who can tell?

The Wingate fowl are, then, ginger and brown-red in color. They have dark legs, and their plumage is heavy, as will be seen by the cut already referred to. They run from 4.08 to 6.12 on their walks. Like all fowl properly bred, they are bred to a standard—medium station, full bosom, broad shoulders, strong backs, quick, nervy and game. A conspicuous point of great importance in the Wingate fowl and one that accounts for their cutting ability, is big thigh and short shank, points that cannot be too highly valued in any strain!

Mr. Wingate reports a case among his Roundheads that is the most remarkable exhibition of youthful pugnacity in our knowledge. A chick *sixteen days old* fought until his head was pecked into a bloody mat of scabs, but continued to fight every day for seven days in that condition. Finally he left the brood and staid to himself. Of course cases sometimes occur among game fowl where the little stag chicks will begin fighting at four weeks, though rarely. Here we have a persistent game fighter at just two days over two weeks old. With our knowledege of Mr. Wingate, no matter how marvelous this case may appear, we readily endorse his report, and set it down among the game chicken curiosities of our day. Mr. Wingate has perpetuated the Tom Heathwood fowl so well known in years gone by, which, however, were always a cross-bred and not a pure strain. They are in color yellow-legged light reds similar in appearance to the Kearney Whitehackles.

ALLEN COCKS.

Hon. William L. Allen, of Mississippi, has no equal in the Southern States as a combination breeder, feeder and fighter of cocks since Col. Grist has devoted his time entirely to breeding. Wm. Allen is held in highest esteem by his home people, having been recently elected mayor of his town, as I am informed, by the unanimous choice of his fellow citizens. Mr. Allen has pinned his faith to his famous "Roundheads" and "Knobcombs,", with which he has met and defeated almost every prominent breeder and feeder in the Gulf States. He has barred no man in long heels, has fought his cocks in great numbers against such men as Moore, McGinty, Carr, Maddigan and Hackney often for $100 and $1,000, and he has never lost a heavy main. His are sparring cocks that shuffle high in the air, and are exceptionally smart ring generals. They are game cocks, and with Mr. Mr. Allen's condition and management they have no superiors in the United States.

The Allen Roundheads and Knobcombs run from light reds with light legs to very dark reds, or even blacks, with black legs. They fight from 4.08 to 6.04. They are medium in station, as are all excellent strains, and have medium plumage. These fowl are said to originate from the yards of Col. F. E. Grist. Mr. Allen breeds a number of the Grist Champions besides his Roundheads and Knobcombs.

TASSELS OR TOPPIES.

These fowl show topknots, which may be either a few feathers behind the comb or quite a tuft. After that has been said, *spar sim,* it is unnecessary to add much. The best known Tassels in this country are the Shawlnecks. Mr. Chas. Kenney bred a fine strain of this mark. The Surrey Tassels are among the most popular fowl in some parts of the North. These fowl got their name from having been imported from Surrey, England. Mr. F. G. Henry, of Ohio, banks on a strain of Tassels he has been breeding, and undoubtedly among the handsomest and best fighters on this side of the water are the John Davis Tassels, of South Carolina. We believe this strain of fowl to be a combination of Shawlneck, Eslin Red Horse and Hopkinson Warhorse. They got the tassel from the Shawlneck, which of course got their topknots from the Claibornes. These fowl are brown-reds, black-reds and gingers. The hens have good sized topknots but the cocks have very few feathers in their tassels. They have tremendous plumage, dark eyes, dark legs and are gamey fowl in general appearance. They are winners and are growing in popularity. The "Shenandoahs" spoken of under the "Washington Party," as bred by Geo. S. Smith and Blucher Hansborough, were a Tassel strain of blues. Joe Wingate also breeds a cross of toppies.

HAMMOND GORDONS.

Before he was thirty years old Mr. J. H. Hammond, of South Carolina, had won a place among the first breeders in the South. He belongs to that group of responsible, reliable, prominent gentlemen in the South, who have made the raising of chickens a lucrative business undertaking. Mr. Hammond has named his fowl after the gallant Confederate, General John B. Gordon—a happy choice, for no gamer man ever lived than this battle-scarred chieftan whose bravery called forth the admiration of both North and South.

The Gordons are descendants of a trio of John Stone Irish Gilders sent to Beech Island in 1855, and a cross with

Col. Alfred Aldrich's fowl known at this day as "Mugwumps," but which are Rhett-Morgans with a dash of Warhorse and Baltimore. The Gordons have also the blood of Col. Thomas Bacon's Brown Eye or Black Eye in them. This blood Colonel Bacon purchased in Baltimore, and in all probability was of the oldest Red Horse blood. Nor would this be the first infusion of Red Horse in the Warhorse of the South, for Walter Hopkinson made the cross on his old stock fifteen years ago, using a cock sent him by Chas. Eslin through Geo. S. Smith.

The Gordons are dark-reds, grays and blacks. The hens are brown or black. They usually have dark legs and dark or light eyes. They are quick, strong fighters and have an enviable reputation, for they have marched straight to the front on their merit in the pit. This, no fair man will deny. They are among the most popular cocks of this day and there is one universal voice of commendation for the Gordons from every quarter of the Union. The Gordons weigh about 4.12 to 7.04 on their walks.

KING COCKS.

Dr. Claud King, of South Carolina, has "sprung up and flourished like a green bay tree" in the line of success with game fowl. His fowl have made a phenomenal record, and two victories alone entitle his "Rough and Readys'" to a place in history. One of these was over the McGinty Warhorses and the Whitehackles combined with "Bob" McGinty's feed. Seventeen pair fell in out of a show of twenty-one. The Rough and Readys won in a score of ten to seven. The King cocks also defeated Mr. Hammond and his Gordons in 1902. The "Rough and Readys" are very fast cocks, Dr. King puts them in good condition for battle, and he is a handler of no mean ability. These fowl are generally dark-reds running from deep black-reds to duckwing reds with green legs and dark or red eyes. They are fowl of medium station and favor the old fashioned Rhett fowl. They range in weight from 4.12 to 7 lbs. Numbers of the Rough and Readys have been shipped to Mexico for slasher fighting, in which style of heel they have been remarkably successful.

The Rough and Readys are the result of combination of several Southern strains on which they have drawn liberally for their many good qualities. Dr. King is assisted in his chicken business and in mains, by Dr. L. Y. King, his brother, who is a skillful surgeon, and by his portner, in the drug business—Dr. Gardner, who breeds a strain he calls "Acorn Eaters."

HUDDLESTON FOWL.

Full of years and ripe experience, G. Perk Huddleston, of Tennessee, continues to breed the strains of game fowl that have made him famous. Considering the merit of Mr. Huddleston's cocks and the heavy demand for them, they have enjoyed a desirable immunity from the unprevoked assaults that are so frequent among competitors for patronage. Everybody has a good word for Perk Huddleston, and he is resorted to freely by the best men in the business as the foundation—head of information on all questions of game chicken history.

For years he has been breeding his "Seven Strain Inside Reds," "Blue Red Gladiators," "Red Lions," "Cuban Dominiques" and "Wellslagers." The Inside Reds are so named from the manner in which they have been bred. Mr. Huddleston hit upon the idea of a happy commingling of the seven strains, then considered the best in America. He crossed so as to combine the blood about in equal proportions and then in-bred the progeny. The result was a fine strain of handsome fowl that won a national reputation in a short time, which they have maintained now for twenty years. These fowl are brown and black-reds, of medium size and station, with all the virtues of in-bred game fowl.

The Blue Reds are a cross of the Irish Reds and are the foundation of one of the most successful strains of cocks ever fought in the United States, viz: D. H. Pierce's Wisconsin Shufflers and Blue Champions. They are also supposed to be the foundation of the best known strain fought in the Chicago pits, viz: Grove's Old Family fought in numbers by John Mackin, the millionaire cocker of the West. With these fowl Mackin whipped Casey, of Boston, for $500 and $5,000.

The Red Lions and Cork Irish are crosses of the Inside Red and all have a splendid record. The Cuban Dominiques come from a cross of imported Cuban blood over Mr. Huddleston's other strains. They are large fowl running in color from White Dominiques with white legs to guinea Doms, either solid or with red backs, with yellow or white legs. They run from 5 lbs. to 7.08. There is no man in the business that has fewer enemies and more friends than C. Perk Huddleston and the unanimous concensus of opinion is emboided in Rip Van Winkle's toast—"May you live long and prosper." Huddleston's "Wellslagers" as they are now called, are descended from fowl he bought of George Woolenslager, of Baltimore, Md., before the war. They are, when true to color, brown-reds.

SHUFFLERS AND CHAMPIONS.

Of the younger set that have jumped into prominence through successful breeding, in the past ten years, none hold a more conspicuous position than Dudley H. Pierce, of far away Wisconsin. The secret of Mr. Pierce's success is easily discovered. Instead of ignoring the experience of past generations and attempting, like most amateurs, to bring something of their own up out of the ground, so that in a spirit of selfish isolation they might not have to credit anybody with any part of such success as might happen to come their way, he does simply take up the task of breeding game cocks where he found it and in a spirit of progress, has utilized what was good to the credit of those whose experience he has accepted as his guide, as well as to his own benefit and honor. All ambitious intelligent young breeders can do the same if they will only adopt Mr. Pierce's plan and exercise his good judgment in the pursuit of that plan.

Mr. Pierce publishes a handsomely illustrated circular terse, neat and to the point. He gives the credit of his start in game fowl almost entirely to the veteran G. Perk Huddleston, of Tennessee. He breeds "Wisconsin Red Shufflers," which are a combination of Inside Reds, McDougall's New Mack, (which blood is in the Inside Reds), Wellslagers and a slight infusion of Gull—all of which are bred by Mr. Huddleston. Mr. Pierce's "Blue Champions" descend from the various Huddleston families with a cross of original Gee Dominique. There are, therefore, two strains of dominique blood in these fowl—Huddleston's Cuban and Dr. Gee's. They are heavily crossed also with "Groves' Old Family."

Pierce's cocks are of medium size. They are black-reds, brown-reds and blues. Mr. Pierce has won twenty-six out of twenty-eight mains with Shufflers and Champions in the past eight years, which is an extraordinarily fine record rarely equalled in the history of cock fighting. It is due Mr. Pierce himself to say, however, that he brings his cocks to the pit in proper condition and has no superior in the feeding or in tactics.

DOMINIQUES.

One of the most popular "off colors" in game fowl are the *Dominiques*. They are known in England as "Cuckoos," and a famous strain of them was bred by Mr. Barnes, an English breeder, who lived about the year 1800. Some have a prejudice against the color, suspecting a distant out cross of dominecker, thus accounting for the color. This is as illogical as the claim that Roundheads come from Japanese because they have "pea combs." Any freak in colors may appear in game fowl just as in pigeons, and that freak can be perpetuated. Hence, the variety in colors. We have already discussed this subject and refer the reader to previous pages. "Dominiques" or "Dominicks" run in colors from a very white, almost pyle or pure white (what the English cockers called a "Smock") with bluish specks here and there, generally in the hackle and saddle feathers, to a perfect guinea or Plymouth Rock color. All these colors may be red more or less, in which case they are called "Red Dominiques." It is impossible to breed a dominique with dark legs; they always have yellow or white legs. No matter what cross is made, they always come, if of the "Dom." feather, with white or yellow legs.

There are numerous so-called game dominiques bred and offered for sale in the United States and so many of these are spurious, worthless strainers that the color has come somewhat into bad repute in many sections. However, it would be a big mistake to say there are no good ones. In this feather the Kentuckians beat the world. That State has been famous for this feather and blues, for a century. Thomas O'Neal, of Louisville, brought the old blood to a high point of excellence and made an easy mark of all comers fighting a draw even with the great Georgia Shawlneck breeder—Chas. F. Brown, nor did there seem to be any check to the triumphant Kentuckian's march till he struck the Kearney Whitehackles in short heels and was whipped nearly every fight. A Dominique fad spread like an epidemic. O'Neal Dominicks were in high request, he selling pullets at $100 a pair. Fakirs as usual "took up the note" and bred imitations fit only for hucksters. Confidence in due time was destroyed, as it was after the great Pacific Railway bubbles began to burst which ended in financial panic in 1873, and dominique game chickens came into bad repute. But out in old Kentucky they still had the right stuff and Roland Minton took up where O'Neal left off. Minton died before O'Neal but not before he had restored general confidence in Kentucky Dominiques. To-day no fowl stand higher in the Chicago pits, and none in the States along the Mississippi have so long a string of victories to their credit. The veteran Henry Flock has whipped all comers with them. Roland Minton's old stock was sold after his death to Mr. F. H. McWhorter, of Chicago, who is breeding them in great numbers and fights them for sums, the mention of which, would frighten the average cock fighter out of ten years growth.

The *Gee Dominiques* so popular twenty years ago, are still bred by a few, and said to be "in their greatest purity." Perhaps a pure Gee Dominique is not to be found, yet the old blood runs in the veins of many of the best known strains in the world, such as Grist's, Huddleston's, Pierce's. Dr. Gee lived in Alabama about 10 years ago, a man over seventy. His fowl were looked after by his daughter, Miss Sue, who continued to sell the old stock several years after her father's death. It was remarkable that a college bred young lady with a mind for those elegancies that usually absorb the cultured female mind, could have mastered the ins and outs of so masculine a subject as the breeding and fighting of game cocks! Dr. Gee Oakey, a nephew, kept the father for a number of years, but we are informed he has practically given up the pure blood entirely. At this day the perpetuation of this famous feather as bred by the Doctor seems to depend upon the efforts of J. L. McLaurin, of Colorado, who makes a specialty of the old Gee blood. Mr. McLaurin is an enthusiastic fancier, the Gee Dominiques are his specialty, he is a breeder of standing and experience, and the fraternity are to be congratulated on his accepting the task of handing down the famous old Gee Dominiques in their purity. See cuts elsewhere in this book.

The *Chappell Dominiques*, of South Carolina, while not so extensively bred today, were a popular strain, and the blood is in many of those private yards in the birthplace of so many famous strains—South Carolina—now. To give some idea of the estimate placed upon game chickens in that part of the Union, a man may travel in some sections a whole day and hear nothing but a game cock crow. Drive into almost any place along the road two miles from everywhere, and you can buy a good game cock from a farmer for a dollar and fifty cents. I saw one of these, a Chappell Dominique cross, fight his fourth battle and die as game as a pebble. There are many birds of the Chappell feather in South Carolina now, but none can truly be said to be pure. The feather has its devoted admirers in every State, and this color seems to have a peculiar fascination for many whose enthusiasm often outruns their judgment, for while the dominiques have some achievements to their credit which are even brilliant, yet their record by no means compares with that of the different shades of red and grey. What a cocker wants is winners and that feather is most desirable which brings the best results. We have already spoken of the Huddleston ½ Dominiques in another connection. From these various sources no doubt nearly all the dominiques in the States have sprung.

HENNIES, OR HEN COCKS.

In the pursuit of no other fad in breeding game cocks has so much time and money been spent as in the search for and development of game winning "Hennies." These are freaks in the game chicken world, for while the game species are characterized by long, handsome, beautiful plumage, the cocks of this breed are feathered exactly like hens, hence they are called "Hen Cocks." They come all colors from pure white to solid black, though the most popular of all is the "Grouse Hennies." These are brown and yellow with either dark, yellow or white legs. They run the same in weights as all other cocks, and beyond their oddity, they possess no virtue, not even the birthright of any good game chicken. They cannot whip any battles because they are hen cocks, and the idea that often they win fights because their antagonists take them for hens and give them a chance to strike the first blow, is sheer nonsense. When the king feathers of a cock are cut off for battle, in what respect does a hen cock differ in appearance? It is not difficult to discover the sex of a brawny man with a hoarse voice, even if he has on a woman's dress!

An account is given by the old writers of a main in Ireland in which one of the parties showed a little henny for every battle, winning nine straights and the main! A phenomenal perfomance. Dick Haydon, the famous turfman whose picture appears on another page, is represented with "Peter Jackson," a part henny that won about $80,000. The English magazines published pictures of this cock and enlarged upon his wonderful performances. Mr. Haydon bred some of Lord Lonsdale's Hennies credited with being the best in the world. This English Lord has made a specialty of Hennies and it is claimed that they have not had an out cross for forty years. I saw a pair sent a distinguished newspaper man in New York. The cock was a

7 lb. bird splendidly built, a perfect grouse hen-feathered cock with yellow legs. The hen was a big-boned, large, solid black hen. The after history of these fowl is not sufficient to require further record. Chester A. Lamb is the best known American specialist in Hennies. Rumor says that Mr. Lamb has spent a fortune in the attempt to develop a strain of dead game hennies that can whip any other cocks. Has he done so? He has them all colors and his customers testify to their gameness. His white hennies I have seen severely punished, while they did not win they died game. There seems to be no doubt that a strain of black and gray hennies fought by William Gilliver, of England, are game and fighters. One of these he sent to a gentleman in Virginia after winning a hard battle. This cock was a perfect, black henny, rather shanky—a very cross, nervous cock, with short plumage. He had every appearance of being a game cock. L. A. Jepson, of Massachusetts, has bred some game black hennies in later years. The writer witnessed a main between these black or very dark-red hennies fed by George Wilson and a main of fowl from George S. Smith, of Washington, fed by John D. Evans. While the hennies were game they had not the shoulder, back and power of the Red Horse and Irish cocks and lost the main. Game hennies have been bred around Erie, Pa., for years, and the best I have ever seen are fought in Baltimore at the present day. There was a curiosity in Baltimore, in the shape of an old hen cock that had won fourteen battles in short heels! The writer owned a daughter of this cock and her get had a splendid record.

Some claim that hen cocks are faster than long feathered fowl. There is no reason why they should be nor is it possible for them to be faster than many of the best Southern strains, unless they are electricity itself. There seems no special reason to perpetuate the hen cock except as a fad or curiosity. Many breeders like to have something different from others, and Hennies are certainly of their own kind. It cannot be denied that some specimens are strikingly handsome and attractive.

PYLE COCKS.

From time immemorial Pyles have been bred and fought in England, Ireland and America. King Charles the Second owned a strain of these fowl which he fought with uniform success against all comers at the Westminster cock pit, and although that has been over two hundred years, enthusiasts are still breeding King Charles' Pyles in England. Wm. Gilliver and Herbert Atkinson, of England, are fighting some good game Pyles. One bred by the latter gentleman won a Welsh main in the gamest possible manner three years ago, and in this connection let me say, that there is no method of testing cocks in the states equal to a Welsh main; for testing every quality in a game cock. We should give the subject attention.

Perhaps the most reliable strain of Pyles in recent times are the "Genets" of New York. This strain is the foundation of those game, savage, winning Pyles fought in such numbers in Chicago. The Pyles sold in many states of the Union by P. W. Carew in past years are of this blood and they have been uniformly successful and proven themselves good game cocks. Many of the present generation of New York and New Jersey cockers are fighting the Genets and class them as among the best in the land. The Genets got their name from the gentleman who bred them and brought them into general notice—Hon. Henry Genet, a prominent New York politician. These fowl are being bred more or less crossed with other good blood, by F. W. Maddux, of Virginia; E. G. Winston, of the same state; and by New York and Illinois cockers.

However, it harms nobody to say that as good Pyles as were ever fought in this country are bred around Baltimore by a class of careful breeders whose superiors are not to be found in the world. The first of this feather brought to my notice was the Goss blood. They were large blue-reds, or White Pyles full of snap, and never quit till stone dead. These are game Pyles and very handsome. Of course fresh blood has been infused since Mr. Goss died years ago, but they have been bred right and are good game winners.

Pyles vary in color from pure white with white beak and legs like many of the Genets, to muddy blue flea-bitten fellows that look as if they had been hatched in an ash barrel, with blue, green or black legs. Rarely a perfectly white Pyle will show a solid black eye. The "Cotton Boll," the old "Thompson Whites" and the "Studwick Whites" of the South, also the "Pea Soups" properly belong to the

Often strains of chickens that have white blood in them will begin to crop out pyles, after many years breeding. Redquills crossed on Shenandoahs finally produced the American Pyle family.

The handsomest "White Tails" I have ever seen, the famous Paton White Tails of Texas, are thought to have originated in this way. These cocks generally show bodies of some solid color generally red with brown or robin breast, and often solid red shawl, but a perfectly white tail, whence the name "White Tails." I have known them to be black and show white tails. This was often true of a strain of blacks that trimmed white in the hackle, fought in New York twenty years ago and there were none better! There is no fad in the Pyle feather—they are a standard color and a perfect specimen cannot be surpassed for beauty, by any bird that ever wore feathers. They are always popular in the pit, and the old writers claim that they carry a bloodier heel than dark cocks. Of course this statement must be taken "with a grain of salt."

MUFF GAMES.

There is a strong prejudice against cocks of this marking in some quarters, but that prejudice would soon give place to admiration if the critics would visit the Baltimore pits a few times. The Maryland breeders, especially of Baltimore county, breed a strain of Grey Muffs that have no superiors for gameness. Of this blood are the Pilsons coming into popular favor in Pennsylvania—though Mr. Pilson's Muffs were mostly reds. These people beat the world for Muffs. In Blucher Hansborough's day, he had the medal for Muffs. The Eslins have always bred a few and George S. Smith has bred some of the best Muffs ever fought in the American pits. I saw a little brown-red Muff of his fight one hour on a broken leg and win against a fine Gull cock, in a hard main. Let no man fall into the mistake of condemning cocks because they happen to have side whiskers!

Muff cocks are so called because they show a tuft of feathers on the sides of the face and under the throat. These are always trimmed off when preparing for battle. A very odd looking fowl not a little similar to hooded owls is produced by crossing tassels over Muffs. This was done by Smith, Eslin and Maddux. The cocks showed heavy muffs and topknots giving the head the appearance of being almost as large as a man's fist. They were game fighters and winners. This only shows what odd fowl can be bred if a breeder wishes to make the attempt. The greatest combination among this line is a roundhead-muff-tassel white henny! These additions are easily produced. Breed any roundhead cock—a muff tassel hen and you have all but the henny the first season.

GULLS.

Much is written about a famous old strain of fowl brought into notoriety by Dennis Mahoney, of New York, called "Gulls." These fowl in their purity were yellow-legged, black-breasted reds showing white in wings, tail and hackle. In short they were very similar to the White Hackles. The fowl were never defeated, as fed and fought by "Den" Mahoney. They have always been known as "Mahoney Gulls." P. W. Carew made a specialty of these fowl for years, but finally lost the pure blood entirely. Through him the blood was distributed throughout the Union, as well as into Canada and Mexico. G. Perk Huddleston and Dudley H. Pierce have the blood in their fowl. The Gulls were very game and had the most pronounced "kicking instinct" in the writer's knowledge. Their first impulse seemed always to be to kick when touched in battle and they won many a forlorn hope by kicking while their opponents were "mouthing." The Gulls were a low-set broad shouldered fowl with full breast, and very short shanks. Proportions of the blood are in the veins of many leading American strains. The Gulls run in weight from 4.10 on the walk, to 7 lbs.

GINN COCKS.

The breeder of this well known strain is a well-to-do planter in Georgia. He breeds and walks great numbers of his fowl, and supplies mains to some of the most skillful cockers in the South. In Steve Moore's feed, the Ginn cocks have more than held their own, while they have been equally successful in recent important mains in Texas. Mr. Ginn is a prominent and popular man who enjoys the esteem and confidence of his fellow citizens as he has done for many years. And this reminds us of the fact that honesty and integrity can survive "the slings and darts of outrageous fortune," while prosperity born of deceit and fraud is of short duration. The merciless critics and "small fry of Grubb street" have assaulted Mr. Ginn and his cocks with all the bitterness of pens that are dipped in gall, but in time some fresh victory hushes the voice of the assailants, and the Ginn cocks go on pursuing the even tenor of their way. It appears after all these plousible diatribes, the Ginn cocks live—"a survival of the fittest."

The Ginn fowl come all colors of plumage, and of legs, and of eyes. They run well up in weight, sometimes reaching 8 lbs. They are mostly straight combs, but some are roundheads with pea combs. Mr. Ginn's Grays and Blues with pea combs are considered by many his best. However, if Mr. Ginn has made any specialty in feather it has been of the Grays. He breeds this color in the various shades from the lightest silver duckwing with white legs, to the blackest brindle gray with black legs, and it may justly be said, in greater numbers than any other man in the world.

ORIENTALS.

All that is needed to be said of fowls from China, India, the Peninsula of Malay, and Japan, will be found under "crossing" in a previous part of this book. What are called "Japs" in this country come from Japan and China; Aseels come from India. The word means *high-bred* in the Hindoo tongue, and these fowl have been bred in that country of departed civilization for centuries, to be fought in *pecking matches*. The cocks were confined in boxes with their heads protruding from holes. The purse is put upon the boxes which are placed near enough for the birds to bite each other. This betting continued till one or the other or both quit. Hence, the big heads and beaks of the Aseels. There can be no question than an Aseel cock is a hard customer in naked heels, because of his superior strength in the neck, head and beak, with his extreme toughness and fine wind power. In the crosses, Aseel *hybrids* are quite attractive to amateurs, because they are excellent barn-yard scrappers and three or four days confinement with a little corn and water is all the condition they can receive. These Japs and Aseels are of all colors, but rarely have dark eyes. Aseels are smaller than Japs, lower set, broader in body and shoulder, and tougher. Malays come from the Malay peninsula, and while much more leggy and larger than the other orientals, are of the same general description, viz: short feathered, knob combs, drooing tails and very erect carriage, very large necks and heads. The young are as naked as buff Cochins. While some expert cockers during the period of experimentation, have had some success with crosses of these orientals, no man has even won a main with the pure blood, and the crosses are better the less they contain of the oriental blood. My personal experience has been peculiar with these fowl. I have never seen fowl that would stand greater harships in natural heels than some crosses I made of Japs and Aseels; but steel gaffs seemed to have the most depressing effect on their courage if administered in heavy doses in quick succession.

WELL KNOWN FEEDERS OF THIS GENERATION.

It is almost impossible to name the men of this day who deserve to be named under this caption. Those that stood sufficiently well to deserve historical mention were very few in past generations, but in our day, their name is legion. In the Southern States, a man can be found almost anywhere, that will not only feed against all comers, but will back his skill with his hard earned cash to the last dollar. Perhaps he may not be known across the border of his country but that matters little. If he has the cocks and the money, no man in the world is too big for him to fight. What is more noticeable still, these brave "know nothings" often win against the cocking celebrities.

Perhaps the following are above the average and their names will dwell in the memory of coming generations of cockers for years to come; while they will be perpetuated in the many books on cock fighting that have been published in the past ten years:

Dick Lee, of Washington City, is a Marylander by birth, approaching his three score and ten, but still in the game with the best. Dick's feed made the record of the Eslin fowl. It was he that fed the famous Red Horse cocks in their many brilliant victories. He has fed cocks successfully for mains in New York, Philadelphia, Maryland and Southern Rules. In this respect "Old Dick," as he is familiarly known, surpasses all other feeders of this day. He has fed mains against Mike Kearney and Wm. Morgan with Tom Rogers, in New York Rules, against Pat Carroll and the Blakhackle Ellises in Philadelphia Rules; against Pat Spelman and many others of the best old Maryland feeders;

against Holt, Kearney, Hicks, the Arringtons, Moore, Dr. Gee, and nearly all the famous long heel feeders. There is no living feeder that has fought more or won more mains than Dick Lee, and no man that ever fed cocks had a higher reputation for honesty and fidelity. One thing everybody always knew when in a main with Dick Lee and that is there was no risk of any "crooked business." He is absolutely unapproachable and takes peculiar pride in the fact. Dick lives near Washington City in a secluded place amid a forest of primaeval trees, where he breeds a few of his old favorites and opens his door wide to the visiting fraternity.

Mike Kearney has bred, fed and fought his famous Whitehackles with almost unbroken success for more than twenty years. Mike is straight from "the old sod" and nursed a fondness for game cocks with his mother's milk. He is bordering on sixty and is open to the world for a cocking main at all times. "Mike" stopped the triumphant march of Tom O'Neal and his Kentucky Dominiques in a main for $5,000. It was he that fought the first main "out east" against Anthony Greene and his grade Japanese chickens, which were a great novelty in this country at that time. The main was not fought out, day coming on and the public in sight. Mike runs a retreat for sporting people on Long Island, where he has had a pit for years, in which many of the famous mains of this generation have been fought.

For five years, Mike's place was cocking headquarters for everybody fighting in New York Rules, especially after "Johnie" Erb's place in Newark, N. J., was broken up by overdiligent bloodsuckers of the law. These same type of blue law, conscience burdened officials have run Mike about from one place to another, but he has survived—not that they wish to stop Mike, but the tariff increases too much and "a move is cheaper than to pay the rent." Their methods were beautifully illustrated in the cocking season of 1899, when they received orders at 7 p. m. to stop a main at Guttenburg Race Track, N. Y. They waited until the main was over, about 1:30 a. m. then "pulled the place" and bled the crowd for $800 or $900! Wm Morgan was robbed of his entire cocking outfit. This gang of bowery tramps were under the leadership of a tenderloin dead beat whose face had been pitted by smallpox in the State penitentiary. Mike Kearney is a small, wiry man and looks as if he were good for many more mains before he crosses over to meet Joseph Gilliver, Nick Arrington, Dr. Gee, Pat Spelman, Henry Hicks, and the best of those that have joined the vast majority.

Dennis Mahoney, of New York, became famous just as did Mike Kearney, by feeding, backing and fighting his one strain of cocks. "Mahoney Gulls" are bred in the crosses all over the United States. It is not thought that there are any pure Mahoney Gulls in existence, but they have improved many of the leading strains of American game cocks that stand first as fighters. The Gulls were black-breasted duckwing reds with yellow legs and many showed white feathers in both wing and tail, and trimmed white in hackle. They were very game and elegant claimers. The hardest main of recent times was fought partly by Gulls, in Baltimore. They were whipped by Smith's Black and Tans, but not one was whipped until he was dead as a stone. Perk Huddleston and P. W. Carew have bred Gulls for years but have none of the pure blood at the present day. Mahoney fought also and deserves the credit perhaps of making the reputation of a strain of New York chickens known as "Genet Pyles." Carew bred these fowl to a late day and they have been freely crossed with many of the best fowl in this country. Dennis Mahoney, as his name would indicate, is an Irishman. He is advanced in years and has practically retired, but the name of "Mahoney Gull" will pass down in history, and such is the general admiration for those famous fowl that breeders many generations after our time, will be advertising "Pure Mahoney Gulls, straight from headquarters." The writer's personal experience with this strain of fowls is that they had more "kick" in them than any fowl he has ever seen. Their first impulse seemed always to be to kick, by reason of which they won many phenomenal battles.

Holly Chappell in his day made Detroit famous as a cocking center. "Holly" could out-feed any man in a hundred miles of him and had an easy walk-over in his better days. He was generally considered the peer of any man in inch and a quarter heels. He was also a signally successful breeder. He had a special fondness for Hennies and bred many of that feather that were game fighters, and able to hold their own in any company. Chappell was also very partial to a strain of long feathered cocks that were almost like dubber flecked with black spots, which he called "Pea Soups." These fowl are pretty well scattered throughout the State, and their blood is in the Pierce Wisconsin Champions.

John Evans, of Washington, has been a very successful feeder in the past six years. It was he that won six straight mains with Smith's Black and Tans in one season. Among these mains was one for $200 and $2,000 against a famous combination of cocks known as "The Shenandoah Club," he winning almost every fight. It is said that more money was bet at this main than was ever seen bet on a main before in the Middle States. Evans two nights after this, defeated one of the cleverest feeders in the world—Geo. Wilson, six to four. He has defeated such men as Tom Rogers, of New Jersey, and other well known men. There is no man that knows "the whole game" better than John Evans.

Billie Howard, of New York, is a member of that brilliant group of comparatively young feeders that have won laurels in the past five years. Billie's father fed cocks for Lord Derby, and he very poignantly observed after defeating one of the strongest combinations in York and Jersey, "I don't see why people are surprised that I can feed cocks. My father fed cocks for Lord Derby in England, and I learned from him." Howard is a small, active, faithful feeder and with a crop of healthy, game fighting cocks, he is as hard a man as there is in the short heel business. The Four Hundred and Wall Street sportsmen will back him for a million. Billie Howard fed for Geo. Smith when he whipped the Erie people backed by the Eslins and Maddux, of Virginia. This is often spoken of as the hardest short heel main on record. Without any loss of time to speak of this main of eleven cocks stood six to five in Smith's favor after fighting from 8:30 at night till 6:30 next morning. Billie has whipped Tom Rogers and Wm. Morgan, and is now open for a main in New York Rules with anybody for any amount. Howard breeds and fights a strain of cocks he calls "Fitzsimmons." They are great fighters when in condition, but are not dead game. Less is heard of Billie of late because the blue laws have become bluer and the New York cockers have begun to fight their mains in private. Billie Howard always said that cocks could not be shipped from the Southern States to New York and fed twenty-one days as their cocks are fed. He claimed that seventeen days is all they will stand.

Tom Rogers, of New Jersey, had the reputation of winnig more straight mains. He fed the Morgan Whitehackles for fifteen years. Indeed it was with his feed that they made their splendid record. The history of the Morgan fowl is so closely identified with that of Tom Rogers that to write one is to write the other. Morgan and Rogers have drifted apart in the past two years, and both have been unfortunate. The combination was one of the strongest in the Northern States. Tom Rogers is the most modest and perhaps pleasantest feeder in the business. He is thoroughly courteous, has a remarkably pleasant face and never says a word that could not be repeated from a pulpit. "Tommie" is not yet fifty, and is in perfect health and like nearly all the successful feeders, is a temperate man.

J. W. Goodhart, of Virginia, has the most brilliant record of any feeder in recent times. He has won eleven straight mains, every man he whipped being considered a hard proposition. He has in the past three years, defeated Casey, of Boston, Dick Lee, the Baltimore Club, A. P. O'Connor, Rogers, etc., etc. Goodhart is improving beyond a doubt for when he began upon his brilliant career, he won several mains only by the odd fight. In the past year or two he has won most of his mains by heavy odds. Goodhart has a hotel and saloon at Leesburg, Virginia. No man is better fixed for feeding a main and none takes more pleasure in putting them in fix. He is a young man scarcely thirty, and throws all his energy into his work, which he does with a never-failing enthusiasm. Goodhart has won his reputation with cocks bred in large part by Wm E. Boteler, of Maryland. He has not been whipped in three years, although he has fought many mains against the best in the business.

A. P. O'Connor first came to public notice as the breeder of "O'Connor Red Horse," a family of fowl bred from stock gotten of the Eslins in Washington. O'Connor, while a mere boy, bred and fought cocks against men ripe in experience and that with remarkable success. In recent years he has formed a cocking partnership with Anthony Greene, of California, and is one of the most vigorous champions of the Japanese crosses. Mr. O'Connor's most distinguished performance was the defeat of Moore and Ginn, the big Georgia combination, at Norfolk, Va., December, 1902, by the odd fight. Mr. O'Connor is about thirty years old and represents a large brewing establishment. He is a man of good education and attractive appearance. He has added two brilliant victories to his record in 1904, one being the defeat of J. W. Goodhart by the odd

George Wilson, of Pennsylvania, is about fifty years old. He was born in Ireland and learned the art of cocking from his father in the old country. Wilson is the most active, enthusiastic man in the game fowl business. He is of a mercurial temperament, busy and full of motion as a Frenchman—a most excellent handler as well as feeder. He has defeated many of the best and has a record that would turn the head of most men. George Wilson does not believe there is a man on earth that can whip him in Philadelphia rules, and such is his confidence, that he bars nobody and will fight anybody on fair terms. He is thoroughly alert to the interest of his friends and his deportment towards those that look to him for instructions during the main is highly satisfactory—he is honorable and thoroughly loyal to his friends. One of the worst defeats in recent times was that Casey and his party of Bostonians got at Wilson's hands, February, 1903, in the Baltimore pit. The score was 8 to 1 in Wilson's favor. He won every fight in a main against Pennsylvania cockers, he using Black and Tans direct from Smith. Wilson has been remarkably successful with Aldrich's Mugwumps, which he has used in nearly all of his mains in the past two seasons.

Col. F. E. Grist, the world renowned Georgia breeder, would go down in history as a *feeder* if his reputation were not secure as a *breeder.* The Colonel has published a simple, clear statement of his highly efficient "nine day feed" for long heels. His instructions for heeling cocks are also explicit enough for the most ignorant novice. This system of feeding and heeling has been used by its author for years and has been thoroughly tested by having been used in many mains and thousands of battles. It is doubtful if any other man in the world is fixed so well as Col. Grist is for breeding, feeding and fighting cocks at his *game chicken plant,* representing an outlay of thousands of dollars, at his home in Georgia. He has fifteen acres in yards, and has the handsomest private pit and cock house in America. It is finished off in cherry and is attractive as a well appointed modern bar. Here the Colonel feeds and fights at least one hundred cocks every year. When Charlie Brown, Sledge & Hanna, Dr. Gee and their ilk were at their best, Col. Grist, with his feed, defeated them all. He is one of the few men that can feed cocks for battle and keep them in fix indefinitely. Before his business compelled him to locate, he travelled a complete outfit, like a circus, tent and all, and carried cocks enough to accommodate all that were looking for fight. On one of these campaigns, at the Montgomery Fair, he defeated Sledge & Hanna and fought cocks for a week—pitting some two hundred and fifty cocks of his own. Being an expert feeder assists very much in breeding cocks. A man who has fed and fought a thousand cocks knows what a fighting cock ought to be. The Colonel cannot leave his place to conduct mains, just as no sensible man would do, situated as he is, but his system of fighting numbers of his cocks in his private pit every year answers every purpose of attending and participating in mains as far as practical cockfighting can throw light upon the breeding of game cocks.

Steve Moore, of Atlanta, Ga., has fought a greater number of "big money" mains in Southren Rules in the past ten years than any other one man. Moore has been defeated now and then but when the balance sheet of his record is struck it will be seen that the great Georgia feeder is far ahead of the game. No matter how badly beaten Moore is he never lacks for backers, of whom he has a greater number than any other feeder in the South. Moore plays no favorites and shuns no set of cockers—he is in no sense a "snap hunter." It would be hard to find a man that travels his cocks greater distances than he and who has a greater number of difficulties to overcome in that respect. He is a rather large man, close to sixty, and it is wonderful that he can keep up his zest and energy, but he does, and he yields the palm to no young man in point of strict attention to his business when he has a main in hand. Moore brought a strain of fowl into prominence called "Clabber-Ears" from their having white ear lobes. "Moore's Clabber Ears" are pretty well scattered throughout the union under the advertising boom of Moore's good feeding. What Dick Lee has been to Red Horses, Tom Rogers to Morgan Whitehackles, Kearney to his own Whitehackles, Allen to his Roundheads, Grist to his Gradys and Champions, Pierce to his Shufflers and Champions, Steve Moore has been to his Clabber Ears, and Ginn's cocks. One of Moore's greatest victories was the defeat of Maddux and the Eslins, assisted by Smith with Dick Lee's feed, at Charleston.

Henry Flock, Tom O'Neal and *Roland Minton* were the great trio that gave the Kentucky Dominiques their reputation. Henry Flock is, beyond question, the most successful feeder between the Rockies and the Alleghenies. He is partial to the Minton Dominiques and has fed a number of Patton White Tails, a Texas strain that made an excellent reputation in one year's fighting in long heels. It is hardly more than just to say that Henry Flock is the peer of any living man in long heels. He is also a fluent writer and holds his own among those who sometimes leave the pit and take to the pen to settle their misunderstandings.

Negro Feeders.—Among the curiosities in modern cocking are two negroes—"Bill" Snell and Lucius Tolbert. We Southern gentlemen, so devoted to all lines of sport, as well as, so fond of personal ease, naturally would have entrusted the task and labor of putting cocks in shape for battle to anyone that might prove proficient in the art. The negro has always been the Southern man's major domo, and so yielding is the average Southern gentleman to the allurements of ease that he has been perfectly willing to leave everything in the form of effort to his "body-servant," even to performing his toilet. Hence the opportunity for colored men as feeders has been boundless in the Southern states. Yet only these two have risen so far above the average as to be conspicuous in their day. They have fed a number of independent mains successfully, and are considered by men at the top as being the "best help" in the business. The two are extremes. Bill is a big stout fellow; Lucius is on the slender order. Both know their places, are thoroughly polite, and just exactly fill the Southerner's idea of a cockfeeder. Hence, both Lucius and Bill are very much in request in long heel fighting. Bill claims to be a severe feeder. He claims that he must have fifty cocks to select from if he shows twenty-one. He says, "Boss, I'ze a hard nigger' on roosters; I kills 'em out if dey can't stand the work I gives 'em." Bill's regular name for a cock is "rooster," he rarely applies any other term, and his demeanor in the cockhouse as well as at the pit, is an inexhaustable source of amusement, especially to those who were bred in the South and understand negro character. Bill is also a very successful breeder of game cocks. He pins his faith in large part to the old "Gilders"—an Irish strain imported years ago and recently returning to popularity through the efforts of Southern cockers and those who have fowls heavily crossed with the old Irish Gilder strain. Mr. Hillsman, of Virginia, used a number of the Snell Gilders in his main against J. W. Goodhart and W. E. Boteler, of Maryland, which he won by the odd fight in thirteen matches, Feb. 25th, 1904. It was a severe main—rarely has there been so hard a con-favorite cocks in this main against the Gilders in excellent test in recent times, and nothing but cocks of the highest order could have won against Mr. Goodhart, who had eleven straight mains to his credit and was fighting his condition. A. P. O'Connor fed for Virginia, and he had the Gilders in perfect fix.

Lucius Tolbert is in great request in Charleston, and while not engaged there, he is busy feeding or helping to feed, mains in Georgia. There is always something for a good feeder in Turner's Rules to do in South Carolina and Georgia, during the cocking season. Lucius is also often employed in Texas where cocking is rapidly increasing through the efforts of such men as J. A. Maddigan, who has been remarkably successful with his "Texas Rangers," a strain of dark and brown-reds perhaps equal to any in long heels. The San Antonio pits are regularly licensed and are frequented by wealthy Mexicans who will wager ten thousand dollars on a cock fight with as much stoical indifference as if tossing heads and tails for a copper cent. It was at these famous pits in Texas that Maddigan defeated F. H. Carr, the largest breeder of game cocks in the Indian Territory, the last of February with the assistance of Lucius Tolbert as right hand man to W. B. Cavanaugh, who has come to the front as one of the best long heel feeders in the State of Texas.

Lucius and Bill both figured extensively in the largest cocking carnival of recent times, that at Birmingham, Alabama, December 15, 16, 17, 18 and 19, 1903. Bill conditioned for S. D. Harris who won the tournament, Lucius conditioned for Burke and Cavanaugh who won a large majority of the battles they fought. This was a unique affair. The purpose was to bring together all the best known cockers of the South in a grand five-day tournament. Each party entering put up $100 and the winner of the greatest number of battles during the tournament was to take all the money. There were seven entries: C. L. and A. L. Love, Burnsville, Ala.; Burke and Cavanaugh, Springfield, Mo., and Paris, Texas; Binford and Tanner, Athens, Ala.; Bud Brown, Warrior, Ala.; Faulk and Hayes, Dothan, Ala., and Natchez, Miss.; S. D. Harris, Birmingham. S. S. Granger, of Madison, Miss., had entered but gave up the forfeit. It was estimated that one thousand people were present. Three or four cock fights were in progress nearly all the time, and with mains and hacks, about two hundred cocks were fought in the five days. Bill Snell and Lucius Tolbert were born in slavery and are hardy men in middle life.

A ROYAL BIRD

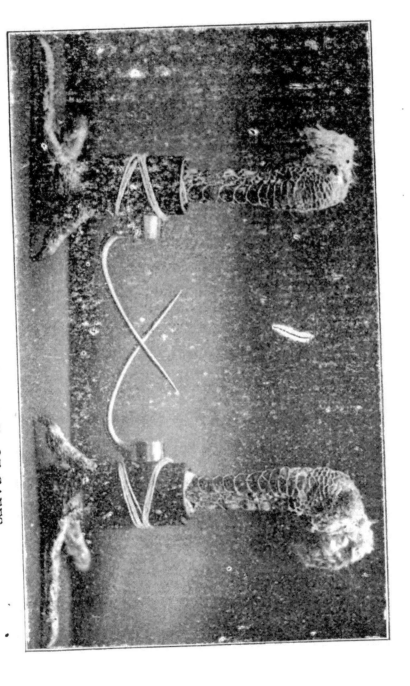

CUT SHOWING HOW TO SET A PAIR OF GAFFS

WM. GILLIVER AND L. HARRIS
TWO ENGLISH COCKERS

DICK HAYDON
OF PLYMOUTH, ENGLAND

JOSEPH E. WINGATE

HON. WM. L. ALLEN

W. E. BOTELER

A. P. O'CONOR

DR. GEE

J. L. McLAURIN

GEORGE WILSON

COL. ALFRED ALDRICH

G. PARK HUDDLESTON

GEO. GILKERSON
AND A WHITEHACKLE COCK

J. C. STURZEL
A CHICAGO COCKER

DR. C. E. KING

S. D. HARRIS

H. B. ("DAD") GLEEZEN
FOUNDER NATIONAL GAME FANCIERS ASSOCIATION

H. E. ESTES

H. C. BENSEMAN

GEO. W. MEANS

C. A. KENNEY

COL. F. E. GRIST

WM. L. MORGAN

Made in the USA
Columbia, SC
06 June 2022